2019 DEVELOPMENT EFFECTIVENESS REVIEW

APRIL 2020

ADB

ASIAN DEVELOPMENT BANK

© 2020 Asian Development Bank
6 ADB Avenue, Mandaluyong City, 1550 Metro Manila, Philippines
Tel +63 2 8632 4444; Fax +63 2 8636 2444
www.adb.org

Some rights reserved. Published in 2020.

ISBN 978-92-9262-216-9 (print), 978-92-9262-217-6 (electronic), 978-92-9262-218-3 (ebook)
Publication Stock No. TCS200145-2
DOI: http://dx.doi.org/10.22617/TCS200145-2

Notes:

1. In this report, "$" refers to United States dollars.
2. The Asian Development Bank's Strategy, Policy and Partnerships Department is the source of all information in tables, figures, boxes, and infographics in this report, unless otherwise stated.
3. Totals may not sum precisely because of rounding.
4. ADB recognizes "Laos" as the Lao People's Democratic Republic.
5. All photos by ADB unless otherwise stated.

Cover design by Stephanie Salazar. On the cover: **Improving access to water.** Family members collect water in Dhunga Village, Doti District, Nepal, one of 100 communities benefiting from water supply and improved water management under the ADB-supported Building Climate Resilience of Watersheds in Mountain Eco-Regions Project (photo by Gerhard Joren).

2019
DEVELOPMENT EFFECTIVENESS REVIEW

APRIL 2020

ASIAN DEVELOPMENT BANK

CONTENTS

INTRODUCTION 2

  A. THE CORPORATE RESULTS FRAMEWORK 4

  B. HOW TO READ THIS REVIEW 6

PERFORMANCE HIGHLIGHTS 8

  SUMMARY PERFORMANCE SCORECARD 2019 10

  A. PROGRESS ON REGIONAL DEVELOPMENT INDICATORS 11

    Level 1: Development Progress in Asia and the Pacific 11

  B. ADB'S ACHIEVEMENTS IN 2019 12

    Level 2: Results from ADB's Completed Operations 12

    Level 3: ADB's Operational Management 14

    Level 4: ADB's Organizational Effectiveness 17

CHAPTER 1: STRATEGY 2030 OPERATIONAL PRIORITIES 18

  SEVEN OPERATIONAL PRIORITIES AND THE SUSTAINABLE DEVELOPMENT GOALS 19

  A. REGIONAL PROGRESS 20

  B. SEVEN OPERATIONAL PRIORITIES: HIGHLIGHTS 25

  SEVEN OPERATIONAL PRIORITIES AND REGIONAL DEVELOPMENT PROGRESS 26

CHAPTER 2: DEVELOPMENT FINANCE AND STRATEGIC ALIGNMENT 42

  A. DEVELOPMENT FINANCE AND STRATEGIC ALIGNMENT 44

  B. PROGRESS ON STRATEGY 2030 TARGETS AND PRIORITIES 45

  C. IN FOCUS 46

    1. Accelerating Gender Equality and Tackling Climate Change 46

    2. Mobilizing Private Sector Resources for Development 49

    3. Expanding Interventions in Social Sectors 50

    4. Poverty Reduction and Inclusiveness 51

    5. Quality Infrastructure: Green, Resilient, Inclusive, and Sustainable 52

    6. Supporting the Sustainable Development Goals 53

CHAPTER 3: SOVEREIGN OPERATIONS **54**

A. READINESS AT DESIGN STAGE 57

B. IMPLEMENTATION PROGRESS 57

C. PERFORMANCE OF COMPLETED OPERATIONS... 57

D. IN FOCUS 58

    1. Main Factors Lowering Sovereign Success Rates 58

    2. Learning from Completed Operations 60

    3. Performance of Completed Concessional Assistance Operations...................62

CHAPTER 4: PRIVATE SECTOR OPERATIONS **64**

A. SCALING UP AND STRATEGIC FIT 67

B. PERFORMANCE AT IMPLEMENTATION.. 67

C. PERFORMANCE AT COMPLETION 67

D. IN FOCUS 68

    1. Newly Committed Nonsovereign Operations..68

    2. Main Factors Lowering Success Rates 70

    3. Learning from Completed Operations..73

CHAPTER 5: ADB AS A KNOWLEDGE ORGANIZATION **74**

A. BENEFITS 76

B. USED 77

C. DELIVERED... 78

D. KNOWLEDGE ORGANIZATION 80

CHAPTER 6: ADB'S SYSTEMS, PROCESSES, AND CAPACITY **84**

A. ORGANIZATIONAL CAPACITY... 87

B. ORGANIZATIONAL SYSTEMS AND PROCESSES... 89

CHAPTER 7: APPLYING DIFFERENTIATED APPROACHES – FRAGILE AND CONFLICT-AFFECTED SITUATIONS, AND SMALL ISLAND DEVELOPING STATES 94

    A. OPERATIONAL FOCUS 97

    B. PERFORMANCE OF COMPLETED OPERATIONS...97

    C. ENHANCING ADB'S CAPACITY TO RESPOND 97

    D. IN FOCUS 99

        1. A Country-Focused Approach to Progressing on the Fragility-to-Stability Continuum 99

        2. Supporting Conflict-Affected Areas 99

        3. Addressing Sources of Fragility in the Pacific 101

ACTIONS TO ADDRESS CHALLENGES... **102**

    A. MANAGEMENT ACTION RECORD SYSTEM...104

    B. ACTIONS TO ADDRESS 2018 CHALLENGES...105

        1. Actions to Improve Success Rates of Completed Sovereign Projects.........................105

        2. Actions to Improve Success Rates of Completed Nonsovereign Operations.....................107

        3. Focus on Social Protection 107

    C. KEY CHALLENGES TO ADDRESS IN 2020 AND ONWARD 108

APPENDIXES **110**

    1. INDICATOR INDEX 112

    2. SELECTED RESULTS OF 2019 COMPLETED OPERATIONS BY SUSTAINABLE DEVELOPMENT GOAL 121

    3. ADB DEVELOPING MEMBER COUNTRIES..122

    4. UPDATES TO THE CORPORATE RESULTS FRAMEWORK, 2019–2024......................124

ENDNOTES... **132**

SCORECARD AND RELATED INFORMATION

SIGNALS AND SCORING METHODS

ALIGNMENT WITH THE SUSTAINABLE DEVELOPMENT GOALS.. 2

RESULTS FRAMEWORK INDICATORS LEVEL 1: SIGNALS.. 2

RESULTS FRAMEWORK INDICATORS LEVELS 2–4: SIGNALS 3

RESULTS FRAMEWORK INDICATORS LEVELS 2–4: COMPOSITE SIGNALS 4

RESULTS FRAMEWORK INDICATORS LEVELS 2–4: SCORING METHODS FOR 2019–2023 4

RESULTS FRAMEWORK INDICATORS LEVELS 2–4: SCORING METHODS FOR 2024 5

RESULTS FRAMEWORK INDICATORS

LEVEL 1: DEVELOPMENT PROGRESS IN ASIA AND THE PACIFIC 8

LEVEL 2: RESULTS FROM COMPLETED OPERATIONS 12

LEVEL 3: ADB'S OPERATIONAL MANAGEMENT 18

LEVEL 4: ADB'S ORGANIZATIONAL EFFECTIVENESS 22

TRACKING INDICATORS

LEVEL 1: DEVELOPMENT PROGRESS IN ASIA AND THE PACIFIC 26

LEVEL 2: RESULTS FROM COMPLETED OPERATIONS 32

LEVEL 3: ADB'S OPERATIONAL MANAGEMENT 48

LEVEL 4: ADB'S ORGANIZATIONAL EFFECTIVENESS 56

LINKED DOCUMENTS

1. ADB CORPORATE RESULTS FRAMEWORK, 2019–2024
2. RESULTS FRAMEWORK INDICATOR DEFINITIONS
3. TRACKING INDICATOR DEFINITIONS
4. TECHNICAL NOTE ON THE DEVELOPMENT EFFECTIVENESS REVIEW RATING SYSTEM

WEB-LINKED RESOURCES

Download the scorecard and related information, and linked documents from

https://www.adb.org/documents/development-effectiveness-review-2019-report.

ABBREVIATIONS

ADB	–	Asian Development Bank
COBP	–	country operations business plan
CRF	–	corporate results framework
CSO	–	civil society organization
DEfR	–	development effectiveness review
DMC	–	developing member country
DMF	–	design and monitoring framework
EGM	–	effective gender mainstreaming
FCAS	–	fragile and conflict-affected situation
GDP	–	gross domestic product
GEN	–	gender equity theme
IAE	–	internal administrative expense
ICT	–	information and communication technology
IED	–	Independent Evaluation Department
kg	–	kilogram
KPS	–	knowledge products and services
MAKE	–	Most Admired Knowledge Enterprise
MARS	–	Management Action Record System
OP	–	operational priority
PRC	–	People's Republic of China
RY	–	reporting year
SDG	–	Sustainable Development Goal
SGE	–	some gender elements
SIDS	–	small island developing state
TA	–	technical assistance

OVERVIEW OF ADB'S SUITE OF ANNUAL CORPORATE PERFORMANCE REPORTS

The Asian Development Bank (ADB) prepares a suite of three complementary yet distinct corporate performance reports annually. **All three reports share the common goals of learning, and accountability to ADB shareholders and other stakeholders.** This overview summarizes the unique focus, purpose, and value addition of each report. It maps their common areas of focus to cross-refer the reader between the reports for information about common topics.

	FOCUS	PURPOSE AND VALUE ADDITION
Annual Evaluation Review	The Board-required report of the Independent Evaluation Department (IED) is produced to promote accountability and learning. It focuses on the operational performance and results of ADB and provides a synthesis of the evaluations prepared by IED in the preceding year and an in-depth analysis of performance trends of completed operations. It includes a special topic to strengthen results, and reports on Management's acceptance and implementation of IED recommendations.	An evidence-based evaluation of performance that is independent and provides recommendations for improvement.

COMMON FOCUS ↕ performance of completed operations

	FOCUS	PURPOSE AND VALUE ADDITION
Development Effectiveness Review	The review is Management's flagship report on ADB's performance in achieving the priorities of its corporate strategy, using indicators in the corporate results framework as the yardstick. Focusing on operations financed by ADB, it assesses ADB's development effectiveness, highlights actions ADB has taken to improve, and identifies areas where ADB's performance needs to be strengthened.	The findings provide the Board of Directors and ADB Management with performance information to guide ADB's strategic and operational directions and resource planning.

COMMON FOCUS ↕ performance of active portfolio

	FOCUS	PURPOSE AND VALUE ADDITION
Annual Portfolio Performance Report	The report provides a strategic overview and analysis of the performance trends, size, composition, and quality of ADB's active portfolio based on key indicators. It includes all operations and projects, including those funded by special funds and cofinancing fully administered by ADB. It identifies key issues, actions taken by departments to support improvement, and lessons for future ADB interventions, and makes recommendations for improvement to ADB Management.	The report provides ADB Management with evidence-based recommendations grounded in an in-depth analysis, including by region, of ADB's full portfolio of active committed sovereign and nonsovereign operations and projects.

Water for all. A girl waits to use the taps from the ADB–supported Emergency Assistance Project in Bangladesh (photo by Abir Abdullah).

INTRODUCTION

The Development Effectiveness Review is ADB's primary tool for monitoring and reporting on its performance in achieving the priorities of its corporate strategy. The 2019 review is the first to use the 60 indicators in the corporate results framework, 2019–2024 as its yardstick. The new framework was approved in 2019 to align with ADB's Strategy 2030 and to assess overall development progress in Asia and the Pacific and ADB's effectiveness in delivering development results.

1.   The 2019 Development Effectiveness Review (DEfR) is the 13th annual performance report of the Asian Development Bank (ADB). The DEfR is based on ADB's corporate results framework (CRF), a management tool used to track and monitor ADB's progress in implementing its corporate strategy. Preparing the DEfR is ADB's annual review and reflection exercise. This yearly process enables it to spot and analyze trends in corporate effectiveness, identify underlying issues, and develop actions to improve. The DEfR's findings inform ADB's operational directions and resource planning through the President's planning directions and the 3-year corporate work program and budget framework process.

2.   The 2019 DEfR is the first to assess ADB's performance in achieving the priorities of ADB's latest long-term strategic framework, Strategy 2030, and to use the CRF, 2019–2024.[1] The 2019 DEfR adopts a new structure and style to reflect this strategic evolution.

A. THE CORPORATE RESULTS FRAMEWORK

3.   The CRF, 2019–2024 covers ADB operations overall and the subset of ADB operations and countries that receive concessional assistance.[2] It contains 60 indicators organized into four performance levels arranged in two sections. Section 1, comprising Level 1, tracks the collective regional development progress made by ADB's developing member countries (DMCs) throughout Asia and the Pacific. These indicators are aligned with the Sustainable Development Goals (SDGs). Section 2, containing levels 2–4, assesses ADB's performance in executing Strategy 2030. Level 2 focuses on the results of ADB operations that supported the seven Strategy 2030 operational priorities and were completed over the preceding 3 years. Level 3 tracks ADB's performance in selecting, designing, financing, and implementing operations that align with Strategy 2030 priorities.

Level 4 examines ADB's performance in managing the internal resources and processes that support its operations. The CRF indicators are complemented and reinforced by 157 tracking indicators.

4.   Among the notable features of the CRF, 2019–2024 are its integration of indicators that reflect the SDGs and key aspects of Strategy 2030. The new CRF strengthens the focus on development outcomes of the seven operational priorities in Level 2. Some indicators have been added to better monitor the performance of nonsovereign operations. Others have been changed to harmonize with indicators used by other multilateral development banks and international finance institutions (Appendix 4).

Future harvest. A farmer in Luang Namtha Province, Lao People's Democratic Republic shows his rice seedlings (photo by Xaykhame Manilasith).

B. HOW TO READ THIS REVIEW

5.　The 2019 DEfR continues the practice of using signals to communicate performance. However, the report's main body is now organized by themes to reflect the new directions of Strategy 2030 and the CRF, 2019–2024.

6.　**Understanding performance signals.** The use of arrows and check mark symbols and green, amber, and red signals to illustrate the status of performance continues in the 2019 DEfR. These signals indicate the direction of change for Level 1 indicators, and performance against targets for the indicators in levels 2–4. Performance on indicators with 2024 targets is expected to show the progress necessary from the baseline values to reach these targets. Signals for indicators with annual or periodic performance targets reflect performance on meeting the minimum and/or maximum threshold values set for each year during 2019–2024. Performance on some indicators is monitored rather than scored. In these cases, arrow signs indicate any improvement or deterioration, but no color signals are assigned. The table on the opposite page summarizes the signals for indicators in levels 2–4.

7.　**Where to find performance results.** The Performance Highlights section and the scorecard in the web-linked resources summarize performance on all indicators across the four levels of the CRF. The scorecard explains each performance signal.

8.　**Where to find a particular indicator.** The indicator index in Appendix 1 shows where to find details on performance for each indicator discussed in the report. Some indicators are featured across several chapters.

9.　**The new thematic structure.** The 2019 DEfR is divided into seven thematic chapters that group indicators according to the priorities and overall objectives of Strategy 2030. An infographic introduces the theme at the beginning of each chapter. Performance signals and key related data are then provided graphically alongside brief commentaries on overall thematic performance followed by deeper examination of particular areas and notable results. The thematic chapter focused on the seven Strategy 2030 operational priorities and the SDGs (Chapter 1) covers all Level 1 indicators and relevant indicators from levels 2 and 3. The six other thematic chapters cluster and discuss results for indicators from levels 2–4 according to theme.

10.　**Reporting key ADB actions.** ADB has a system in place to identify and monitor actions for improvement and undertook important actions during 2019 to address major performance challenges identified in the 2018 DEfR. Actions to address challenges that remain relevant to Strategy 2030 priorities are summarized in the closing section.

11.　**Complementing the two other ADB corporate performance reports.** The DEfR complements and refers to the two additional corporate performance reports ADB prepares each year—the Annual Portfolio Performance Report prepared by the Procurement, Portfolio and Financial Management Department; and the Annual Evaluation Review prepared by the Independent Evaluation Department. An overview of the focus and purpose of each review is illustrated in the diagram at the beginning of this report.

Levels 2–4 Signals Explained

Scoring Method	Signal	Annual Change[a]
At or above target—performance at or above target	✓	
On track—performance exceeded desired progress to attain target	↑	Improved
	■	Remained constant
	↓	Deteriorated
On track but watch—performance met desired progress to attain 2024 target but requires close monitoring	↑	Improved
	■	Remained constant
	↓	Deteriorated
Off track—performance fell short of desired progress to attain target	↑	Improved
	■	Remained constant
	↓	Deteriorated
Monitor—no performance assessment	↑	Increased
	■	Remained constant
	↓	Decreased

[a] An arrow indicates a significant (≥ 3%) change from previous performance.

PERFORMANCE HIGHLIGHTS

This section summarizes the main findings for the 60 indicators in the corporate results framework, 2019–2024, organized by indicator level. The 10 indicators at Level 1 track regional development progress and challenges in Asia and the Pacific. Level 2 measures the results from completed operations, including 22 indicators monitoring delivery of results for the 7 operational priorities in Strategy 2030 and 5 assessing the quality of completed operations. The 15 indicators at Level 3 gauge how ADB manages its operations, focusing on design and implementation quality, development finance, and strategic alignment. Level 4 includes 8 indicators that measure ADB's organizational effectiveness in terms of systems, processes, and capacity.

SUMMARY PERFORMANCE SCORECARD 2019

REGIONAL DEVELOPMENT PROGRESS (SECTION I)						
Development Progress in Asia and the Pacific (Level 1)						
	ADB DMCs Overall			ADB Concessional Assistance DMCs		
	⬆	⬌	⬇	⬆	⬌	⬇
Strategy 2030: Achieving a Prosperous, Inclusive, Resilient, and Sustainable Asia and the Pacific	3	4	0	1	3	3

ADB'S DEVELOPMENT EFFECTIVENESS (SECTION II)		
Results from ADB's Completed Operations (Level 2)		
	ADB	CA
Strategy 2030 Operational Priority Results	🟢	🟢
Quality of Completed Operations	🔴	🔴
ADB's Operational Management (Level 3)		
Design and Implementation Quality	--	--
Development Finance	🟢	--
Strategic Alignment	🟢	--
ADB's Organizational Management (Level 4)		
Organizational Systems and Processes	🟢	--
Organizational Capacity	⚪	--

🟢 = good, 🟡 = mixed, 🔴 = poor, ⚪ = not available until end of 2020, -- = not scored, ⬆ = number of results framework indicators (RFIs) that have improved since the prior year, ⬌ = number of RFIs that have remained constant since the prior year, ⬇ = number of RFIs that have deteriorated since the prior year.

ADB = Asian Development Bank, CA = concessional assistance, DMC = developing member country.

Hard at work. A student checks on her equipment at the Mongolian University of Life Sciences in Ulaanbaatar, Mongolia (photo by Eric Sales).

A. PROGRESS ON REGIONAL DEVELOPMENT INDICATORS

Level 1: Development Progress in Asia and the Pacific

12. Asia and the Pacific has made important progress on many critical development agendas, but the advances to date are inadequate if the region is to meet the ambitious Sustainable Development Goals (SDGs). For Level 1 regional progress indicators, ADB tracks whether results have improved, stayed constant, or regressed relative to the last year of available data.

13. **Poverty and inequality reducing but persistent despite robust economic growth.** While poverty in the region has decreased dramatically, 7% of the population, or 264 million people, still live in extreme poverty, and 29% of the population, or 1.1 billion people, live very close to the poverty line on less than $3.20 per day. Poverty persists even though average growth rates of gross domestic product (GDP) per capita have remained robust at more than 5%. Inequality remains a major issue, although data suggest some improvement as the income growth rates of the poorest 40% of the population are slightly higher than those of the general population. Social protection system coverage and access to health, education, and other basic services have expanded but remain inadequate.

14. **Women's economic empowerment remains to be strengthened.** Unemployment rates for women were slightly higher than those for men (3.8% versus 3.5%), and the gap was wider in concessional assistance countries (4.4% for women versus 2.7% for men). A much higher proportion of young women are not in education, employment, or training (42% compared with 13% for men). Women also spend substantially more of their time doing unpaid care work (12.0% compared with 4.2% for men).

15. **Managing climate change, disaster risk, and environmental sustainability remains a challenge.** The carbon intensity of the region's economies continued to decline slightly overall, from 1.04 kilograms (kg) per dollar of GDP in 2014 to 0.90 kg in 2017, although it increased slightly in concessional assistance countries. Emissions continued to grow in absolute terms. Millions of people were affected and displaced by natural hazards in 2019, with more than 4,800 deaths. Pressures on the region's forest and marine ecosystems remain high, and there is a recognized need to focus on attaining the environmental SDGs in the region.

16. **Development challenges in increasingly prosperous urban hubs.** Air quality in ADB developing member countries (DMCs) was categorized as moderate in 2017, with a mean annual exposure to fine suspended particles less than 2.5 micrometers in diameter of about 61 micrograms per cubic meter. This is symptomatic of urban planning and service delivery challenges and is linked to an urgent need for more sustainable transport and the use of cleaner fuels for cooking and electricity generation, which can also support climate change mitigation.

17. **Rural–urban development disparities and inadequate food security result in poor health outcomes for many.** In 2016, about 20% of the region's children under the age of 5 were stunted. However, this scarcity sits alongside problems of plenty, such as food wastage. In South Asia and Central Asia about one-fifth of food goes to waste. Rural areas lag urban areas in access to basic services including health, water, sanitation, and electricity.

18. **Governance requires further strengthening.** ADB DMCs' scores on the World Governance Index generally improved, although overall scores remain low.

19. **Regional cooperation and integration unchanged.** ADB's Asia-Pacific Regional Cooperation and Integration Index showed stable levels of regional cooperation and integration, but with lower scores in the concessional assistance countries. Amid continued global trade tensions and weakening demand, indicators related to trade and investment deteriorated.

B. ADB'S ACHIEVEMENTS IN 2019
Level 2: Results from ADB's Completed Operations

20. Completed operations displayed uneven performance in 2019. While most achieved their expected outcomes across the seven operational priorities, success rates for sovereign and nonsovereign operations declined and were below target. A smaller proportion of projects closed on time, but the delivery of gender equality results remained relatively stable.

Strategy 2030 Operational Priority Results

21. **Strong delivery of results.** The corporate results framework, 2019–2024 introduced a new generation of outcome indicators for measuring the results of ADB's sovereign and nonsovereign operations and technical assistance in support of the seven operational priorities of Strategy 2030. In 2019, completed operations delivered 80% or more of their expected results for 18 of the 22 new indicators. Three indicators had shortfalls below the 80% target, and achievement for one other indicator was too early to assess. Selected results from operations completed in 2019 by SDG are highlighted in Appendix 2.

Sovereign Operations Performance

22. **Lower success rates.** The share of completed sovereign operations rated *successful* fell to 71% in reporting years (RY) 2017–2019, a decline of 6 percentage points compared with RY2016–2018. The success rate of operations financed by concessional assistance was also *off track*, declining to 70% from 77% in RY2016–2018. These declines were mainly caused by weaker performance of transport sector operations and, to a lesser extent, finance and education sector operations.

23. **Weaker performance across modalities.** The 3-year average success rates dipped for both policy-based operations (from 89% to 84%) and investment projects (from 75% to 69%), with the share of investment projects rated *successful* reaching a 6-year annual low of 64% in 2019.

24. **Strong relevance and persistently weaker sustainability ratings.** Across the four evaluation criteria, as in the past, sovereign operations scored lowest for sustainability (62%) followed by effectiveness (68%), but better for efficiency (75%), and relevance (82%).

25. **Lower success rates for fragile and conflict-affected situations and small island developing states.** Only 54% of the 13 sovereign operations completed in countries with fragile and conflict-affected situations (FCAS) were rated *successful*. In small island developing states (SIDS) (19 operations), only 42% achieved the same rating. Volatility of this indicator is high because of the small number of operations.

26. **Fewer projects closed on time.** Only 36% of projects in 2017–2019 closed on time, a drop of 4 percentage points compared with 2016–2018, putting ADB's performance *off track* to achieve the 2024 target. Issues related to safeguards, procurement, and performance of contractors and consultants contributed to the delays. Concessional assistance projects were also *off track* on this indicator. They recorded a steeper decline of 10 percentage points, with only 30% closing on time in 2017–2019.

Nonsovereign Operations Performance

27. **Success rate further *off track*.** Only 52% of nonsovereign operations were rated *successful* in RY2017–2019 compared with 54% in RY2016–2018 and a 2024 target of 70%. The smaller share of better-performing infrastructure projects and weak performance of private equity funds were the main factors behind this *off-track* performance.

28. **Lower ratings for development results and ADB work quality.** Ratings for development results, which is the most important criterion determining success rates, remained low (52%) because of underachievement against ambitious targets, absent or insufficient data, and other shortcomings in design and monitoring frameworks. Among other evaluation criteria, investment profitability remained the strongest (73%), additionality lagged (55%), and ADB's work quality was the weakest (39%).

Gender Equality Results

29. **Relatively stable achievement of gender equality results.** For ADB as a whole, the share of completed operations that were assessed as having achieved their envisaged gender equality results declined by 1 percentage point to 74% from the RY2016–2018 baseline, putting the indicator *on track but watch* to meet the 80% target by 2024. Operations financed by concessional assistance recorded an increase of 1 percentage point from the baseline to 77% and were also rated *on track but watch*. For the first time, sovereign and nonsovereign operations were both included in the assessment.

Level 3: ADB's Operational Management

30. The implementation readiness of sovereign projects was *on track* in 2019. ADB piloted enhanced methodologies for measuring and monitoring the performance of operations under implementation. Performance was good overall on indicators measuring financing mobilized and transferred to DMCs. Financing for education fell short of the target. ADB made a strong start on aligning its new operations with Strategy 2030 priorities, especially gender equality.

Design and Implementation Quality

31. **Continuing strong design and procurement readiness.** The share of sovereign infrastructure projects that were design-ready was 83%, 3 percentage points above the annual target. The share of sovereign infrastructure projects that were procurement-ready increased by 4 percentage points to 50% in 2019, putting the performance of the indicator *on track* to reach the 2024 target of 60%.

32. **Monitoring of active portfolio enhanced.** In 2019, ADB piloted an enhanced methodology for rating the performance of sovereign projects under implementation, and a new indicator to measure the share of nonsovereign operations under implementation that are at risk of not delivering their intended development results. Based on provisional data, 52% of sovereign operations under implementation were rated *satisfactory* and 23% of nonsovereign operations sampled were rated *at risk* of not achieving development results. Both methodologies will be finalized and fully rolled out in 2020.

Mobilization and Transfer of Development Finance

33. **Sovereign disbursement rate *on target*.** ADB disbursed 93% ($9.5 billion) of its targeted $10.2 billion of financing for sovereign projects and results-based lending to its DMCs, exceeding the target of 90%.

34. **Nonsovereign cofinancing ratio higher.** The volume of long-term cofinancing for nonsovereign operations signed in 2017–2019 totaled $10.1 billion. Every $1.00 in financing ADB committed for its nonsovereign operations was matched by $1.43 in long-term cofinancing, achieving a 143% cofinancing ratio. This performance puts ADB *on track* to reach a ratio of 200% by 2024 and brings it closer to the Strategy 2030 target of 250% by 2030.

35. **Education financing share lower.** Education commitments made up 5.23% of total ADB commitments in 2019, which was slightly below the strong baseline of 5.43% and triggered a status of *off track* to meet the 2024 target range of 6%–10%. With $1.1 billion committed for 16 loans and grants, 2019 saw more operations but less financing committed than the record $1.6 billion in 2018.

36. **Health finance *on track*.** Financing for health reached 2.95% of total ADB commitments in 2019, a significant increase from the baseline of 1.75%, and close to the 2024 target range of 3%–5%. Health financing reached a record high of $636 million in 2019 with 13 loans and grants committed.

37. **Steady commitments in fragile and conflict-affected situations and small island developing states.** Operations committed in FCAS DMCs and SIDS as a share of total ADB commitments remained constant at 8% in 2019. FCAS DMCs accounted for 7% of commitments, while SIDS, some of which are also classified as FCAS, made up 2%.

38. **Project start-up time shortened.** The average time from concept approval to first disbursement in sovereign projects shortened by 1 month in 2019 to 30.5 months. The average start-up time for nonsovereign operations remained steady at 16.3 months in 2019. The longest processing stage is from concept approval to Board approval, which took 18.0 months for sovereign operations and 8.4 months for nonsovereign operations.

Alignment with Strategy 2030 Priorities

39. **Operational priorities.** During ADB's first full year of implementing Strategy 2030, 75% of committed operations were aligned with operational priority (OP) 1: Addressing remaining poverty and reducing inequalities; 92% with OP2: Accelerating progress in gender equality; 59% with OP3: Tackling climate change, building climate and disaster resilience, and enhancing environmental sustainability; 23% with OP4: Making cities more livable; 27% with OP5: Promoting rural development and food security; 68% with OP6: Strengthening governance and institutional capacity; and 22% with OP7: Fostering regional cooperation and integration.

40. **Increased focus on poverty reduction and inclusiveness.** The proportion of committed ADB operations contributing to poverty reduction and inclusiveness increased to 74% in 2017–2019 from a baseline of 70%, based on a provisional methodology. As in 2016–2018, 5% of committed ADB operations supported social protection. The share of operations committed in 2019 considered disability-inclusive or creating enabling conditions for disability inclusion was 22%.

Extra income. When not farming, Wang Bao and Mei Chunzhi help with the maintenance of roads built through an ADB-supported project in Yunnan Province, People's Republic of China (photo by Lu Jingwen).

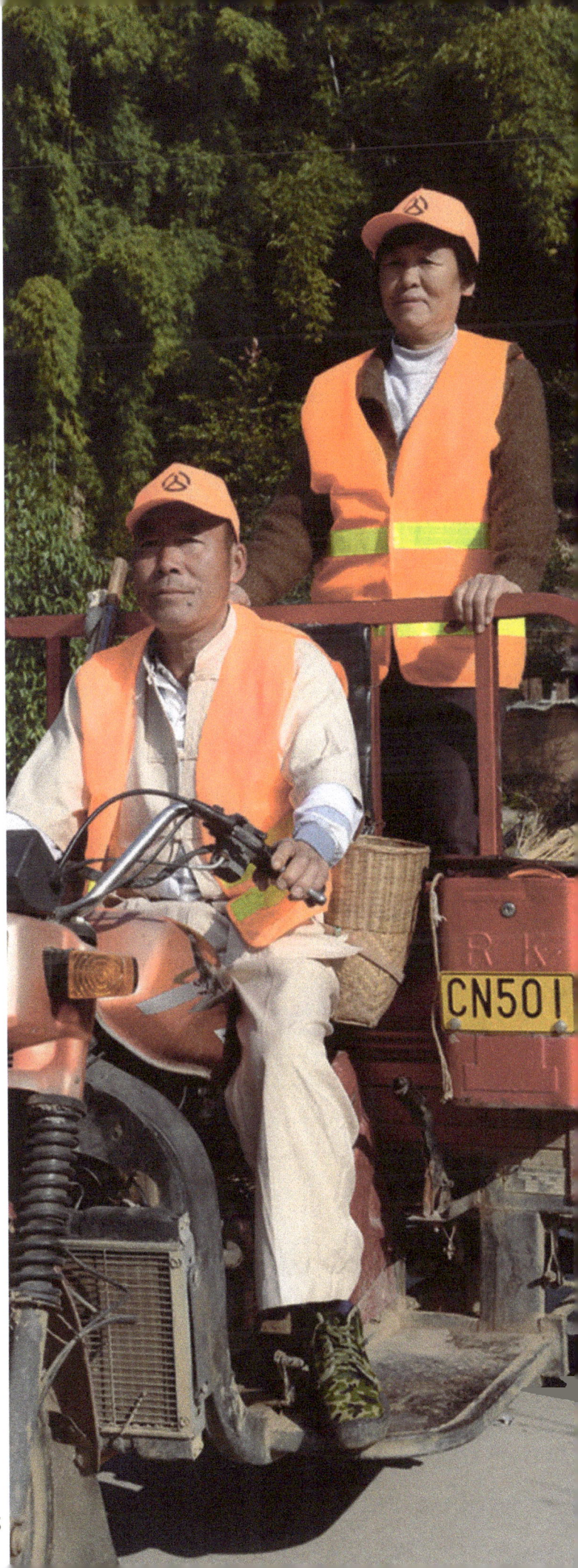

41. **Record gender mainstreaming commitments and financing.** The share of committed operations classified *gender equity theme* (GEN) or *effective gender mainstreaming* (EGM) reached 55% in 2017–2019 and the share classified GEN, EGM, or *some gender elements* (SGE) rose by 10 percentage points to 80%. Performance on both indicators exceeded the 2024 targets of 50% (for GEN or EGM) and 71% (for GEN, EGM, or SGE) and represented rapid early progress toward the Strategy 2030 targets of 55% (GEN and EGM) and 75% (GEN, EGM, and SGE). The share of financing for GEN and EGM operations reached historic highs of 51% of total ADB financing in 2017–2019 and 71% for the concessional assistance subset.

42. **Positive start on climate change mitigation and adaptation.** The proportion of ADB operations supporting climate change mitigation and/or adaptation increased to 59% during 2017–2019 from the 56% baseline. This indicator was rated *on track but watch* to achieve the 2024 target of 65% and the ambitious 2030 target of 75%. The share of operations supporting both mitigation and adaptation increased from 12% in 2016–2018 to 17% in 2017–2019, while support for adaptation alone declined by 2 percentage points to 26% and support for mitigation alone declined by 1 percentage point to 16%. For the concessional assistance subset, the share of operations supporting climate change mitigation and/or adaptation increased to 63% during 2017–2019 from the 58% baseline.

43. **Early headway toward climate financing target.** Strategy 2030 targets committing a cumulative total of $80 billion for climate change mitigation and/or adaptation from 2019 to 2030. In 2019, ADB committed $6.5 billion, or 30% of the total financing ADB committed that year. This was almost 50% more in total annual financing than ADB committed in any previous year. Operations supporting both mitigation and adaptation received total commitments of $3.3 billion, which was more than double the 3-year average of $1.2 billion committed in 2016–2018 and exceeded the total cumulative amount committed in the same period. Financing for operations supporting only mitigation declined slightly to $2.4 billion, while the volume supporting only adaptation increased marginally to $0.8 billion.

44. **Strong growth of the nonsovereign portfolio.** The share of nonsovereign operations in ADB's portfolio grew to 24% in 2019 from 20% in 2018 and was *on track* to reach the Strategy 2030 target of 33% by 2024. The volume of financing for nonsovereign operations declined to 17.5% of total ADB financing in 2019 from 19.3% in 2018. These results were in line with ADB's private sector operations strategy, which focuses on delivering more smaller-budget, higher-quality operations in a variety of frontier economies and new sectors.

45. **Target met for nonsovereign operations in frontier economies and new sectors.** In 2019, 61% of committed nonsovereign operations were in frontier economies and/or nontraditional sectors, up from the baseline of 48% and exceeding the 2024 target of 55%. Of these operations, 65% were in underserved markets (group A and B DMCs [Appendix 3]) and 35% were in sectors that are more challenging but have a higher potential for development impact.

Level 4: ADB's Organizational Effectiveness

Organizational Systems and Processes

46. **Budget utilization improved.** The quality of budget management was *on target,* with unutilized internal administrative expenses at 0% at the end of 2019, including 1.8% carryover to 2020.

47. **Robust capitalization.** The loan portfolio continued to grow in 2019, utilizing more cofinancing to optimize growth. Loan portfolio growth outpaced capital formation, resulting in a decline in the equity–loan ratio to 45.32% in 2019 from 47.48% in 2018.

48. **Nonsovereign credit quality largely unchanged.** Both the impaired loans ratio (4.8%) and the weighted average risk rating of nonsovereign operations (9.3 or B+) remained almost unchanged in 2019.

49. **Procurement time remained steady.** The proportion of procurement transactions for sovereign operations of $10 million or more that were processed within the target time of 40 days remained steady at 67% in 2019. There was a marked improvement in procurement processing time for concessional assistance operations, with 71% of procurement transactions processed within the target time compared with 60% in 2018. The indicator is rated *on track but watch* for ADB overall and *on track* for the concessional assistance subset.

50. **Representation of women *on track but watch.*** Women's share of ADB's international staff positions grew to 36.7% from 36.3% in 2018, although their representation in leadership roles (levels 7–8) declined to 24.1% from 26.1%.

51. **Increased One ADB collaboration.** Eight projects brought together private sector and sovereign operations expertise and knowledge in a "One ADB" approach. Progress was *on track* to meet the cumulative target of 18 projects by 2024.

Enhancing Organizational Capacity

52. **Digital transformation in progress.** A total of 27 digital products were completed in 2019, including the Partner Fund Management System, the e-Procurement system, and the Treasury System Improvement for Pricing.

53. **Slight reduction in staff share in field offices and slight increase in fragile and conflict-affected situations and small island developing states.** The share of ADB staff in field offices and assigned outposted positions declined by 3 percentage points to 45% in 2019, while ADB staff in FCAS and SIDS increased from 82 positions in 2018 to 84 in 2019. A strengthened field presence is needed to respond to Strategy 2030's calls for greater resident mission capacity and improving business processes in the field.

54. **Gradual transformation into knowledge and learning institution taking place.** Starting in 2005, ADB has conducted the globally benchmarked Most Admired Knowledge Enterprise (MAKE) survey. In 2019, ADB scored 65%, an improvement of 2 percentage points from 2018, and was rated *on track but watch* to achieve the 2024 target of 75%.

CHAPTER 1
STRATEGY 2030 OPERATIONAL PRIORITIES

SEVEN OPERATIONAL PRIORITIES AND THE SUSTAINABLE DEVELOPMENT GOALS

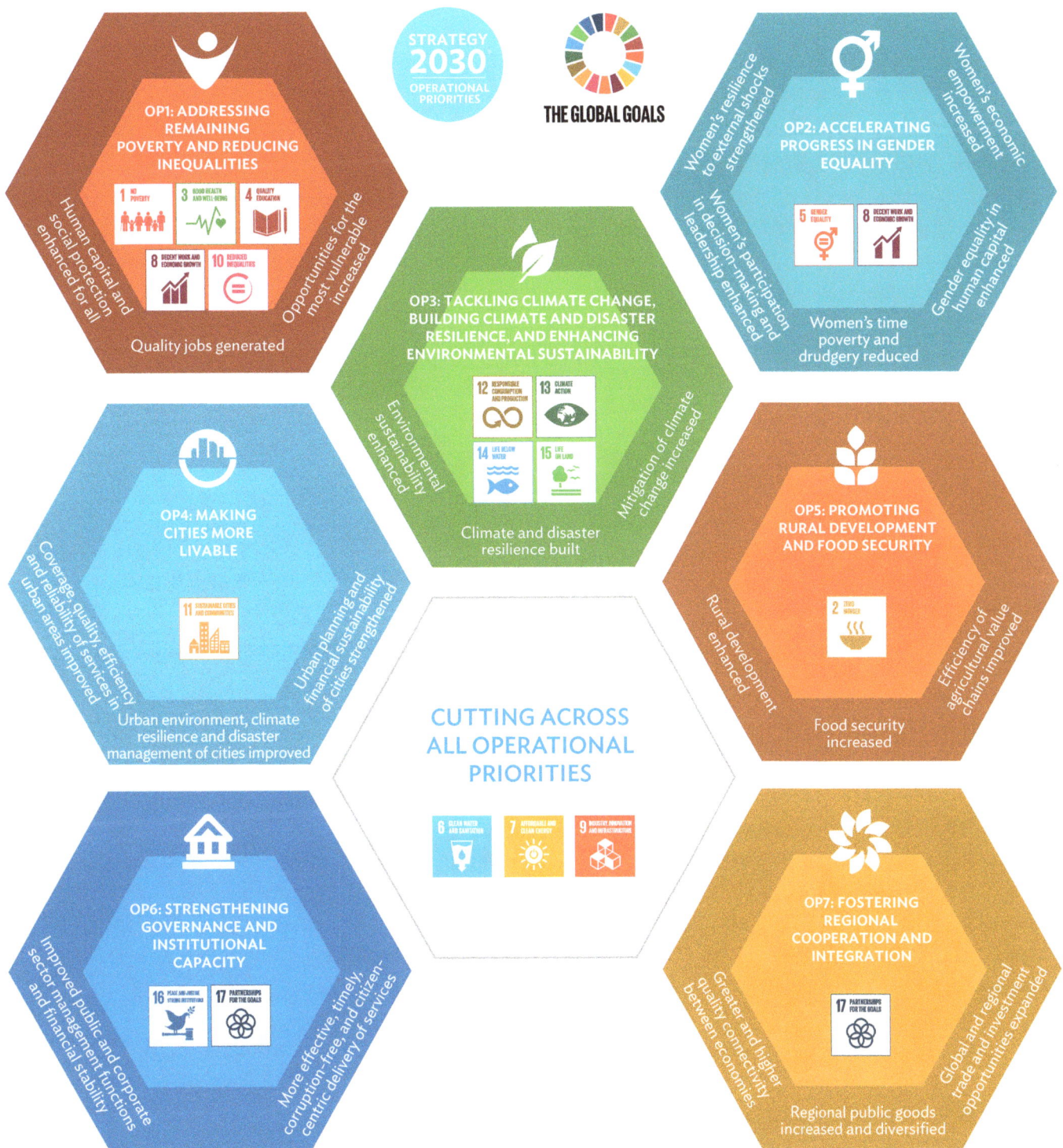

STRATEGY 2030 OPERATIONAL PRIORITIES

THE GLOBAL GOALS

OP1: ADDRESSING REMAINING POVERTY AND REDUCING INEQUALITIES

1 NO POVERTY
3 GOOD HEALTH AND WELL-BEING
4 QUALITY EDUCATION
8 DECENT WORK AND ECONOMIC GROWTH
10 REDUCED INEQUALITIES

Human capital and social protection enhanced for all

Opportunities for the most vulnerable increased

Quality jobs generated

OP2: ACCELERATING PROGRESS IN GENDER EQUALITY

5 GENDER EQUALITY
8 DECENT WORK AND ECONOMIC GROWTH

Women's resilience to external shocks strengthened

Women's participation in decision-making and leadership enhanced

Women's economic empowerment increased

Gender equality in human capital enhanced

Women's time poverty and drudgery reduced

OP3: TACKLING CLIMATE CHANGE, BUILDING CLIMATE AND DISASTER RESILIENCE, AND ENHANCING ENVIRONMENTAL SUSTAINABILITY

12 RESPONSIBLE CONSUMPTION AND PRODUCTION
13 CLIMATE ACTION
14 LIFE BELOW WATER
15 LIFE ON LAND

Environmental sustainability enhanced

Mitigation of climate change increased

Climate and disaster resilience built

OP4: MAKING CITIES MORE LIVABLE

11 SUSTAINABLE CITIES AND COMMUNITIES

Coverage, quality, efficiency and reliability of services in urban areas improved

Urban planning and financial sustainability of cities strengthened

Urban environment, climate resilience and disaster management of cities improved

OP5: PROMOTING RURAL DEVELOPMENT AND FOOD SECURITY

2 ZERO HUNGER

Rural development enhanced

Efficiency of agricultural value chains improved

Food security increased

CUTTING ACROSS ALL OPERATIONAL PRIORITIES

6 CLEAN WATER AND SANITATION
7 AFFORDABLE AND CLEAN ENERGY
9 INDUSTRY INNOVATION AND INFRASTRUCTURE

OP6: STRENGTHENING GOVERNANCE AND INSTITUTIONAL CAPACITY

16 PEACE AND JUSTICE STRONG INSTITUTIONS
17 PARTNERSHIPS FOR THE GOALS

Improved public and corporate sector management functions and financial stability

More effective, timely, corruption-free and citizen-centric delivery of services

OP7: FOSTERING REGIONAL COOPERATION AND INTEGRATION

17 PARTNERSHIPS FOR THE GOALS

Greater and higher quality connectivity between economies

Global and regional trade and investment opportunities expanded

Regional public goods increased and diversified

Strategy 2030 envisions a prosperous, resilient, inclusive, and sustainable Asia and the Pacific, and states that ADB's future operations will help developing member countries meet the Sustainable Development Goals. To achieve this vision, the strategy introduced seven operational priorities that take integrated thematic approaches reflecting the 2030 Agenda and align with the 17 Sustainable Development Goals. This chapter takes stock of the region's development progress as it relates to the operational priorities. It then highlights results delivered and new efforts initiated for each of the priorities in 2019.

A. REGIONAL PROGRESS

55.	Countries in Asia and the Pacific have made important progress on many critical development agendas, but that progress remains inadequate to meet the ambitious Sustainable Development Goals (SDGs).[3] Many parts of the region were affected by torrential flooding, heat waves, severe air pollution, episodes of unrest and violence, and escalating trade tensions. Realizing the Strategy 2030 vision of a prosperous, inclusive, resilient, and sustainable Asia and the Pacific is critical in a vulnerable region where rising affluence alone does not assure the attainment of the SDGs.

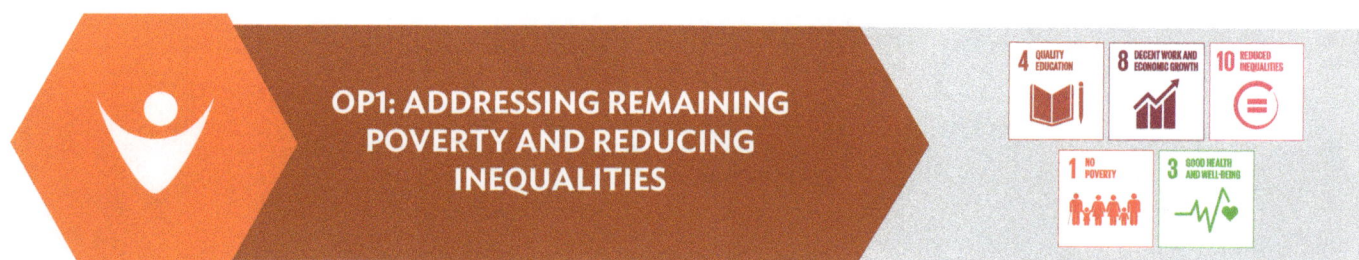

OP1: ADDRESSING REMAINING POVERTY AND REDUCING INEQUALITIES

56.	Despite dramatic reductions in recent decades, poverty is far from eliminated in the region. Extreme poverty still affects about 7% of the population, or 264 million people who live on less than $1.90 a day. About 29%, or 1.1 billion, live very close to the poverty line on less than $3.20 a day. Poverty persists even though average growth of gross domestic product (GDP) per capita across the region has remained robust at more than 5%.

57.	Inequality, although still largely entrenched, shows some improvement. Historical data on the official SDG indicator of inequality indicate that the income growth of the poorest 40% of households has narrowly outstripped that of the overall population. The region's average Gini coefficient of income distribution has also improved slightly since 2012 to a little over 34. Income inequality is particularly severe in South Asia, Southeast Asia, and in the most populous countries in the Pacific.

58.	Persistent impoverishment and inequities underline the critical need to expand the region's social protection systems and improve access to health care and other basic services. Universal health care coverage in the region has risen to an average score of 64.31 against a maximum of 100 on the World Health Organization index. About 47% of the region's population had access to basic social assistance in 2014, up from 40% in 2013. The proportion of the region's youth that were not in school, training, or employment also fell from about 22.3% in 2017 to 19.9% in 2018.

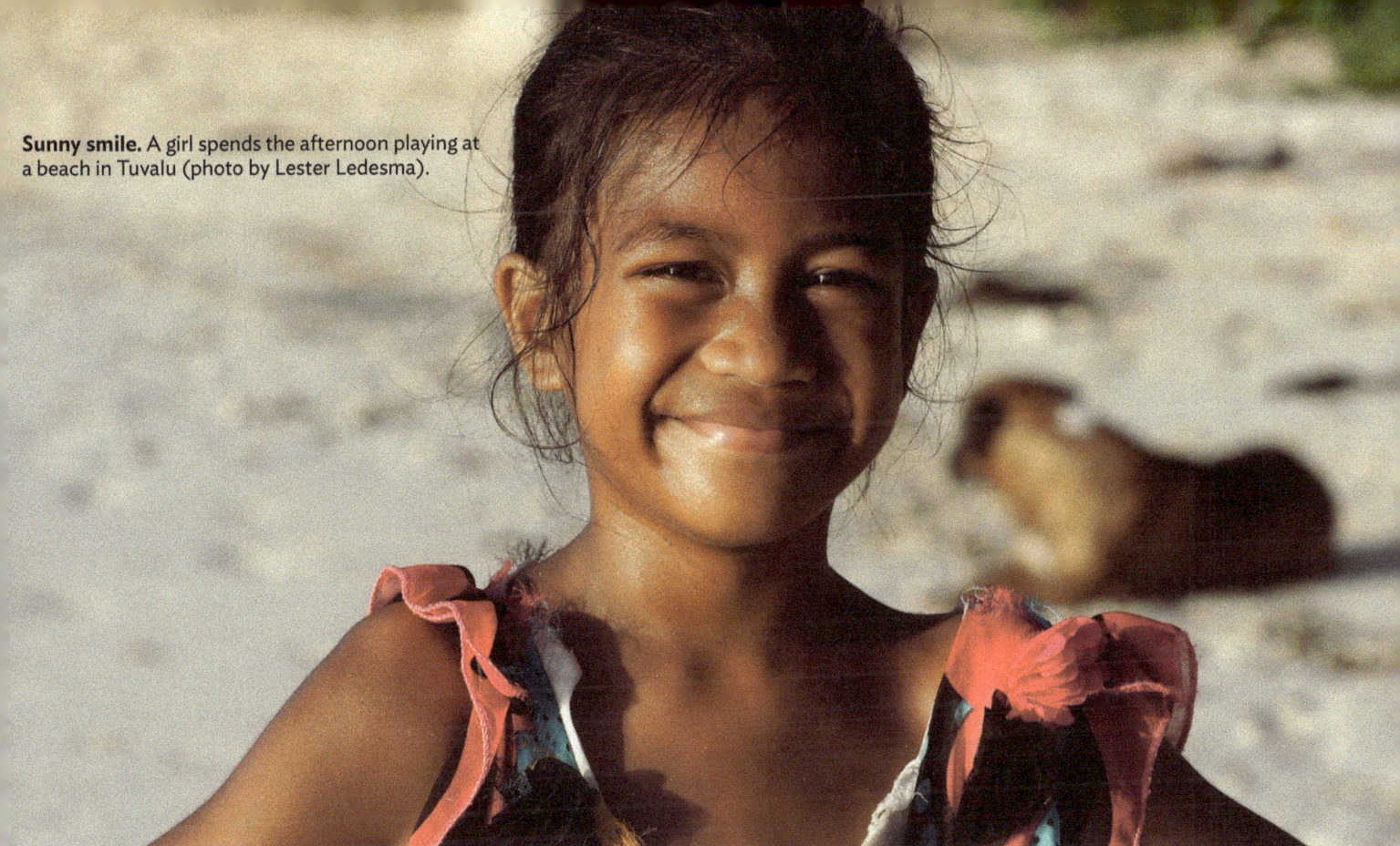

Sunny smile. A girl spends the afternoon playing at a beach in Tuvalu (photo by Lester Ledesma).

OP2: ACCELERATING PROGRESS IN GENDER EQUALITY

59. The SDGs will not be achieved without improving gender equality and realizing the enormous untapped potential of the region's women and girls. Only 50% of women participate in the formal labor force compared with 82% of men; unemployment rates in the formal labor force are higher among women (3.79%) than among men (3.51%), especially in ADB's concessional assistance countries (4.36% for women versus 2.69% for men); and a much higher percentage of young women than young men are not employed or in education or training (about 42% versus 13%).

60. A contributing socioeconomic factor is the greater amount of time women spend on unpaid care, some of which could be available for paid work, education, or improved quality of life. Limited data suggest women devote 12.3% of their time to unpaid care work, compared with 4.2% for men, while the International Labour Organization estimates women do four times more unpaid care work than men in Asia and the Pacific.[4] The statistics for financial inclusion show a large gap between the region overall and the concessional assistance countries: in Asia and the Pacific as a whole, 66% of women had access to financial services in 2017, compared with 73% of men; in the concessional assistance countries, only 26% of women and 42% of men had access.

21

OP3: TACKLING CLIMATE CHANGE, BUILDING CLIMATE AND DISASTER RESILIENCE, AND ENHANCING ENVIRONMENTAL SUSTAINABILITY

61. The overall carbon intensity of the region's economies continued to gradually decline, from 1.04 kilograms (kg) per dollar of GDP in 2014 to 0.90 kg in 2017. In the concessional assistance countries, however, it increased slightly from 0.64 kg to 0.68 kg in the same period. In absolute terms, greenhouse gas emissions continued to grow, tripling since 1990, and in 2018 developing countries in Asia and the Pacific were responsible for about half of global emissions.[5] Afforestation efforts have helped maintain overall forest cover, and marine protected area coverage has also remained steady, although pressure on ecosystems and biodiversity are high and continue to increase. As the region has grown richer, indicators of domestic material consumption have significantly worsened, and encouraging responsible consumption has emerged as a major challenge. Plastic pollution is now recognized as a critical issue, and countries in the region are a major source of the problem.[6]

62. The devastating effects of the 2019 monsoon season on communities across South Asia and Southwest Asia, compounded by record-breaking heat waves in May and June of that year, underscored the region's exposure to natural hazards and events brought on by climate change. Climate change linked to El Niño disruptions led to a harsh dry season that triggered severe fires in Indonesia's forests.[7] Climate-related hazards, including tropical storms and typhoons, hit some of the richest and poorest countries, causing significant damage and displacing or otherwise impacting millions of the region's people. However, the overall number of deaths attributed to such events was significantly lower at 4,815, than the 8,761 reported in 2018, because the geophysical hazards in 2019 were less severe. In concessional assistance countries, however, deaths increased.

OP4: MAKING CITIES MORE LIVABLE

63. Most people in Asia and the Pacific live in burgeoning cities that are hubs of growing prosperity but also face severe development constraints. Air quality has emerged as a major issue, taking a heavy toll on health and highlighting major shortcomings in urban planning and service delivery. While access to basic services is high, there is an urgent need for more sustainable transport, and the use of cleaner fuels for cooking and electricity generation, which can also support climate change mitigation. In 2019, all but one of the world's 100 most-polluted cities were in Asia and Pacific developing member countries (DMCs).[8] An ADB-supported study found that 61% of the region's large and medium-sized cities suffer from poor to critically poor air quality.[9] The air quality in ADB's DMCs was moderate overall in 2017, and the mean annual exposure to particulate matter 2.5 microns in diameter remained at about 61 micrograms per cubic meter for the region overall, and 49 micrograms per cubic meter in the concessional assistance countries.

OP5: PROMOTING RURAL DEVELOPMENT AND FOOD SECURITY

64. As the region urbanizes, poverty remains prevalent in many rural areas, particularly in localities that are not well connected to urban markets.[10] Rural people often move to cities because they cannot make ends meet, an issue that is linked to agricultural productivity and a lack of access to economic opportunities. Access to basic services, including infrastructure, health care, and education, is also generally lower in rural areas (Box 1.1). Food security and malnutrition are crucial problems for the region, where about 20% of children under the age of 5 were stunted in 2016, although this was less than the 2010–2016 average baseline of 29%. A 2018 United Nations report put the number of stunted children at 77.2 million and estimated that 32.5 million were wasted.[11] Yet this scarcity sits alongside evidence of plenty: one-fifth of food goes to waste in South Asia and Central Asia.[12] Progress needs to be made on SDG 2 (Zero Hunger) targets of halving global consumer and retail food waste, including in production and supply chains.

Box 1.1: Access to Infrastructure Is Improving, but Rural Areas Lag Urban Areas in Asia and Pacific Developing Member Countries

By 2017, urban access to basic water services had increased substantially to 97% and access to basic sanitation had risen to 87%. Despite improvement, rural areas still lag urban areas: only 49% of rural populations had basic water services and 63% had access to basic sanitation. In addition, much more effort will be required in all areas to reach the Sustainable Development Goal targets for the proportion of the population using safely managed drinking water, safely managed sanitation services, and a hand-washing facility with soap and water. About 94% of the population had access to electricity, but access was higher in urban areas (98%) than rural areas (89%). Access to clean cooking fuel is also a major challenge: in 2016, nearly 50% of people still relied on polluting fuels such as kerosene and biomass.

OP6: STRENGTHENING GOVERNANCE AND INSTITUTIONAL CAPACITY

65. Improving governance and establishing more capable and accountable institutions are central to solving the region's development issues. DMCs' scores on the World Governance Index improved compared with the preceding year, but the aggregate scores were negative on all six of the index pillars (Figure 1.1). Weak regulatory quality particularly affects private sector development in the region.

Figure 1.1: ADB Developing Member Country Scores on World Governance Indicators

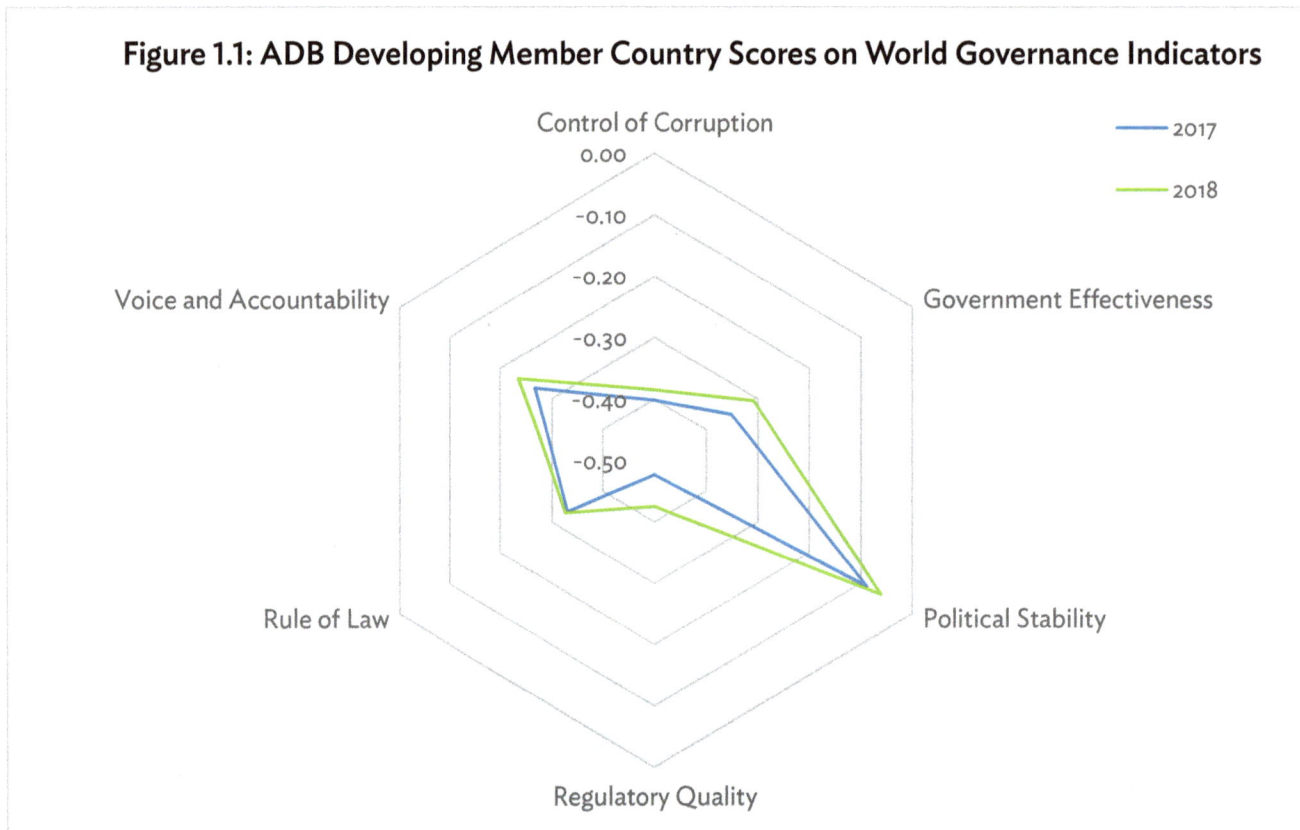

66. The problems of limited institutional capacity and mobilizing domestic resources and financing are closely linked in many DMCs. After many years with some of the lowest rates of tax collection in the world, tax revenue as a share of GDP in ADB DMCs rose slightly from 12% in 2017 to 14% in 2018.

OP7: FOSTERING REGIONAL COOPERATION AND INTEGRATION

67. In an increasingly interconnected world, regional cooperation and integration can play a central role in enabling progress toward the SDGs and realizing ADB's vision. Constant scores on the ADB Asia-Pacific Regional Cooperation and Integration Index suggest that overall cooperation has been stable (Figure 1.2). While infrastructure and connectivity have improved, in a global context of trade tensions and weakening global demand, scores for trade and investment, and regional value chains were adversely affected, particularly in concessional assistance countries. The data also suggest that financial and monetary cooperation fell slightly in the DMCs.

**Figure 1.2: Asia-Pacific Regional Cooperation and Integration Index
ADB Developing Member Country Scores, 2017**
(0= not integrated, 1= fully integrated)

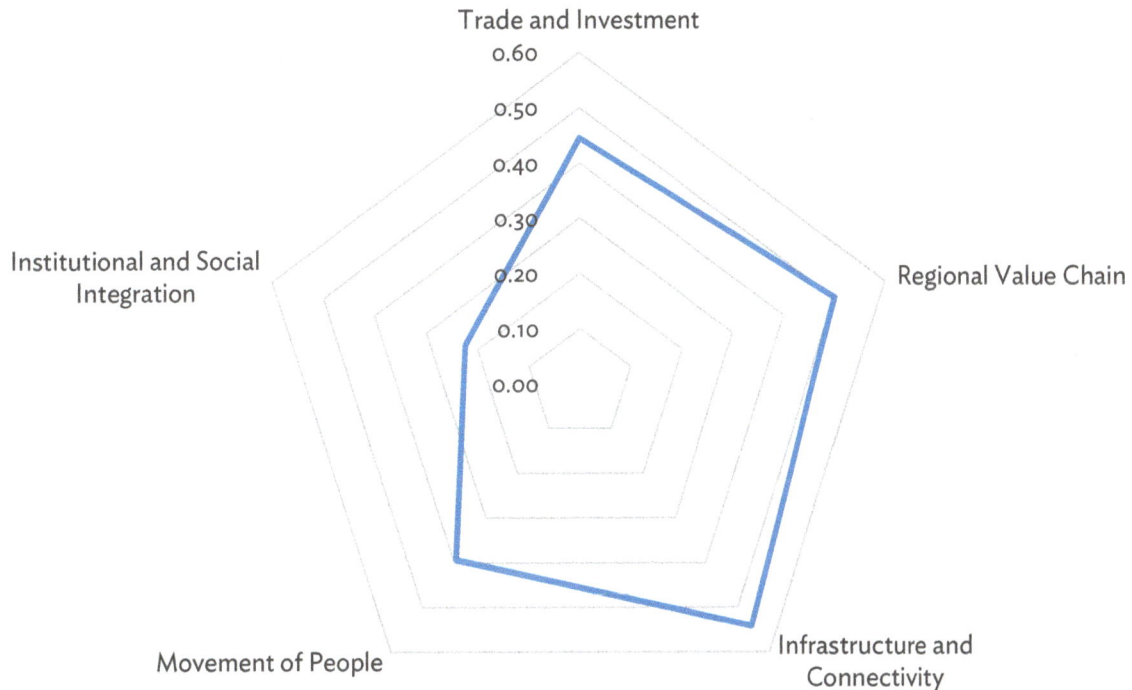

B. SEVEN OPERATIONAL PRIORITIES: HIGHLIGHTS

68.   Asia and the Pacific faces pressing development challenges related to the seven operational priorities of Strategy 2030. ADB is responding to these challenges, and this section highlights early efforts to implement the operational priorities. Pages 26–41 provide the results of completed operations, new operations committed in 2019, and selected project synopses that bring ADB's efforts to life.

SEVEN OPERATIONAL PRIORITIES AND REGIONAL DEVELOPMENT PROGRESS

OP 1 ADDRESSING REMAINING POVERTY AND REDUCING INEQUALITIES

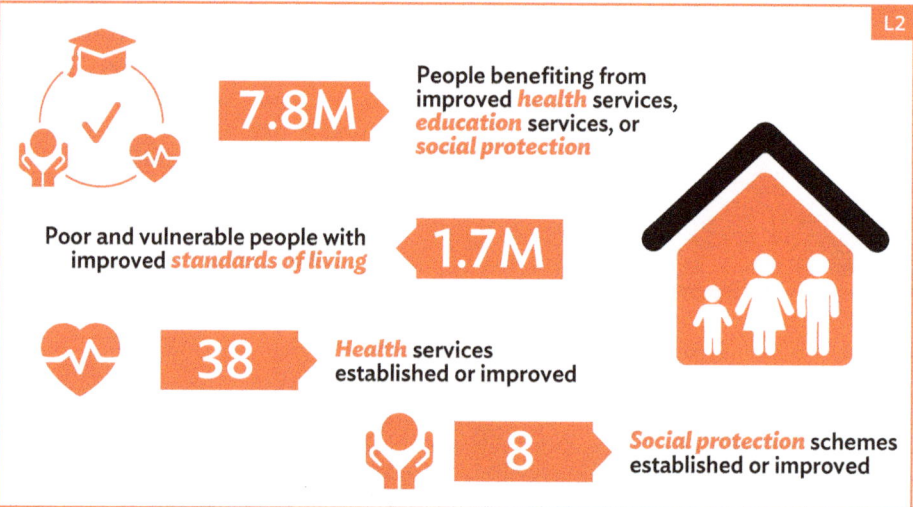

L1

1.1B
(29% of the population)
People living under $3.2 per day

264M
People living under $1.9 per day

47%
Social assistance coverage

L2

7.8M People benefiting from improved *health* services, *education* services, or *social protection*

1.7M Poor and vulnerable people with improved *standards of living*

38 *Health* services established or improved

8 *Social protection* schemes established or improved

OP 2 ACCELERATING PROGRESS IN GENDER EQUALITY

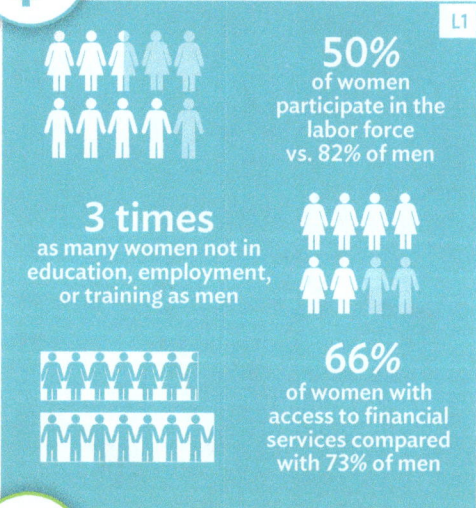

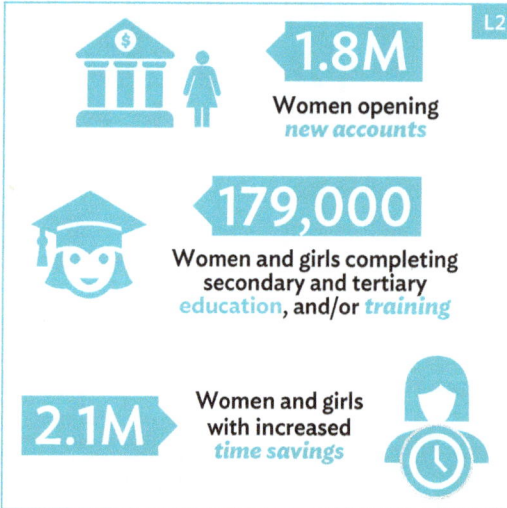

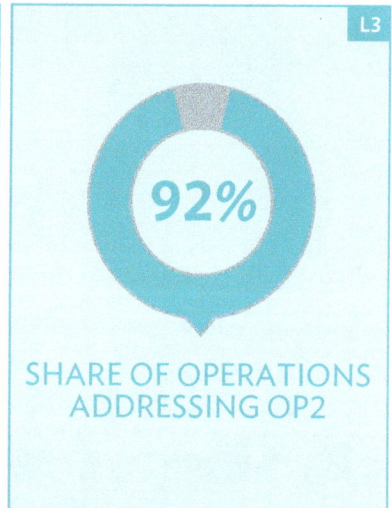

L1

50% of women participate in the labor force vs. 82% of men

3 times as many women not in education, employment, or training as men

66% of women with access to financial services compared with 73% of men

L2

1.8M Women opening *new accounts*

179,000 Women and girls completing secondary and tertiary *education*, and/or *training*

2.1M Women and girls with increased *time savings*

L3

92%

SHARE OF OPERATIONS ADDRESSING OP2

OP 3 TACKLING CLIMATE CHANGE, BUILDING CLIMATE AND DISASTER RESILIENCE, AND ENHANCING ENVIRONMENTAL SUSTAINABILITY

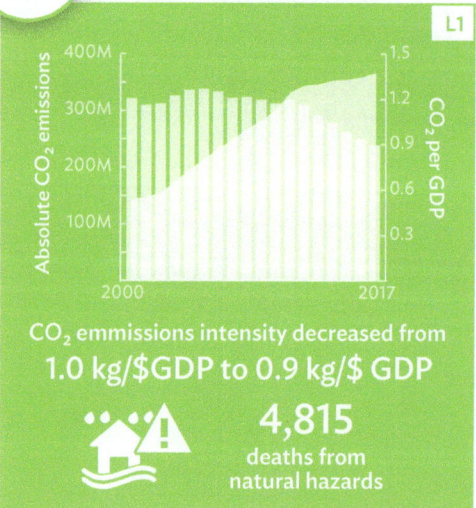

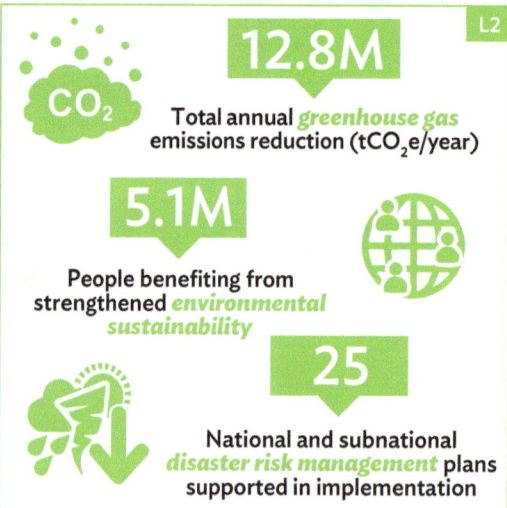

L1

Absolute CO_2 emissions
400M
300M
200M
100M
2000   2017

CO_2 per GDP
1.5
1.2
0.9
0.6
0.3

CO_2 emmissions intensity decreased from 1.0 kg/$GDP to 0.9 kg/$ GDP

4,815 deaths from natural hazards

L2

CO_2

12.8M Total annual *greenhouse gas* emissions reduction (tCO_2e/year)

5.1M People benefiting from strengthened *environmental sustainability*

25 National and subnational *disaster risk management* plans supported in implementation

L3

59%

SHARE OF OPERATIONS ADDRESSING OP3

OP 4 MAKING CITIES MORE LIVABLE

L1

Pollution stayed at PM 2.5 of 60.65 µg per m³

Region hosts 99 of the world's 100 most polluted cities

Urban access to

WATER	97%
SANITATION	87%

L2

2.8M People benefiting from improved *services* in *urban* areas

37 Zones with improved urban *environment*, climate *resilience*, and *disaster risk* management

L3

23%

SHARE OF OPERATIONS ADDRESSING OP4

OP 5 PROMOTING RURAL DEVELOPMENT AND FOOD SECURITY

L1

20% of children stunted

Access to basic

WATER	49%
SANITATION	63%
ELECTRICITY	89%

L2

6.6M People benefiting from increased *rural investment*

176,000 Hectares of *land* with higher *productivity*

L3

27%

SHARE OF OPERATIONS ADDRESSING OP5

OP 6 STRENGTHENING GOVERNANCE AND INSTITUTIONAL CAPACITY

L1

World Governance Index

-0.29

-0.5   +2.5

Tax to GDP Ratios 11.6% in 2017 to 13.9% in 2018

L2

1,700 Entities with improved *management functions* and financial stability

33 *Transparency* and *accountability* measures supported in implementation

L3

68%

SHARE OF OPERATIONS ADDRESSING OP6

OP 7 FOSTERING REGIONAL COOPERATION AND INTEGRATION

L1

Asian Regional Cooperation and Integration Index (ARCII)

0.43

0   1

ARCII score remained stable despite trade tensions

L2

$237.4M *Trade* and *investment* facilitated

16 Measures to improve the *efficiency* and/or *connectivity* supported in implementation

L3

22%

SHARE OF OPERATIONS ADDRESSING OP7

µg/m3 = micrograms per cubic meter, B = billion, CO₂ = carbon dioxide, GDP = gross domestic product, kg = kilogram, L1 = Level 1: Development Progress in Asia and the Pacific, L2 = Level 2: Results from ADB Completed Operations, L3 = Level 3: ADB Operations Committed in 2019, M = million, OP = operational priority, PM2.5 = particulate matter less than 2.5 microns in diameter, tCO₂e/year = tons of carbon dioxide equivalent per year.

✅ **7.8M**
PEOPLE

BENEFITING FROM IMPROVED HEALTH SERVICES, EDUCATION SERVICES, OR SOCIAL PROTECTION

76,000
PEOPLE ENROLLED IN IMPROVED EDUCATION AND/OR TRAINING

38
HEALTH SERVICES IMPROVED

✅ **313,000**
JOBS

DIRECTLY GENERATED

720
INFRASTRUCTURE ASSETS ESTABLISHED OR IMPROVED

✅ **1.7M**
PEOPLE

POOR AND VULNERABLE PEOPLE WITH IMPROVED STANDARDS OF LIVING

Results are from project completion reports, extended annual review reports, and technical assistance completion reports circulated from 1 January 2019 to 15 November 2019.

OPERATIONS COMMITTED IN 2019

% OF TOTAL 2019 COMMITMENTS

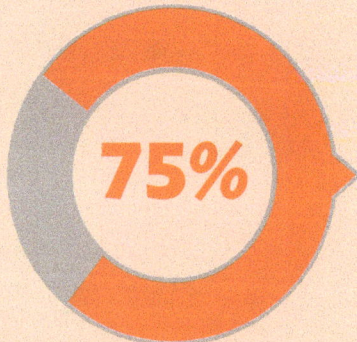

75%

109 OF 146 PROJECTS

BY SECTOR

Sector	Share of operations supporting OP1	Number of operations supporting OP1
TRANSPORT	25%	27
ANR	22%	24
WUS	22%	24
FINANCE	19%	21
EDUCATION	15%	16
ENERGY	12%	13
HEALTH	12%	13
PSM	10%	11
INDUSTRY AND TRADE	4%	4
ICT	3%	3

■ Share of operations supporting OP1
■ Number of operations supporting OP1

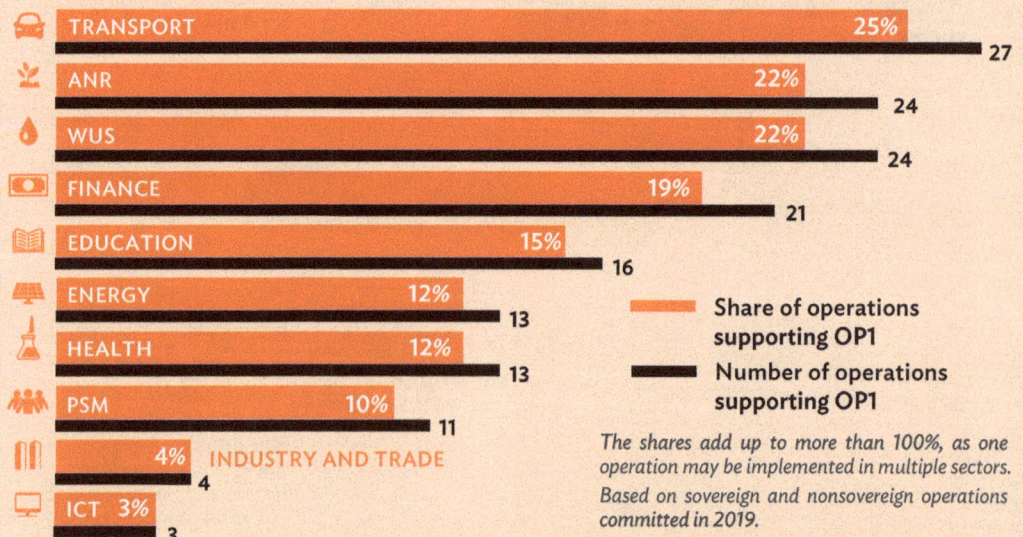

The shares add up to more than 100%, as one operation may be implemented in multiple sectors. Based on sovereign and nonsovereign operations committed in 2019.

ANR = agriculture, natural resources, and rural development, ICT = infomation and communication technology, M = million, OP = operational priority, PSM = public sector management, WUS = water and other urban infrastructure and services.

Lack of electricity in Viet Nam's remote mountain provinces has greatly limited opportunities for some of the country's poorest and most vulnerable people. With ADB support of more than $150 million through the **Renewable Energy Development and Network Expansion and Rehabilitation for Remote Communes Sector Project**, the government was able to finance rural electrification and the development of renewable energy in remote communes, particularly in northern and central Viet Nam. New mini hydropower plants and expanded or rehabilitated grids brought power to 3,119 villages. With reliable and affordable electricity, about 768,000 poor and vulnerable people are now empowered to create and pursue opportunities for a more productive and better life.

The mountains of Nepal are breathtaking, but the people living in these areas suffer from pervasive poverty, partly because of poor road connectivity. ADB supported inclusive growth in the country with $65 million in loans and grants focused on 18 very remote hill and mountain districts.

The **Decentralized Rural Infrastructure and Livelihood Project** and its additional financing generated jobs for more than 150,000 residents, of which 36% were women and 22% were from marginalized ethnic and social groups. A total of 776 kilometers of roads and 422 trail bridges were rehabilitated or newly built and about 640,000 people now have much smoother and more reliable access to markets and social services.

Reducing poverty and tackling inequalities remain at the core of ADB's activities. Projects completed in 2019 helped millions of poor and vulnerable people increase their standard of living, mainly by providing better infrastructure services. Operations committed in 2019 are introducing new solutions for tackling poverty and reducing inequalities, including through better elderly care. ADB also began developing an approach to better identify potential projects that support poverty reduction and inclusiveness, particularly disability inclusion.

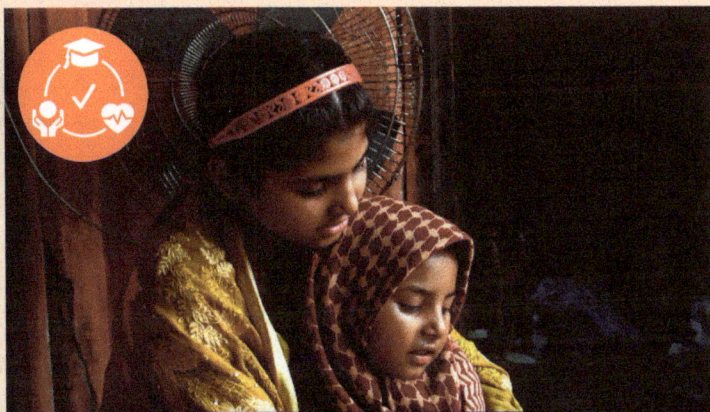

Despite impressive progress, a quarter of Pakistan's 200 million people remain poor. This is mainly because of poor health outcomes, lack of education, and overall low human capital investment. To overcome this challenge, the government sustains its flagship Benazir Income Support Program (BISP)—one of the largest social protection programs in South Asia. ADB has been supporting the BISP since 2013 with the **Social Protection Development Project,** and in 2019 it added a further $200 million to help expand the coverage of the BISP's cash transfer program. Such programs can provide a financial cushion for the poor and boost human capital development by improving health, education, and nutrition. The additional assistance will help increase health insurance coverage, bringing the total number of beneficiaries to 5.6 million.

The People's Republic of China has the largest elderly population in the world, and the growing demand for elderly care far outpaces existing services. In 2019, ADB committed a $150 million loan for the **Hubei Yichang Comprehensive Elderly Care Demonstration Project** to develop a comprehensive elderly care system in Yichang, a city of 4.14 million people, 22% of whom are over 60 years of age. It is envisioned that the project will serve as a model for similar developments in other towns and cities as part of the government's drive for elderly care reform. The activities that the project will support include the construction or rehabilitation of 16 community-based elderly care centers, construction of one dementia care center, and elderly care training.

☑ **179,000**
WOMEN AND GIRLS

COMPLETING EDUCATION, AND/OR OTHER TRAINING

☑ **59,000**
SKILLED JOBS

GENERATED FOR WOMEN

☑ **14,000**
WOMEN

REPRESENTED IN DECISION-MAKING STRUCTURES AND PROCESSES

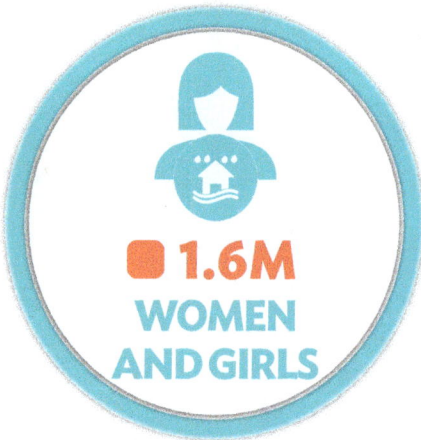

☑ **1.6M**
WOMEN AND GIRLS

WITH INCREASED RESILIENCE TO CLIMATE CHANGE, DISASTERS, AND OTHER EXTERNAL SHOCKS

☑ **2.1M**
WOMEN AND GIRLS

WITH INCREASED TIME SAVINGS

75% IN 2018   **74% IN 2019**   **80% BY 2024**

OPERATIONS

COMPLETED OPERATIONS DELIVERING GENDER RESULTS

Results are from project completion reports, extended annual review reports, and technical assistance completion reports circulated from 1 January 2019 to 15 November 2019.

OPERATIONS COMMITTED IN 2019

% OF TOTAL 2019 COMMITMENTS

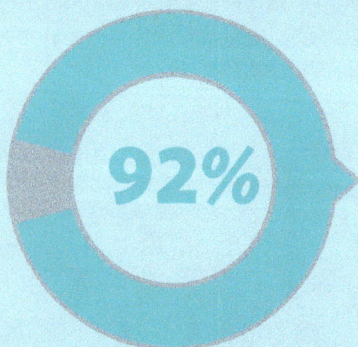

92%

134 OF 146 PROJECTS

BY SECTOR

Sector	Share of operations supporting OP2	Number of operations supporting OP2
TRANSPORT	22%	29
FINANCE	18%	24
ENERGY	17%	23
ANR	16%	22
WUS	16%	21
EDUCATION	12%	16
PSM	12%	16
HEALTH	10%	13
INDUSTRY AND TRADE	5%	7
ICT	1%	2

■ Share of operations supporting OP2
■ Number of operations supporting OP2

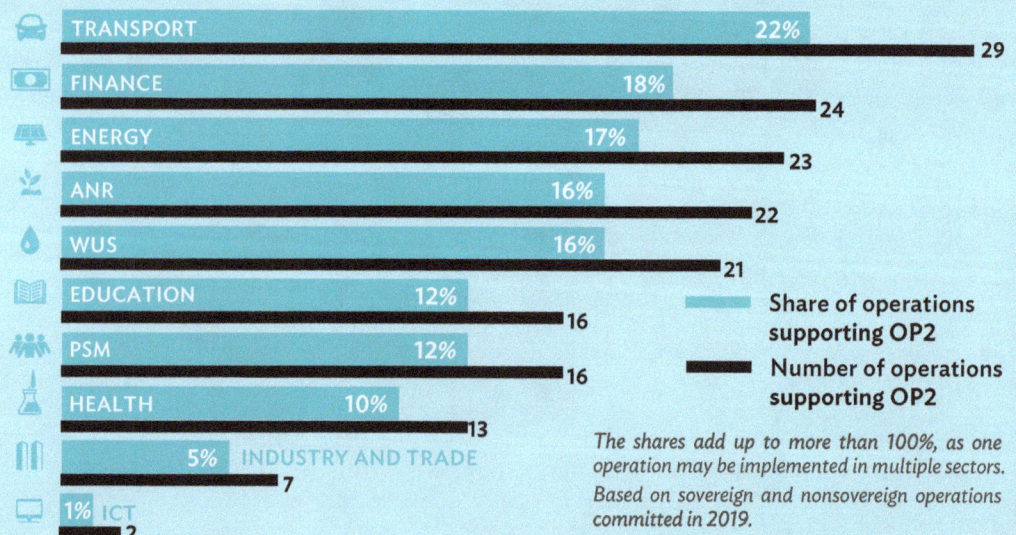

The shares add up to more than 100%, as one operation may be implemented in multiple sectors.
Based on sovereign and nonsovereign operations committed in 2019.

ANR = agriculture, natural resources, and rural development, ICT = information and communication technology, M = million, OP = operational priority, PSM = public sector management, WUS = water and other urban infrastructure and services.

Completed Operations Delivering Gender Equality Results

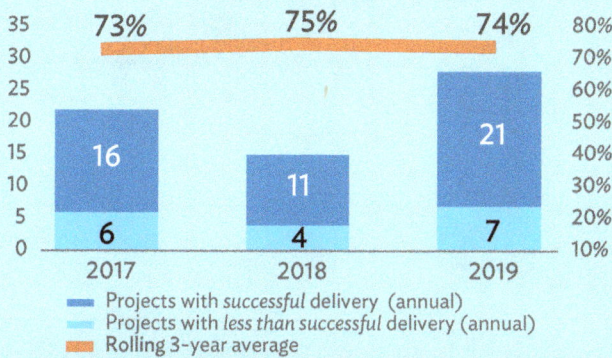

	2017	2018	2019
Rolling 3-year average	73%	75%	74%
Projects with successful delivery (annual)	16	11	21
Projects with less than successful delivery (annual)	6	4	7

- Projects with *successful* delivery (annual)
- Projects with *less than successful* delivery (annual)
- Rolling 3-year average

For the first time, the 2019 Development Effectiveness Review reports the delivery of gender equality results for both sovereign and nonsovereign completed operations. It also tracks progress toward the more ambitious 2024 target of 80%.

Of the 28 operations completed in 2019, 21 (75%) successfully delivered their intended gender results, bringing the 3-year average for 2017–2019 to 74%—slightly lower than in 2016–2018. All operations in water and urban development, transport, and energy were *successful*. Two of three nonsovereign operations completed in 2019 failed to achieve gender results in part because of the client's lack of awareness of the gender action plan. This underscores the importance of constant engagement and awareness-raising among private sector clients.

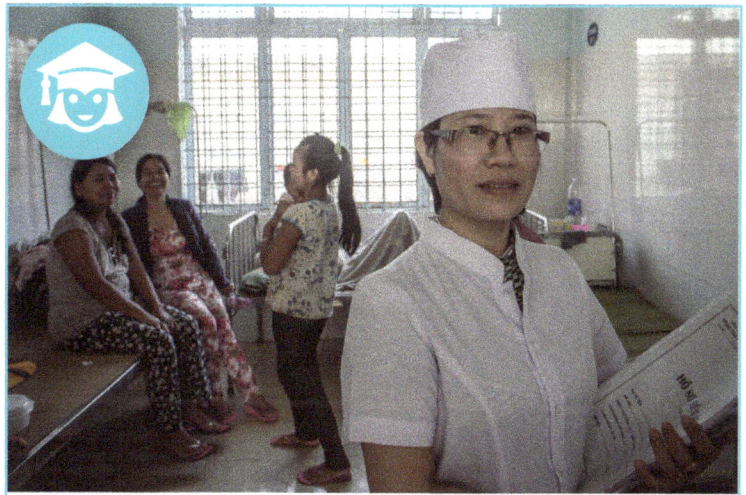

ADB's **Health Human Resources Sector Development Program** supported key reform actions in health workforce management in Viet Nam to help the government make health benefits more equitable and widely available across the country. The program developed new care pathways for quality inpatient services for women, provided scholarships and training programs to enhance the quality of sexual and reproductive health services, and expanded practitioner licensing and registration to all nurses and doctors. More than 9,000 women received scholarships and financial support for training programs for hospital services, and 28,000 female doctors and 94,000 female nurses have been licensed and are providing superior health care services nationwide.

ADB made headway in promoting gender equality in 2019. Record numbers of ADB operations committed in 2019 mainstream gender, addressing key gender gaps related to women's safety, mobility, access to services, and decision-making. Operations completed in 2019 helped women and girls save time, find employment, and get a better education.

● *Roads were only partially climate-proofed through a completed project in Viet Nam, leading to a shortfall in the number of women beneficiaries with improved climate resilience.*

Overcrowding and accidents on Mumbai's suburban rail system cause more than 3,000 deaths every year, endangering more than 7.5 million daily passengers. Women are not only particularly affected by these issues, but also face challenges related to personal safety.

To improve commuters' welfare and security, the **Mumbai Metro Rail Systems Project** will fund 63 six-car trains, as well as signaling and safety systems. The project will introduce women-only carriages, mobile applications to enhance women's security, and a station with an all-female staff. Commercial spaces in metro stations will be allotted to women-led businesses, and a multi-stakeholder committee will be established to support a gender equality policy for the Mumbai Metro Operations Organization.

Microenterprises can promote private sector-led economic growth by developing forward links and creating self- and wage-employment opportunities. But women entrepreneurs in Bangladesh face numerous hurdles. Limited access to finance is one of the greatest challenges for women entrepreneurs there, along with lack of business management skills, equal opportunities, and business networking support.

The **Microenterprise Development Project** in Bangladesh is improving microenterprises' access to finance through the Palli Karma Sahayak Foundation, an apex development finance and capacity building not-for-profit company that promotes poverty reduction through sustainable employment generation. The foundation will onlend funds to partner organizations to finance about 40,000 microenterprises, 70% of them women-owned.

RESULTS DELIVERED IN 2019

CO_2
☑12.8M
TCO$_2$E/YEAR

19
LOW-CARBON SOLUTIONS PROMOTED AND IMPLEMENTED

TOTAL ANNUAL GREENHOUSE GAS EMISSIONS REDUCED

18
LOW-CARBON INFRASTRUCTURE ASSETS ESTABLISHED OR IMPROVED

49,000
HECTARES OF AREA WITH REDUCED FLOOD RISK

3.2M PEOPLE

5.1M PEOPLE

26
POLLUTION CONTROL ENHANCING INFRASTRUCTURE ASSETS ESTABLISHED OR IMPROVED

WITH STRENGTHENED CLIMATE AND DISASTER RESILIENCE

BENEFITING FROM STRENGTHENED ENVIRONMENTAL SUSTAINABILITY

25
DISASTER RISK REDUCTION AND MANAGEMENT PLANS SUPPORTED IN IMPLEMENTATION

Results are from project completion reports, extended annual review reports, and technical assistance completion reports circulated from 1 January 2019 to 15 November 2019.

OPERATIONS COMMITTED IN 2019

% OF TOTAL 2019 COMMITMENTS

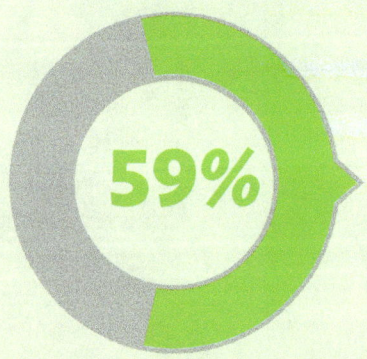

59%

86 OF 146 PROJECTS

BY SECTOR

Sector	Share	Number
TRANSPORT	35%	30
ENERGY	29%	25
WUS	27%	23
ANR	24%	21
EDUCATION	7%	6
HEALTH	6%	5
FINANCE	5%	4
PSM	5%	4
INDUSTRY AND TRADE	3%	3
ICT	1%	1

- Share of operations supporting OP3
- Number of operations supporting OP3

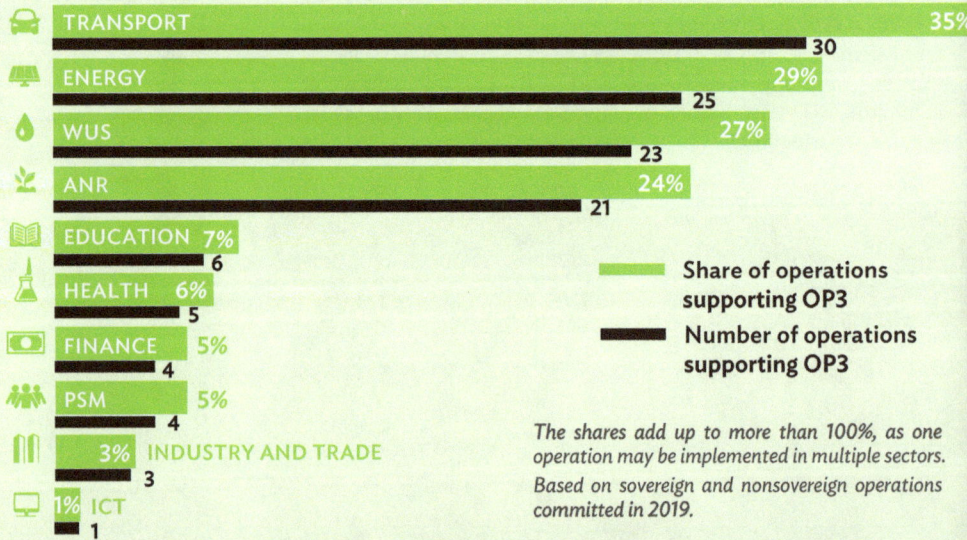

The shares add up to more than 100%, as one operation may be implemented in multiple sectors. Based on sovereign and nonsovereign operations committed in 2019.

ANR = agriculture, natural resources, and rural development, ICT = infomation and communication technology, M = million, OP = operational priority, PSM = public sector management, tCO$_2$e/yr = tons of carbon dioxide equivalent per year, WUS = water and other urban infrastructure and services.

The Philippines is estimated to have 250,000 megawatts (MW) of untapped renewable energy resources. The Department of Energy is targeting 2,870 MW of additional installed capacity from these sources by 2030 to reduce reliance on fossil fuels.

The nonsovereign **150-Megawatt Burgos Wind Farm Project** constructed 50 3.0 MW wind turbines in Burgos in Ilocos Norte Province, along with a substation and ancillary facilities. Actual net power generation from the project reached 376 gigawatt-hours in 2018, surpassing expectations by 30%. The project supported the government's push to diversify its energy sources and reduce harmful greenhouse gas emissions, avoiding about 174,000 tons of carbon dioxide equivalent annually.

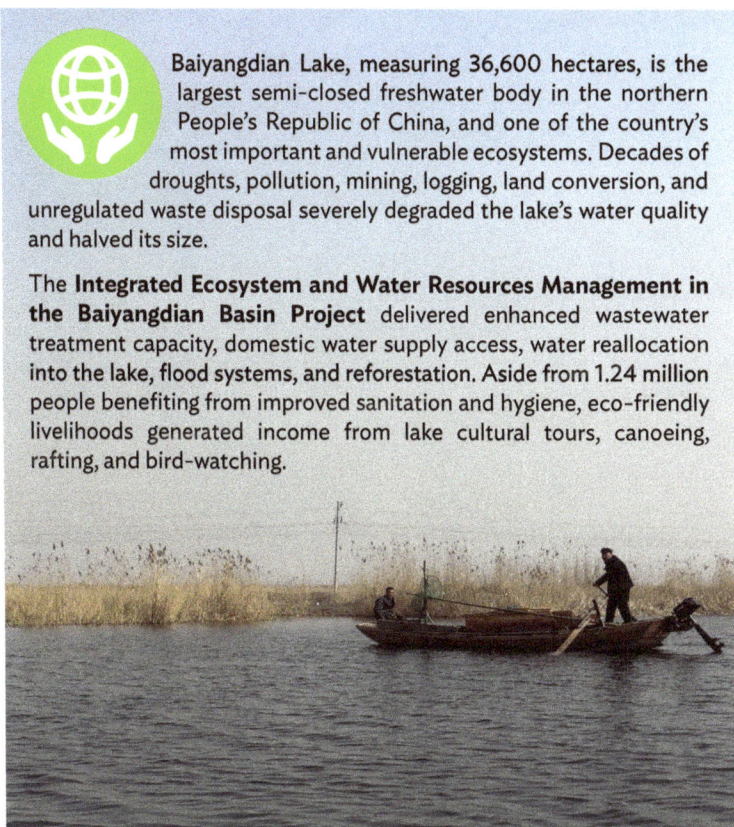

Baiyangdian Lake, measuring 36,600 hectares, is the largest semi-closed freshwater body in the northern People's Republic of China, and one of the country's most important and vulnerable ecosystems. Decades of droughts, pollution, mining, logging, land conversion, and unregulated waste disposal severely degraded the lake's water quality and halved its size.

The **Integrated Ecosystem and Water Resources Management in the Baiyangdian Basin Project** delivered enhanced wastewater treatment capacity, domestic water supply access, water reallocation into the lake, flood systems, and reforestation. Aside from 1.24 million people benefiting from improved sanitation and hygiene, eco-friendly livelihoods generated income from lake cultural tours, canoeing, rafting, and bird-watching.

Climate change, natural disasters, and deteriorating environments pose increasing risks to many countries in Asia and the Pacific. Strategy 2030 puts the climate agenda at the forefront of its activities, setting ambitious targets for climate mitigation and adaptation operations, and aiming to decouple economic growth from environmental degradation. In 2019, ADB stepped up its interventions in this area and delivered important contributions to reducing emissions and improving environmental sustainability for millions of people.

Carbon dioxide emissions reduction targets were not fully achieved for the concessional assistance subset—the outputs for two projects were not completed, while the assumptions made at the design stage for a third project were no longer valid at completion.

The Khuvsgul Lake and Onon-Balj national parks in Mongolia are among the government's ecotourism priorities. However, the unexpectedly rapid rise in tourists has created severe seasonal congestion and damaged natural resources, while providing fewer than expected benefits for local residents.

The **Sustainable Tourism Development Project** aims to help promote community-based tourism in these two national parks by providing the residents training on touring camps and livelihood programs focused on local products, as well as implementing infrastructure subprojects such as the improvement of ecotourism trails and sanitation facilities. These will benefit visitors and more than 11,000 people in the project areas, while helping the Khuvsgul Lake and Onon-Balj national parks meet the social, environmental, and sustainability criteria of the International Union for Conservation of Nature.

Rural livelihoods in Myanmar are heavily dependent on weather patterns. Climate change disrupts agriculture, the main source of income, affecting people's quality of life and exposing them to hazards and vulnerabilities.

The $195 million loan and grant for the **Resilient Community Development Project** will focus on 17 of the poorest townships in the Ayeyarwady, Chin, Sagaing, and Tanintharyi regions that are exposed to climate and disaster risks. It will help identify, develop, and fund 3,000 infrastructure subprojects covering climate- and disaster-resilient farm roads, bridges, water supply, and electricity connections. About 15,000 resilient livelihood subprojects on climate-smart agricultural practices will benefit 1.8 million people in 3,000 villages.

✅ 2.8M
PEOPLE

BENEFITING FROM IMPROVED SERVICES IN URBAN AREAS

86
URBAN INFRASTRUCTURE ASSETS ESTABLISHED OR IMPROVED

✅ 37
ZONES

WITH IMPROVED URBAN ENVIRONMENT, CLIMATE RESILIENCE, AND DISASTER RISK MANAGEMENT

17
SOLUTIONS TO ENHANCE URBAN ENVIRONMENT IMPLEMENTED

✅ 98
ENTITIES

WITH IMPROVED URBAN PLANNING AND FINANCIAL SUSTAINABILITY

12
MEASURES TO IMPROVE REGULATORY, LEGAL, AND INSTITUTIONAL ENVIRONMENT FOR BETTER PLANNING SUPPORTED IN IMPLEMENTATION

Results are from project completion reports, extended annual review reports, and technical assistance completion reports circulated from 1 January 2019 to 15 November 2019.

% OF TOTAL 2019 COMMITMENTS

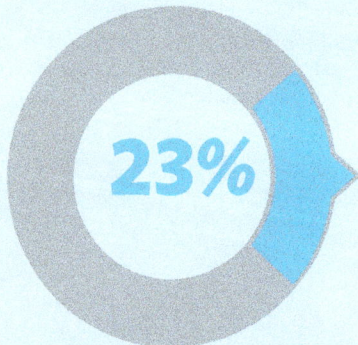

23%

34 OF 146 PROJECTS

BY SECTOR

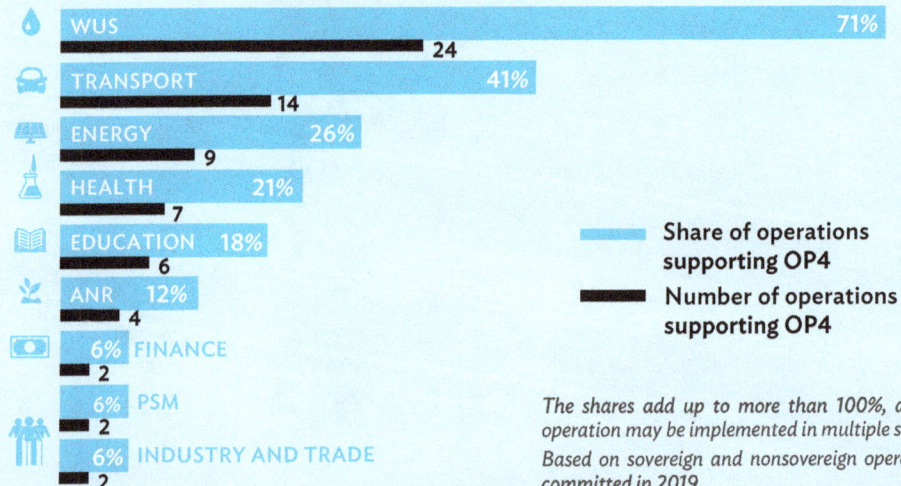

Sector	Share of operations supporting OP4	Number of operations supporting OP4
WUS	71%	24
TRANSPORT	41%	14
ENERGY	26%	9
HEALTH	21%	7
EDUCATION	18%	6
ANR	12%	4
FINANCE	6%	2
PSM	6%	2
INDUSTRY AND TRADE	6%	2

■ Share of operations supporting OP4
■ Number of operations supporting OP4

The shares add up to more than 100%, as one operation may be implemented in multiple sectors. Based on sovereign and nonsovereign operations committed in 2019.

ANR = agriculture, natural resources, and rural development, M = million, OP = operational priority, PSM = public sector management, WUS = water and other urban infrastructure and services.

The harsh, arid climate in Rajasthan, northern India, makes it more difficult to provide adequate basic services, including water supply, in its cities. The urban poor, who make up 11% of the state's population, suffer most.

ADB has been supporting the state's drive for more livable cities through the **Rajasthan Urban Sector Development Investment Program**. The $170 million ADB loans for the second and third tranches benefited about 900,000 residents by supporting the installation of 1,163 kilometers of water pipeline, 90,000 household water meters, and two bridges. It also supported the preservation of six heritage sites and training of 200 staff in urban service delivery.

Lake Issyk-Kul in the Kyrgyz Republic, the world's second-largest saline lake, attracts about 1 million tourists every year. This has put pressure on already inadequate infrastructure for water, sanitation, solid waste management, and other basic services in the Issyk-Kul area.

The $30 million **Issyk-Kul Sustainable Development Project** supported sustainable environmental management and urban service delivery by investing beyond physical infrastructure improvements. ADB helped develop the capacity of agencies and service providers to operate and manage the improved urban resources. Better systems for accounting and information management were set up and staff were trained, improving the revenue collection rate to almost 90%.

As cities in Asia and the Pacific grow in number and density, ADB is playing an important role in making them more livable. Cross-sector solutions from projects committed in 2019 will improve the quality of urban services and enhance cities' resilience. Projects completed in 2019 benefited millions of urban dwellers and improved local government capacity to deliver urban services.

Metro Manila and other business centers in the Philippines drive economic growth, but heavy road traffic costs residents and businesses dearly. ADB has been supporting government efforts to improve transportation efficiency and capacity.

The **Malolos–Clark Railway Project** will connect the regional center of Clark in Central Luzon with Metro Manila and Calamba City by 2025. ADB is funding the construction of 53 kilometers of this planned 163-kilometer railway network. This support will help provide affordable, reliable, and safe public transport, reduce greenhouse gas emissions, and is expected to shave 2 hours off Manila-to-Clark travel time, helping decongest Metro Manila and directing growth to other urban areas in the country.

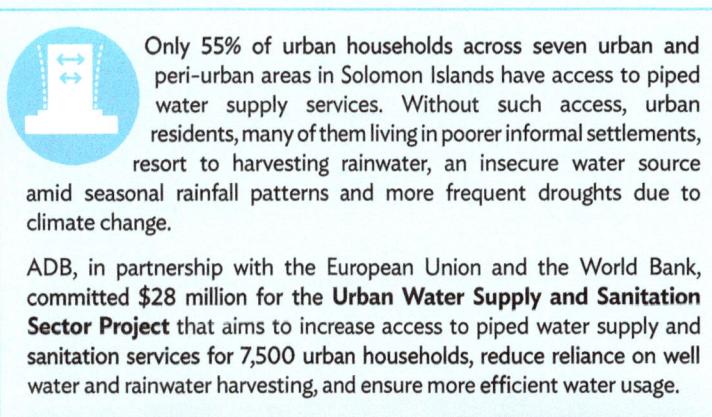

Only 55% of urban households across seven urban and peri-urban areas in Solomon Islands have access to piped water supply services. Without such access, urban residents, many of them living in poorer informal settlements, resort to harvesting rainwater, an insecure water source amid seasonal rainfall patterns and more frequent droughts due to climate change.

ADB, in partnership with the European Union and the World Bank, committed $28 million for the **Urban Water Supply and Sanitation Sector Project** that aims to increase access to piped water supply and sanitation services for 7,500 urban households, reduce reliance on well water and rainwater harvesting, and ensure more efficient water usage.

✅ 6.6M PEOPLE

610 RURAL INFRASTRUCTURE ASSETS ESTABLISHED OR IMPROVED

BENEFITING FROM INCREASED RURAL INVESTMENT

2 RURAL ECONOMIC HUBS SUPPORTED

■ 62,000 FARMERS

WITH INCREASED MARKET ACCESS

4,000 STORAGE, AGRI-LOGISTICS, AND MODERN RETAIL ASSETS ESTABLISHED OR IMPROVED

✅ 176,000 HECTARES

OF LAND WITH HIGHER PRODUCTIVITY

Results are from project completion reports, extended annual review reports, and technical assistance completion reports circulated from 1 January 2019 to 15 November 2019.

OPERATIONS COMMITTED IN 2019

% OF TOTAL 2019 COMMITMENTS

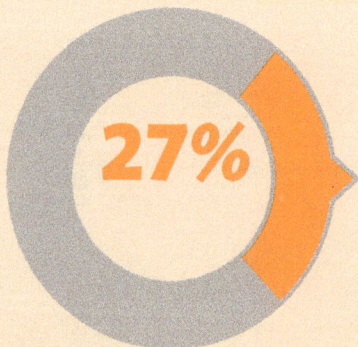

27%

39 OF 146 PROJECTS

BY SECTOR

Sector	Share of operations supporting OP5	Number of operations supporting OP5
ANR	62%	24
TRANSPORT	26%	10
FINANCE	15%	6
WUS	10%	4
ENERGY	10%	4
EDUCATION	5%	2
HEALTH	3%	1
INDUSTRY AND TRADE	3%	1
ICT	3%	1

■ Share of operations supporting OP5
■ Number of operations supporting OP5

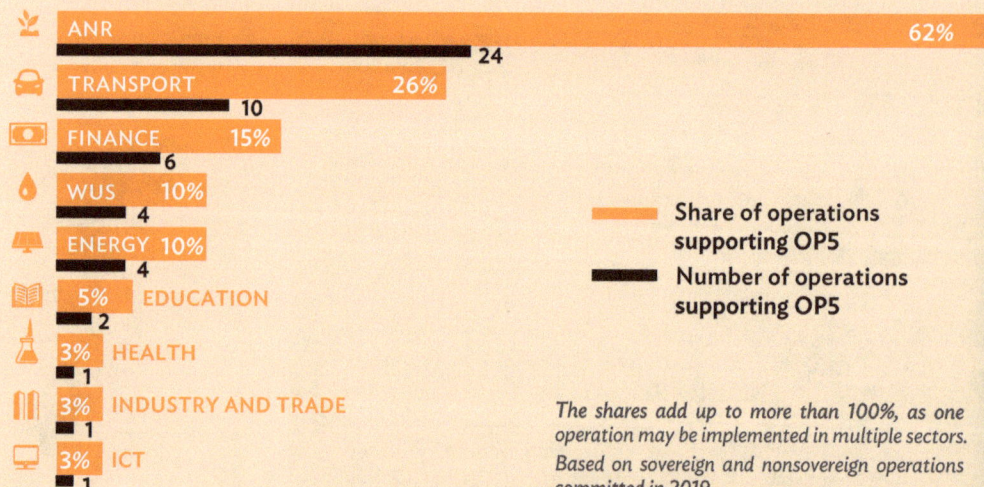

The shares add up to more than 100%, as one operation may be implemented in multiple sectors.

Based on sovereign and nonsovereign operations committed in 2019.

ANR = agriculture, natural resources, and rural development, ICT = infomation and communication technology, M = million, OP = operational priority, WUS = water and other urban infrastructure and services.

In Cambodia, nearly 5 million people, especially in the rural areas, do not have access to a reliable source of electricity. This leaves them reliant on automobile batteries, kerosene, woody biomass, and candles for cooking and lighting.

The **Rural Energy Project** supported the government's ambitious electrification program by helping to provide access to a 24-hour supply of electricity for more than 46,000 individuals in Svay Rieng Province. Sei Song, a widow who lives with her seven grandchildren, is very happy to be connected. "I have been waiting for many years," she says. "Electricity saves me a lot of time and eases the burden of everyday household chores."

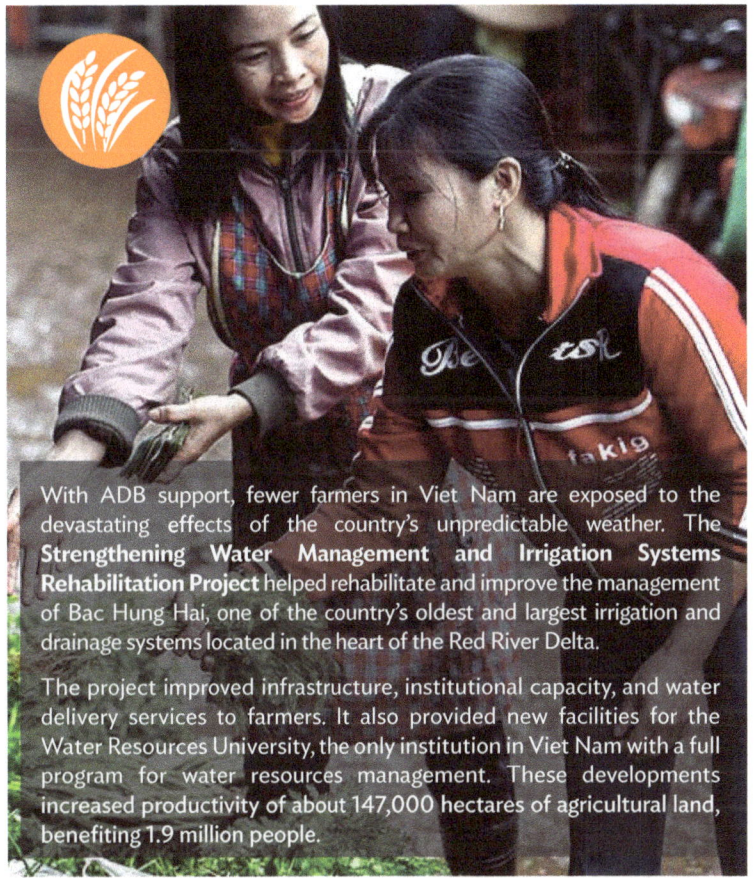

With ADB support, fewer farmers in Viet Nam are exposed to the devastating effects of the country's unpredictable weather. The **Strengthening Water Management and Irrigation Systems Rehabilitation Project** helped rehabilitate and improve the management of Bac Hung Hai, one of the country's oldest and largest irrigation and drainage systems located in the heart of the Red River Delta.

The project improved infrastructure, institutional capacity, and water delivery services to farmers. It also provided new facilities for the Water Resources University, the only institution in Viet Nam with a full program for water resources management. These developments increased productivity of about 147,000 hectares of agricultural land, benefiting 1.9 million people.

More than half of the population of Asia and the Pacific lives in rural areas, and these people lack access to services and opportunities compared with their urban peers. Through new and completed projects in 2019, ADB is helping developing member countries provide better infrastructure and social services to millions of rural inhabitants. ADB also focused its efforts on addressing food security concerns and working to improve agricultural productivity, optimize value chains, and strengthen the capacity of farmers across the region.

The establishment of integrated value chains through a project in India did not materialize and therefore did not result in increased market access for the more than 110,000 planned beneficiary farmers.

A third of Mongolia's population lives in rural areas, where livelihoods are anchored on animal husbandry and milk production. Milk is the most important income source for many households. In 2019, ADB approved its first private sector loan in the country, worth $7.5 million, to support the dairy production expansion of the Teso group, Mongolia's leading food and beverage company.

Smallholder farmers and herders, most of them women, will be the beneficiaries of the **Gender Inclusive Dairy Value Chain Project** as main suppliers. Tsogtgerel Odon, president of the Teso group, says ADB's assistance "underpins the mutual aims of Teso and ADB to support rural livelihoods, especially for women."

In Afghanistan, water is scarce, erratic, and highly seasonal amid frequent and worsening droughts. Agriculture is the country's major source of livelihood, employing 62% of its labor force. Reliable and integrated water resources management is essential.

In 2019, ADB approved the **Arghandab Integrated Water Resources Development Project**, a $349 million Asian Development Fund grant, to help develop water resources in Kandahar Province by expanding the Dahla Dam, Afghanistan's second-largest dam. The support will also train about 300 farmers—at least 30% of them women—in climate-smart farming technologies. This project will increase water security and improve agricultural productivity for 1.25 million people in seven rural districts.

OP6
GOVERNANCE

✅ **1,700 ENTITIES**

70,000 GOVERNMENT OFFICIALS WITH INCREASED CAPACITIES

GOVERNMENT AND PRIVATE INSTITUTIONS WITH IMPROVED MANAGEMENT FUNCTIONS AND FINANCIAL STABILITY

120 MEASURES SUPPORTED IN IMPLEMENTATION TO PROMOTE THE PRIVATE SECTOR AND FINANCE SECTOR

✅ **390 ENTITIES**

43 MEASURES SUPPORTED IN IMPLEMENTATION TO STRENGTHEN STATE-OWNED ENTERPRISES' GOVERNANCE

GOVERNMENT AND PRIVATE INSTITUTIONS WITH IMPROVED SERVICE DELIVERY

46 BETTER SERVICE DELIVERY STANDARDS ADOPTED

Results are from project completion reports, extended annual review reports, and technical assistance completion reports circulated from 1 January 2019 to 15 November 2019.

OPERATIONS COMMITTED IN 2019

% OF TOTAL 2019 COMMITMENTS

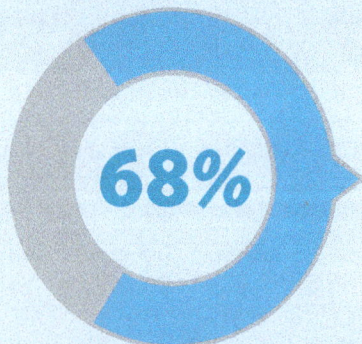

68%

99 OF 146 PROJECTS

BY SECTOR

Sector	Share of operations supporting OP6	Number of operations supporting OP6
TRANSPORT	26%	26
WUS	22%	22
PSM	19%	19
ANR	17%	17
FINANCE	15%	15
ENERGY	13%	13
EDUCATION	13%	13
HEALTH	12%	12
INDUSTRY AND TRADE	7%	7

■ Share of operations supporting OP6
■ Number of operations supporting OP6

The shares add up to more than 100%, as one operation may be implemented in multiple sectors.

Based on sovereign and nonsovereign operations committed in 2019.

ANR = agriculture, natural resources, and rural development, OP = operational priority, PSM = public sector management, WUS = water and other urban infrastructure and services.

While the Philippines was an early adopter of decentralization principles in Southeast Asia, lack of sufficient revenue, an outdated regulatory framework, and diluted accountability hampered effective delivery of services such as health, education, and housing.

The **Local Government Finance and Fiscal Decentralization Reform Program** helped address these constraints and sustainably widen the own-source revenue base of the local government units (LGUs) by strengthening tax collection efficiency, access to debt capital markets, and public financial management systems; and creating a more equitable fiscal framework. Rolling out bottom-up planning and budgeting in more than 1,200 LGUs across the country helped almost double LGUs' property tax collections and increase recurrent expenditure by one-third.

The 2014–2015 crash in oil prices severely depressed Azerbaijan's economic growth, and in the first quarter of 2016, the economy fell into recession. With the sharp depreciation in the local currency, people's real incomes tumbled as the prices of goods climbed.

The **Countercyclical Support Facility Program** helped mitigate these negative economic impacts by contributing to the government's countercyclical stimulus package. The program supported social assistance programs for 3.7 million people, an increase in government employees' wages and benefits, the implementation of measures to create 84,000 additional jobs in the public and private sectors, and incentives for private investors in sectors that diversify the economy away from the hydrocarbon industry.

Achieving sustainable growth is impossible without effective governance and adequate institutional capacity in the developing member countries. In 2019, ADB continued to provide strong support for improving governance and promoting institutional reforms to increase public sector efficiencies and enhance service delivery to people. Operations completed in 2019, including policy-based lending and technical assistance, helped thousands of local and national public institutions improve their functions and service delivery.

Bhutan's impressive economic performance since the late 1980s has mainly been driven by state-led hydropower development. Its small private sector largely consists of micro, small, and medium-sized enterprises that suffer from high financing costs.

To promote broad-based economic growth, the **Financial Market Development Program** is helping the government develop a finance sector that offers strong financial intermediation to enable efficient resource mobilization for productive investments. The program is also strengthening the regulatory and supervisory framework to better manage financial risks and promote access to finance by disadvantaged groups.

Papua New Guinea has the highest maternal and child mortality rates and lowest life expectancy among Pacific island countries. With about 85% of its population living in remote rural areas, access to quality health care is a major challenge.

The second subprogram of the **Health Services Sector Development Program** is supporting policy reforms to make quality health services available to all citizens. The program is building a stronger public financial management foundation to improve service delivery and ensure adequate resources are available for family, maternal, and child health services. It is also establishing six additional provincial health authorities and developing a framework for human resources, financial management, and governance.

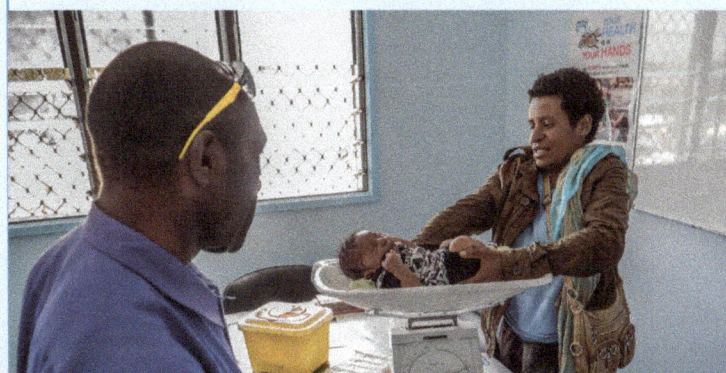

OP7 REGIONAL COOPERATION

☑ $219.3M CARGO & ENERGY
TRANSPORTED AND TRANSMITTED ACROSS BORDERS

16 MEASURES SUPPORTED IN IMPLEMENTATION FOR CROSS-BORDER CONNECTIVITY

1,000 MW OF CLEAN ENERGY CAPACITY FOR POWER TRADE INSTALLED

☑ $237.4M INVESTMENTS
TRADE AND INVESTMENT FACILITATED

10 REGIONAL MECHANISMS TO ENHANCE COORDINATION AND COOPERATION AMONG DMCs

3 INITIATIVES
REGIONAL PUBLIC GOODS INITIATIVES

For initiatives, scoring is only conducted when a cumulative planned result of 20 or more has been recorded. Results are from project completion reports, extended annual review reports, and technical assistance completion reports circulated from 1 January 2019 to 15 November 2019.

OPERATIONS COMMITTED IN 2019

% OF TOTAL 2019 COMMITMENTS

22%

32 OF 146 PROJECTS

BY SECTOR

Sector	Share	Number
TRANSPORT	47%	15
WUS	19%	6
INDUSTRY AND TRADE	19%	6
FINANCE	16%	5
ANR	13%	4
ENERGY	13%	4
PSM	6%	2
HEALTH	6%	2
EDUCATION	3%	1
ICT	3%	1

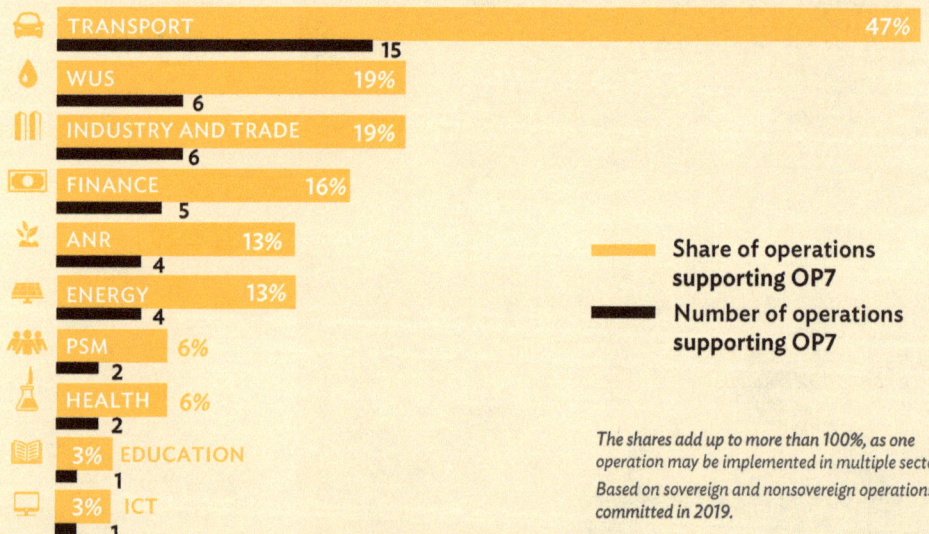

— Share of operations supporting OP7
— Number of operations supporting OP7

The shares add up to more than 100%, as one operation may be implemented in multiple sectors.

Based on sovereign and nonsovereign operations committed in 2019.

ANR = agriculture, natural resources, and rural development, DMC = developing member country, ICT = infomation and communication technology, MW =megawatt, M = million, OP = operational priority, PSM = public sector management, WUS = water and other urban infrastructure and services.

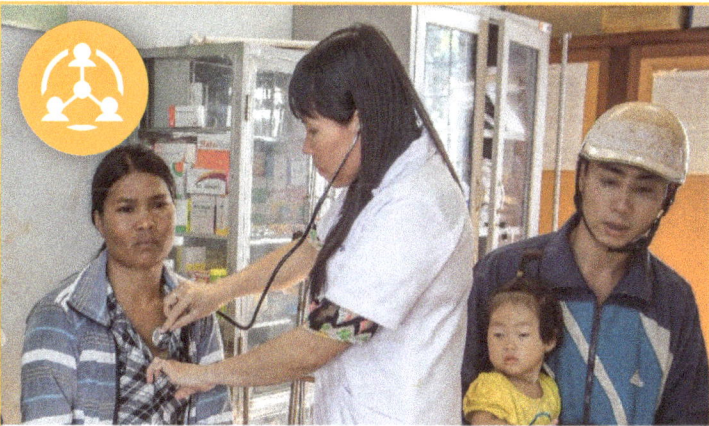

Infectious diseases pose a constant threat not only to millions of people in the Greater Mekong Subregion (GMS), but also to its productivity, trade, and tourism. Controlling these diseases requires strong surveillance systems, community prevention and preparedness, and quick response capacities.

The **Second Mekong Communicable Disease Prevention Program** delivered measures to improve regional public health through the development of cross-border action plans to control the spread of malaria in Cambodia, the Lao People's Democratic Republic, and Viet Nam. It also promoted better communicable disease control practices in these countries' communities, and effective use of technology to support the communicable disease control surveillance system. Agreements were made between GMS countries on joint disease prevention activities and interventions.

Uzbekistan is a key transit point for trade among Central Asian countries and with the rest of Asia and Europe. The Central Asia Regional Economic Cooperation Program plans to develop six transport corridors to improve connectivity and cut transport costs. As part of these efforts, the **Central Asia Regional Economic Cooperation Corridor 2 Road Investment Program** built 175 kilometers of the A380 highway in Karakalpakstan and in Khorezm and Bukhara provinces. The program facilitated $122 million of external trade with Kazakhstan, reduced the border-crossing time from 2 hours to 20 minutes, and cut the accident rate from 150 accidents per year in 2017 to 9 in 2018.

Regional cooperation and integration is an effective tool to promote shared economic interests and address common challenges, including those related to disease outbreaks and disasters. In 2019, ADB continued to support DMCs in expanding regional connectivity, investment, and trade opportunities, and enhancing the provision of regional public goods. ADB continued to work closely with and strengthen subregional integration initiatives, while also providing knowledge solutions and technical assistance to promote greater integration and cooperation among DMCs.

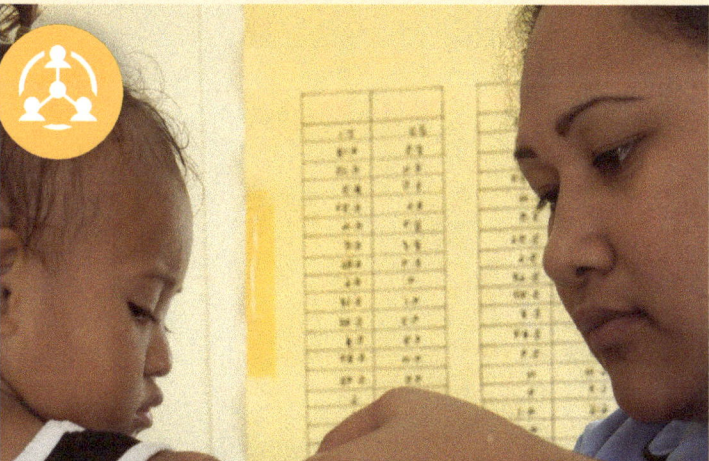

Vaccination is among the most effective and practical public health investments. Cervical cancer, pneumonia, and diarrhea, which pose a challenge to Pacific countries, are all preventable through immunization.

The **Systems Strengthening for Effective Coverage of New Vaccines in the Pacific Project** is financing the pooled procurement of vaccines against the human papillomavirus, rotavirus, and pneumococcus that cause these diseases through the Vaccine Independence Initiative of United Nations Children's Fund (UNICEF). Samoa, Tonga, Tuvalu, and Vanuatu will benefit from global procurement and safe administration of quality, safe vaccines by upgrading the countries' cold chains and training health workers in vaccine administration, waste management, and reporting.

At least 2 billion people in Asia and the Pacific lack access to reliable internet because of network limitations or the high cost of services. The nonsovereign **Asia-Pacific Remote Broadband Internet Satellite Project,** ADB's first satellite financing venture, is an agreement with Kacific Broadband Satellites International Limited to provide affordable, satellite-based, high-speed broadband internet connections to countries in the region, especially in remote and underserved areas.

"ADB's involvement has helped secure the necessary financing for this highly developmental project," says Kacific's chief executive Christian Patouraux. "The benefits of connectivity are life-changing for many remote communities in the region across a number of areas, including increased tourism, access to information, financial services, health care, and education."

Energy from the sun. Daily operations at the 15-megawatt Sermsang Khushig Khundii solar plant in Khushig Valley, Tuv *aimag*, which is located 40 kilometers from Mongolia's capital, Ulaanbaatar (photo by Ariel Javellana).

CHAPTER 2

DEVELOPMENT FINANCE AND STRATEGIC ALIGNMENT

DEVELOPMENT FINANCE AND STRATEGIC ALIGNMENT

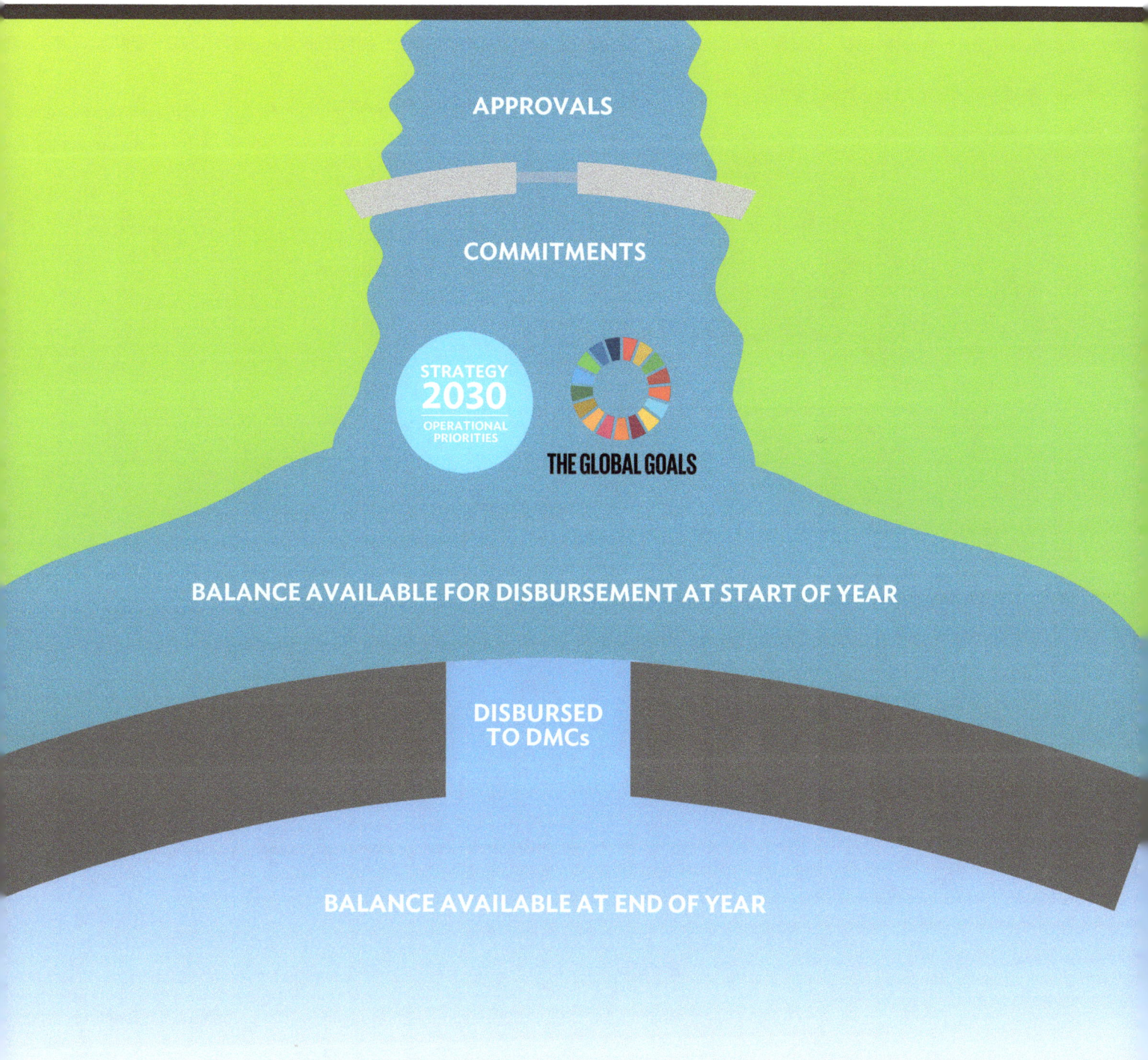

APPROVALS

COMMITMENTS

STRATEGY **2030** OPERATIONAL PRIORITIES

THE GLOBAL GOALS

BALANCE AVAILABLE FOR DISBURSEMENT AT START OF YEAR

DISBURSED TO DMCs

BALANCE AVAILABLE AT END OF YEAR

As a development bank, ADB provides needed finance to its developing member countries in line with its vision of a prosperous, inclusive, resilient, and sustainable Asia and the Pacific free of extreme poverty. Strong and diverse partnerships with private and public financing institutions and traditional and new development partners help catalyze and mobilize financial resources for this development.

ADB is focusing its investments on Strategy 2030's seven operational priorities in alignment with the Sustainable Development Goals, and is working to efficiently disburse financing to its developing member countries.

A. DEVELOPMENT FINANCE AND STRATEGIC ALIGNMENT

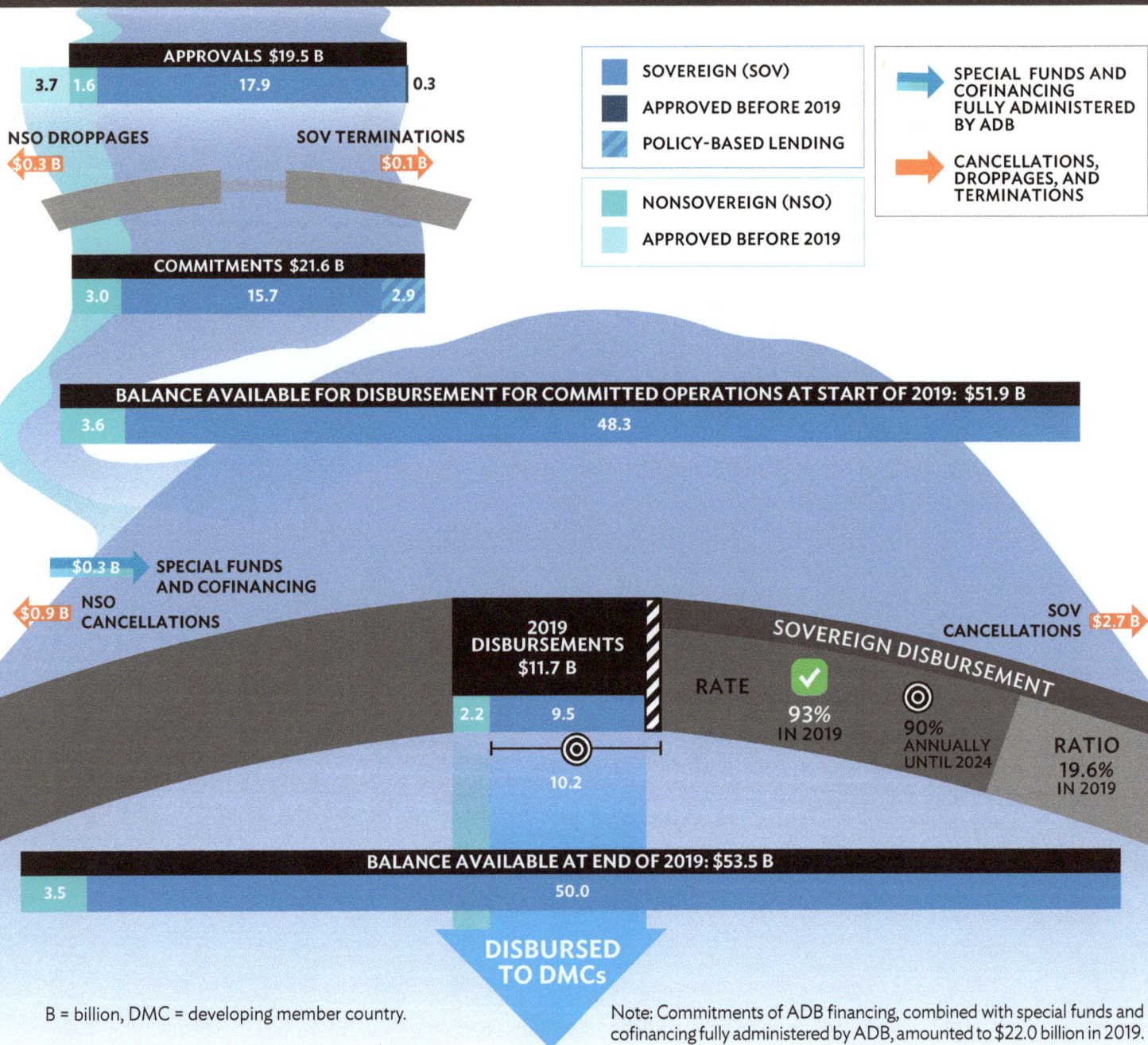

Legend:
- SOVEREIGN (SOV)
- APPROVED BEFORE 2019
- POLICY-BASED LENDING
- NONSOVEREIGN (NSO)
- APPROVED BEFORE 2019
- SPECIAL FUNDS AND COFINANCING FULLY ADMINISTERED BY ADB
- CANCELLATIONS, DROPPAGES, AND TERMINATIONS

APPROVALS $19.5 B
3.7 | 1.6 | 17.9 | 0.3

NSO DROPPAGES $0.3 B
SOV TERMINATIONS $0.1 B

COMMITMENTS $21.6 B
3.0 | 15.7 | 2.9

BALANCE AVAILABLE FOR DISBURSEMENT FOR COMMITTED OPERATIONS AT START OF 2019: $51.9 B
3.6 | 48.3

$0.3 B SPECIAL FUNDS AND COFINANCING
$0.9 B NSO CANCELLATIONS
SOV CANCELLATIONS $2.7 B

2019 DISBURSEMENTS $11.7 B
2.2 | 9.5
10.2

SOVEREIGN DISBURSEMENT
RATE 93% IN 2019
90% ANNUALLY UNTIL 2024
RATIO 19.6% IN 2019

BALANCE AVAILABLE AT END OF 2019: $53.5 B
3.5 | 50.0

DISBURSED TO DMCs

B = billion, DMC = developing member country.

Note: Commitments of ADB financing, combined with special funds and cofinancing fully administered by ADB, amounted to $22.0 billion in 2019.

69. ADB total approvals and commitments increased in volume during 2019. A volume increase over 2018 in the sovereign category outpaced a decrease on the nonsovereign side. Of the total ADB financing committed, 40.3% ($8.7 billion) was for 90 operations in concessional assistance countries. Of the 156 ADB operations committed overall, 108 were sovereign, 38 nonsovereign, and 10 were project readiness financing facilities.

70. ADB disbursed 93% of the targeted $10.2 billion in financing for sovereign projects and results-based lending to its DMCs, exceeding its sovereign disbursement rate target of 90%. The total of $9.5 billion disbursed from the $48.3 billion balance available for disbursement for committed sovereign operations at the beginning of 2019 resulted in a 2019 sovereign disbursement ratio of 19.6%. The *2019 Annual Portfolio Performance Report* provides further details.[13]

B. PROGRESS ON STRATEGY 2030 TARGETS AND PRIORITIES

2019 PROGRESS ON STRATEGY 2030 TARGETS

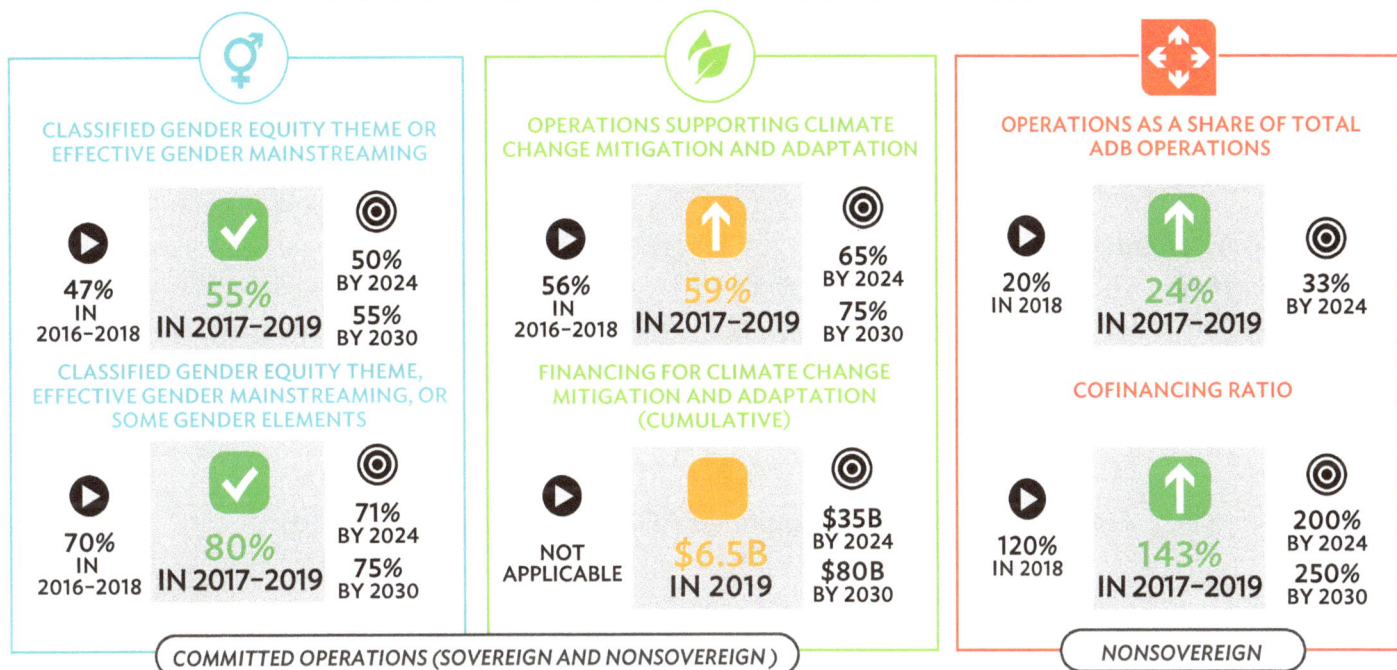

CLASSIFIED GENDER EQUITY THEME OR EFFECTIVE GENDER MAINSTREAMING

47% IN 2016–2018   ✓ 55% IN 2017–2019   50% BY 2024 / 55% BY 2030

CLASSIFIED GENDER EQUITY THEME, EFFECTIVE GENDER MAINSTREAMING, OR SOME GENDER ELEMENTS

70% IN 2016–2018   ✓ 80% IN 2017–2019   71% BY 2024 / 75% BY 2030

OPERATIONS SUPPORTING CLIMATE CHANGE MITIGATION AND ADAPTATION

56% IN 2016–2018   ↑ 59% IN 2017–2019   65% BY 2024 / 75% BY 2030

FINANCING FOR CLIMATE CHANGE MITIGATION AND ADAPTATION (CUMULATIVE)

NOT APPLICABLE $6.5B IN 2019 $35B BY 2024 / $80B BY 2030

COMMITTED OPERATIONS (SOVEREIGN AND NONSOVEREIGN)

OPERATIONS AS A SHARE OF TOTAL ADB OPERATIONS

20% IN 2018   ↑ 24% IN 2017–2019   33% BY 2024

COFINANCING RATIO

120% IN 2018   ↑ 143% IN 2017–2019   200% BY 2024 / 250% BY 2030

NONSOVEREIGN

71. ADB has made a good start on meeting its Strategy 2030 targets.[14] Committed operations had a record level of gender mainstreaming in 2017–2019. Progress was also good on increasing the focus on climate change mitigation and adaptation. Nonetheless, meeting Strategy 2030's targets of 75% of ADB operations committed being gender mainstreamed and 75% supporting climate change mitigation and adaptation will remain challenging as ADB moves closer to the target date. Progress was *on track* for expanding private sector operations and long-term cofinancing. Chapter 4 provides details on the growing share of nonsovereign operations in ADB's portfolio.

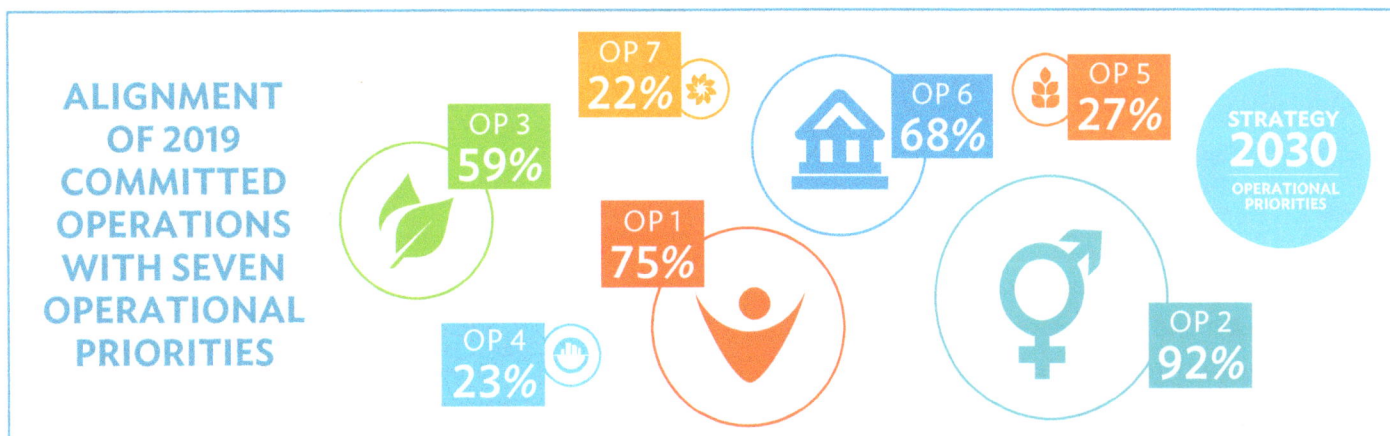

ALIGNMENT OF 2019 COMMITTED OPERATIONS WITH SEVEN OPERATIONAL PRIORITIES

OP 7 22%

OP 3 59%

OP 6 68%

OP 5 27%

STRATEGY 2030 OPERATIONAL PRIORITIES

OP 1 75%

OP 4 23%

OP 2 92%

72. ADB aligned its committed operations with the seven operational priorities of Strategy 2030 in 2019—the strategy's first full year of implementation. It developed operational plans for the individual priorities and began enhancing the methodology for identifying the alignment of its operations with each. Results for 2019 were calculated using an interim methodology, to be replaced in 2020. Details on the Strategy 2030 operational priorities, including the sector breakdown, are provided in Chapter 1.

C. IN FOCUS

1. Accelerating Gender Equality and Tackling Climate Change

Gender Mainstreaming

73. **Record attention to gender equality across ADB portfolio.** The share of ADB operations committed in 2017–2019 and classified *gender equity theme* (GEN) or *effective gender mainstreaming* (EGM) rose by 8 percentage points. Those classified GEN, EGM, or *some gender elements* (SGE) increased by 10 percentage points (Figure 2.1). The share of financing for GEN and EGM operations reached a historic high of 51% of total ADB financing in 2017–2019, including 71% for the concessional assistance subset. This was due to the steep increase in gender mainstreaming from 2016 to 2019.

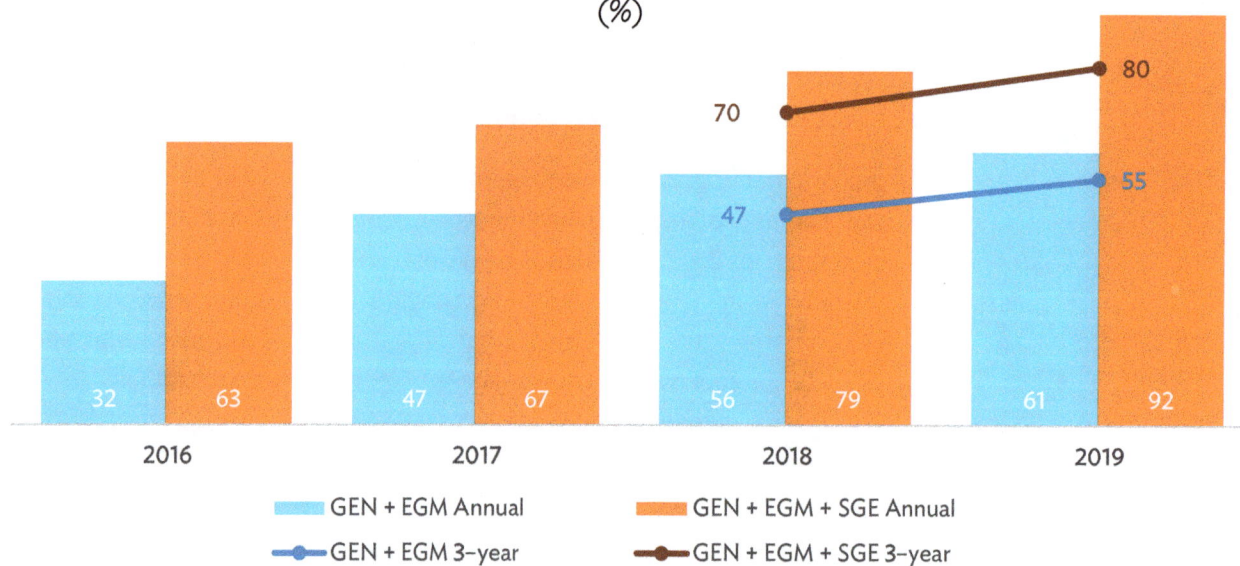

Figure 2.1: Gender Mainstreamed ADB Operations, 2016–2019
(%)

ADB = Asian Development Bank, EGM = effective gender mainstreaming, GEN = gender equity theme, SGE = some gender elements.
Source: ADB Sustainable Development and Climate Change Department.

74. ADB's focus on gender equality intensified in both its sovereign and nonsovereign operations. The share of sovereign operations classified EGM increased by 10 percentage points in 2017–2019 to 54%. The ratio for SGE dropped slightly to 21%. The GEN share was steady at 8% (Figure 2.2). The nonsovereign portfolio showed improvements in all categories. Shares of committed operations designated SGE rose 7 percentage points to 35% and were up 4 percentage points to 16% for EGM classifications. The GEN ratio increased slightly to 13%.

75. **Actions supporting strong 2019 mainstreaming.** The record gender mainstreaming performance in 2019 was due to concerted efforts by Management and staff and changes in portfolio composition. Project teams significantly reduced operations with no gender elements, guided by gender specialists. ADB staff and implementing and executing agency officials were given additional gender mainstreaming training.

Figure 2.2: ADB Operations Supporting Gender Equality by Classification, 2016–2019
(%)

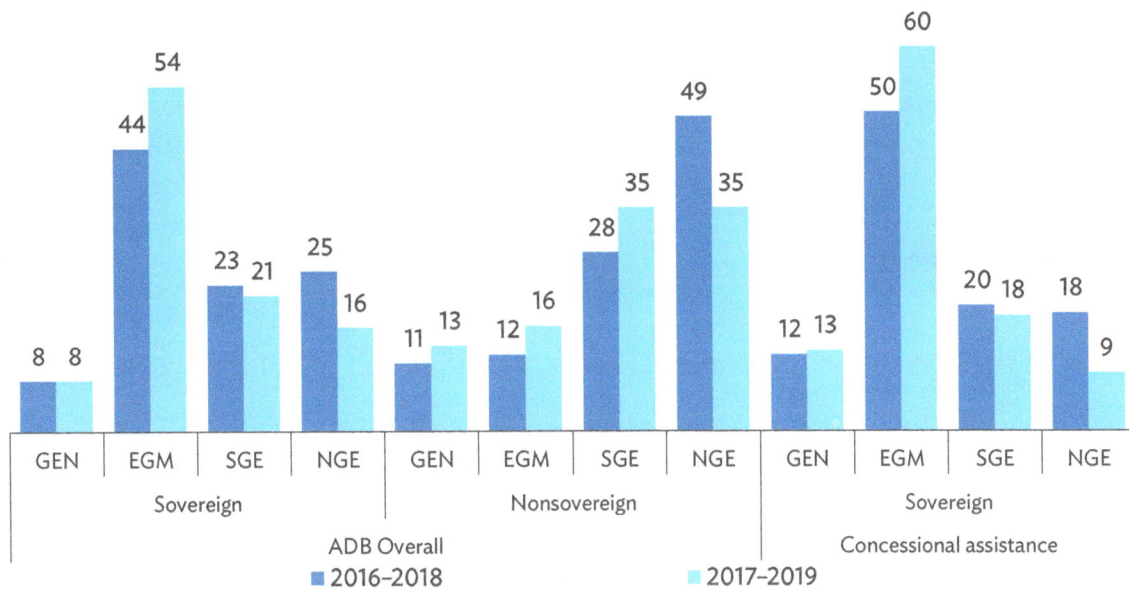

ADB = Asian Development Bank, EGM = effective gender mainstreaming, GEN = gender equity theme, NGE = no gender elements, SGE = some gender elements.
Source: ADB Sustainable Development and Climate Change Department.

76. **Performance enhanced by portfolio shift.** Gender mainstreaming was accelerated further by internal shifts in the portfolio. Infrastructure projects, including those in the energy and transport sectors, have historically had low rates of gender mainstreaming. Their share of committed operations declined in 2019, and that of the more readily mainstreamed social sector operations increased, supporting an increase in the overall EGM ratio. Nevertheless, operations departments increased the gender focus of many infrastructure projects as well. The share of gender mainstreamed energy projects rose from 15% in 2018 to 31% in 2019. Ratio upswings in 2019 for gender mainstreaming in finance (39% to 48%) and public sector management (44% to 53%) were notable, given the two sectors' historically low gender focus.

77. **Nonsovereign operations challenge.** ADB intends to increase the portfolio share of nonsovereign operations, which have much lower historical rates of gender mainstreaming than sovereign operations. ADB's concerted efforts to mainstream gender, especially in more challenging sectors and in nonsovereign operations, will therefore need to be sustained to meet the 2030 target. In 2019, ADB's Private Sector Operations Department created two positions for gender specialists. Work began on revising ADB's gender category guidelines. This is designed to help improve the quality as well as the quantity of gender mainstreaming—another Strategy 2030 commitment. For details on the achievement of gender equality results, refer to Chapter 1.

Supporting Climate Change Mitigation and Adaptation

78. **Moderate increase in share of operations tackling climate change.** The proportion of ADB operations committed in 2017–2019 that support climate change adaptation and/or mitigation increased by 3 percentage points from the baseline to 59%. A smaller share of operations focused on tackling climate change in 2019 than in 2018, but this did not depress the 3-year average because the 2019 figure replaced the lower 2016 performance in the moving average (Figure 2.3). The pattern was similar but more pronounced in the concessional assistance subset. The share of these operations committed and tackling climate change in 2017–2019 increased by 5 percentage points to 63% from the baseline of 58% even though the ratio dipped to 58% in 2019 from 79% in 2018. More operations supported both climate change mitigation and adaptation in 2019 than in the 3 prior years.

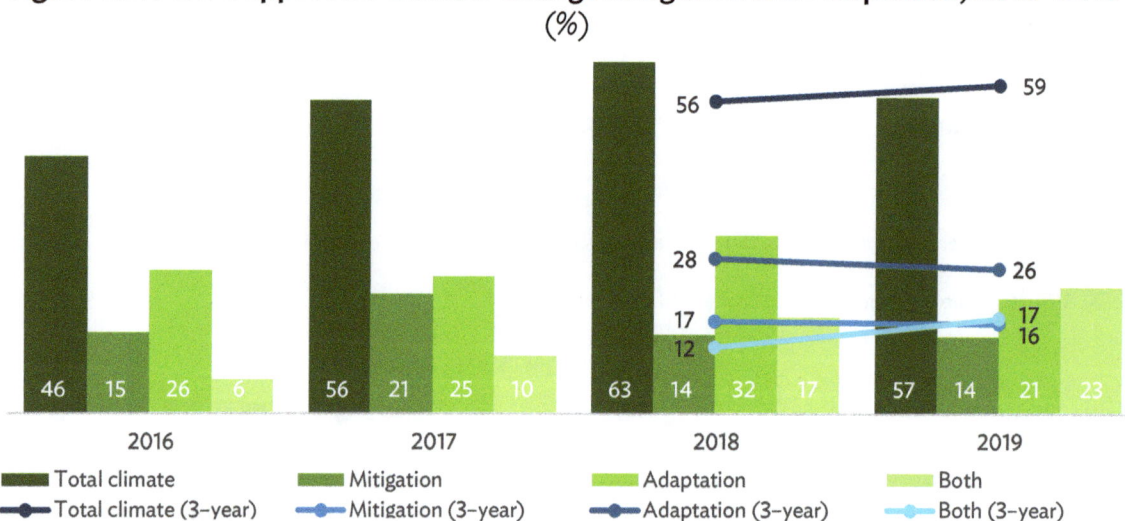

Figure 2.3: ADB Support for Climate Change Mitigation and Adaptation, 2016–2019
(%)

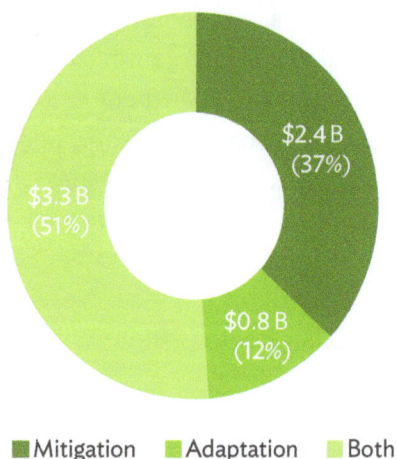

Figure 2.4: ADB Financing for Climate Change Mitigation and Adaptation, 2019

ADB = Asian Development Bank, B = billion.
Source: ADB Sustainable Development and Climate Change Department.

79. **Early headway toward Strategy 2030 climate financing target.** In 2019, ADB committed $6.5 billion, or 30% of its total financing, to operations tackling climate change. With this, ADB met its 2015 commitment to double its annual climate investments from $3 billion in 2014 to $6 billion by 2020 a year early.[15] At $3.3 billion, the commitments for operations that support both mitigation and adaptation nearly tripled the $1.2 billion committed in 2018, and also exceeded the cumulative total of $2.8 billion committed during the 3 prior years. Financing to support mitigation alone declined slightly to $2.4 billion in 2019, while increasing marginally to $0.8 billion for adaptation only (Figure 2.4). ADB operations with climate change components dedicated a larger portion of their budgets to the effort in 2019 than in 2018 and allocated an average of $79 million to climate change measures, compared with $44 million a year earlier.

Strategy 2030 Gender and Climate Targets Challenge

Figure 2.5: ADB Operations Supporting Gender and/or Climate in 2017–2019 (%)

80. Although ADB has made good progress toward increasing the share of operations that tackle climate change and promote gender equality, additional efforts will be required to achieve the Strategy 2030 targets of 75% of committed operations supporting each of these two priorities. In 2017–2019, 49% of committed

ADB operations mainstreamed gender and supported climate change mitigation and/or adaptation (Figure 2.5). To achieve both of the 75% 2030 targets, ADB will need to ensure that about 65% of its committed operations support both priorities, recognizing that the share of operations that are not appropriate for either gender mainstreaming or climate change mitigation and/or adaptation will probably need to remain about 10%–15%. To achieve this, operations that integrate climate change mitigation and/or adaptation will have to increase, in particular in sectors and subsectors where there are opportunities for mainstreaming gender equality. In addition, ADB will need to balance this with the Strategy 2030 target of increasing nonsovereign operations to one-third of ADB's portfolio by 2024. Historically, a smaller proportion of these operations have supported gender equality and addressed climate change than sovereign operations.

2. Mobilizing Private Sector Resources for Development

81. ADB was *on track* to achieve the Strategy 2030 nonsovereign cofinancing ratio target of 250%. Parallel loans, equity, guarantees, and risk transfers were among the measures employed during 2019 to increase commercial and official cofinancing for nonsovereign operations. A total of $10.1 billion in long-term cofinancing was mobilized in 2017–2019. Every $1 in financing ADB committed for its nonsovereign operations was matched by $1.43 in long-term cofinancing (Figure 2.6).

Figure 2.6: Long-Term Cofinancing for Nonsovereign Operations, 2017–2019

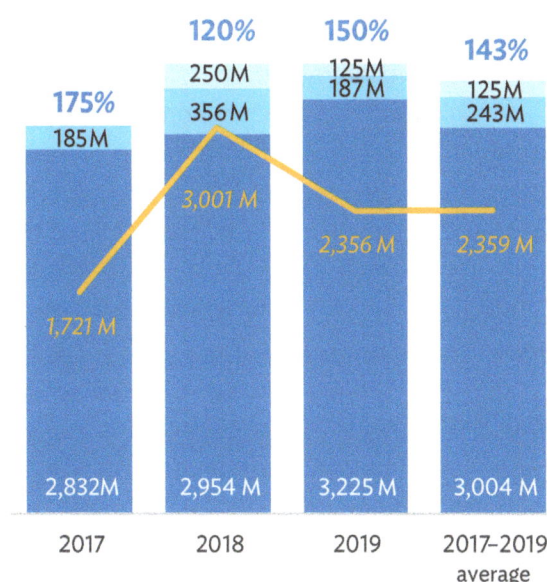

ADB = Asian Development Bank, M = million.
Source: ADB Private Sector Operations Department and Office of Public-Private Partnership.

FINANCING FOR EDUCATION			FINANCING FOR HEALTH			OPERATIONS CONTRIBUTING TO SOCIAL PROTECTION	
5.43% IN 2016–2018	5.23% IN 2019	6%–10% BY 2024	1.75% IN 2016–2018	2.95% IN 2019	3%–5% BY 2024	5% IN 2016–2018	5% IN 2019

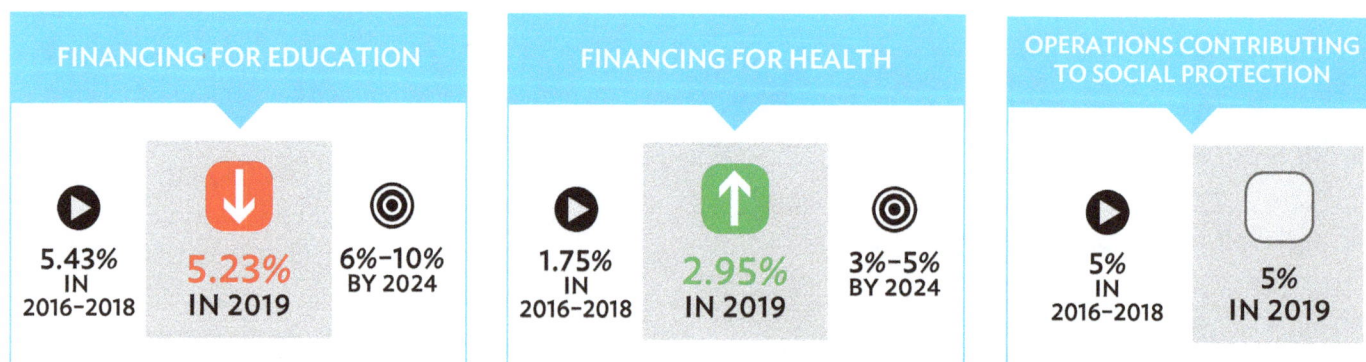

3. Expanding Interventions in Social Sectors

82. Strategy 2030 commits ADB to expanding its investments in the social sectors, including education, health, and social protection. These sectors provide important pathways for operational priority (OP) 1: addressing remaining poverty and reducing inequalities.

83. **Education financing share lower.** Declining education commitments put ADB *off track* to meet the 2024 target. The $1.1 billion committed for 16 loans and grants went to more operations in 2019 but fell short of the record high $1.6 billion achieved in 2018 due to strong demand from DMCs in South Asia. Lending for secondary education (48%) and technical and vocational education and training (42%) was highest. Two regional nonsovereign loans were committed for operations focusing on tertiary education and education sector development. Operations in Southeast Asia accounted for 67% of the financing. The two largest were in the Philippines: a $300 million program to improve the quality of secondary education, and a $150 million program to help young people transition from school to work. Based on ADB's project pipeline, lending for education is expected to increase in 2020.

84. **Health finance *on track*.** Health's financing share was close to the 2024 target range of 3%–5%. The $636 million committed in 2019 for 13 loans and grants was a record high. ADB committed its first health sector multitranche financing facility. It will support improved access to health services for disadvantaged groups in Mongolia. Innovations were pursued to address evolving DMC priorities. Among them was a sovereign operation in the People's Republic of China (PRC) that will employ international public–private partnership principles in a demonstration of integrated elderly and health care services.[16]

85. **Consistent support for social protection.** The number of ADB operations supporting social protection remained constant at seven. Four of those committed in 2019 focused on technical and vocational education and training in Bangladesh, Cambodia, the Philippines, and Viet Nam. Two were social assistance operations in Pakistan. The PRC demonstration project was the seventh and covered both areas. It aims to increase the number of older persons using an expanded range of elderly and health care services. It will also boost the number of service providers through training programs in a local college. The region's social protection issues, including aging populations, require greater ADB investment in such innovative designs. Operations supporting social assistance and social insurance will be essential to reducing poverty and increasing equality and inclusiveness in the DMCs.

Waiting in line. A woman stands in queue at a communal water source in Cox's Bazar, Bangladesh (photo by Abir Abdullah).

4. Poverty Reduction and Inclusiveness

86. **More focus on poverty reduction and inclusiveness.** The proportion of committed ADB operations supporting poverty reduction and inclusiveness was 74% in 2017–2019, based on preliminary calculations using an interim methodology. This was up from 70% in 2016–2018. To qualify, operations had to meet at least one of six criteria. These included the targeting of poor geographic locations or households, a strong focus on rural areas, and implementation in fragile and conflict-affected situations or small island developing states. Operations that devoted at least 15% of their financing to social protection areas (social assistance, social insurance, or labor market programs) also qualified. So did operations that were gender mainstreamed (classified GEN or EGM), and those that allocated at least half of their ADB financing to a sector or subsector that provides a pathway to poverty reduction and inclusion. The qualifying operations were most commonly in the health, education, or inclusive finance sectors. ADB will finalize the development and enhancement of a methodology for this indicator in 2020 and include a focus on generating quality jobs, one of the pillars of OP 1.

87. **Method for ranking disability inclusiveness piloted.** ADB has developed and piloted a methodology for classifying operations as disability-inclusive. The rating system is based on the Organisation for Economic Co-operation and Development's disability marker. It aligns with the United Nations Economic and Social Commission for Asia and the Pacific's 2012 Incheon Strategy and the 2017 Beijing Declaration and Action Plan to Accelerate the Implementation of the Incheon Strategy, which introduced goals, indicators, and targets for implementing the Convention on the Rights of Persons with Disabilities in the Asia and Pacific region.[17]

88. The ranking system's pilot results showed that 32 (22%) of the 146 operations committed in 2019 are disability-inclusive (Figure 2.7). One was rated principally or significantly disability-inclusive. The new urban rail system to be built in India under this project features disability inclusion in its plans for platforms, ticket halls, and carriages.[18] The differently abled will be consulted on the final design and for feedback on the quality of the infrastructure once it is completed. Railway staff will learn how to interface with differently abled customers through a training module the project will develop and deliver. Seven operations (5% of 2019 commitments) have some disability inclusion elements and involve the differently abled in project planning, monitoring, or feedback provision. Most operations rated disability-inclusive (24 of 32, or 16% of 2019 commitments overall) will enable disability inclusion without setting specific disability inclusiveness indicators or explicitly including persons with disabilities in their design, monitoring, or implementation. For example, an administration and operations center to be built under a project in Sri Lanka will include features to provide better services for persons with disabilities using Colombo's port.[19]

Figure 2.7: Committed Operations that are Disability-Inclusive, 2019 (%)

22 IN 2019

1 — CATEGORY 2: PRINCIPALLY OR SIGNIFICANTLY DISABILITY-INCLUSIVE

5 — CATEGORY 1A: SOME DISABILITY INCLUSION ELEMENTS

16 — CATEGORY 1B: ENABLING CONDITIONS FOR DISABILITY INCLUSION

5. Quality Infrastructure: Green, Resilient, Inclusive, and Sustainable

89. ADB will play an important role under Strategy 2030 in supporting the global goal of developing infrastructure to promote social and economic growth. A new ADB methodology piloted in 2019 aims to measure the quality and good practices of an infrastructure project. It assesses the project practices based on four dimensions, starting with whether it is green—i.e., whether it addresses climate change mitigation, pollution, and other emissions; or promotes resource efficiency and/or nature-based solutions and biodiversity. The project's resilience is calculated based on its resilience to climate risks and vulnerability and natural hazards, any positive sustainable development impact it makes, and/ or its use of data to optimize service delivery. Inclusion is assessed in terms of promotion of gender equality and access for the vulnerable, support for job creation and better livelihoods, and contribution to better health and safety. The sustainability assessment examines whether life-cycle cost accounting is used, operation and maintenance optimized, infrastructure governance and anticorruption measures strengthened, and effective strategic financing approaches employed. Based on initial pilot data, 100% of infrastructure projects reviewed met minimum quality standards and included at least one green (75%), resilient (98%), inclusive (94%), and sustainable (91%) good practice.

6. Supporting the Sustainable Development Goals

90. ADB tracks the links between its operations and the Sustainable Development Goals (SDGs), distinguishing between cross-cutting SDGs, which cover critical development themes, and the SDGs tied to sectors and concrete investment areas (Figure 2.8).

Figure 2.8: Alignment of ADB Commitments with the Sustainable Development Goals, 2019

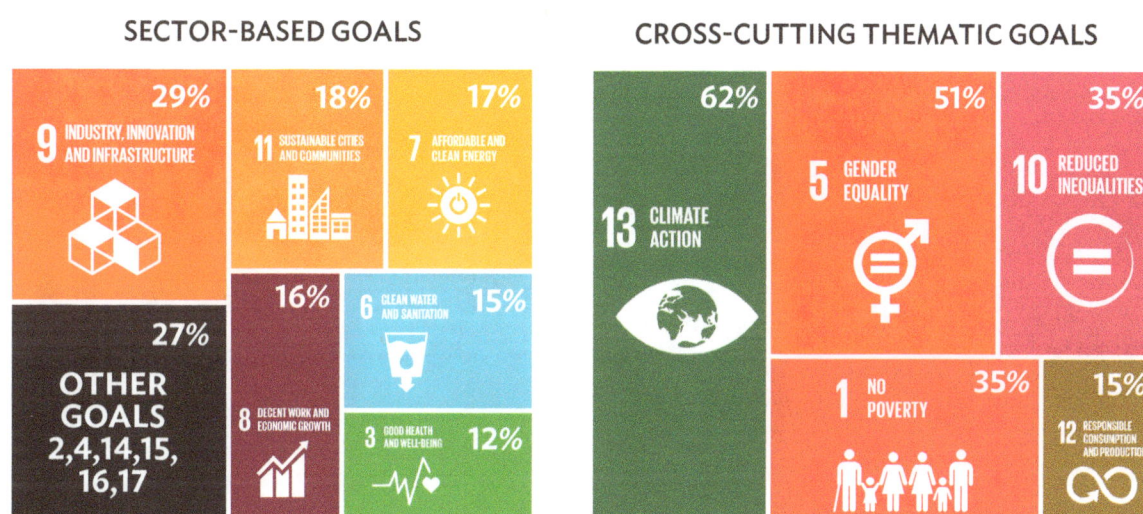

ADB = Asian Development Bank.
Based on enhanced project classification system tagging system rolled out on 1 April 2019.

91. **Alignment with sector or investment area goals.** Reflecting infrastructure's leading role in the ADB portfolio, 2019 commitments were linked most often on a sector basis to SDG 9: Infrastructure, Industry, and Innovation. Transport projects were particularly prominent. In terms of the number of total links, SDG 11 (Sustainable Cities) was next, followed by SDG 7 (Affordable and Clean Energy), and SDG 6 (Clean Water and Sanitation). Several transport and health sector projects were linked to SDG 3, which includes road safety targets. Chapter 1 describes progress toward the SDGs in ADB DMCs, as well as how ADB operations are helping to achieve these global goals through its seven operational priorities.

92. **Alignment with cross-cutting goals.** SDG 13 (Climate Action) and SDG 5 (Gender Equality) were the crossing-cutting SDGs with which ADB's 2019 operations commitments were most commonly linked. Both are priority areas under Strategy 2030. Links were often identified between projects targeting gender equality or featuring effective gender mainstreaming and target 5 of SDG 5: ensuring that women have full and effective participation and equal opportunities for leadership in political, economic, and public life. The 2019 commitments were also frequently linked to SDG 1 (Zero Poverty) and SDG 10 (Reduced Inequalities).

53

Demonstrating techniques. Seamstress Rano Kimsanova cuts fabric with other students who benefited from the ADB-supported Skills for Inclusive Growth Sector Development Program in the Kyrgyz Republic (photo by Danil Usmanov).

CHAPTER 3
SOVEREIGN OPERATIONS

Lessons from **ongoing and completed** operations inform improved selection and design of new ones, in a continuous cycle of **learning and adaptation.**

SOVEREIGN OPERATIONS

ENSURING QUALITY THROUGHOUT THE PROJECT CYCLE

ASSESS PROJECTS APPROVED IN 2019

AT DESIGN

DESIGN QUALITY OPERATIONS THAT ARE IMPLEMENTATION-READY

LESSONS LEARNED

DEVELOPMENT RESULTS DELIVERED TO CLIENTS AND BENEFICIARIES

AT COMPLETION

LESSONS CAPTURED

AT IMPLEMENTATION

ENSURE SATISFACTORY IMPLEMENTATION OF OPERATIONS

ASSESS AND LEARN FROM COMPLETED OPERATIONS VALIDATED IN 2017–2019

MEASURE AND MONITOR PERFORMANCE OF PROJECTS UNDER IMPLEMENTATION IN 2019

ADB is pursuing quality development and growth with its developing member countries. Success in this effort demands high-level performance throughout the project cycle. This chapter assesses the quality of the design and implementation of ADB's sovereign operations in 2019 and examines whether those recently completed performed as planned. The main factors affecting the relevance, efficiency, effectiveness, and likely sustainability of these completed operations are analyzed. The chapter also summarizes the key actions ADB took in 2019, based on lessons learned, to improve its performance.

DESIGN QUALITY OPERATIONS THAT ARE IMPLEMENTATION-READY

INFRASTRUCTURE PROJECTS APPROVED ANNUALLY

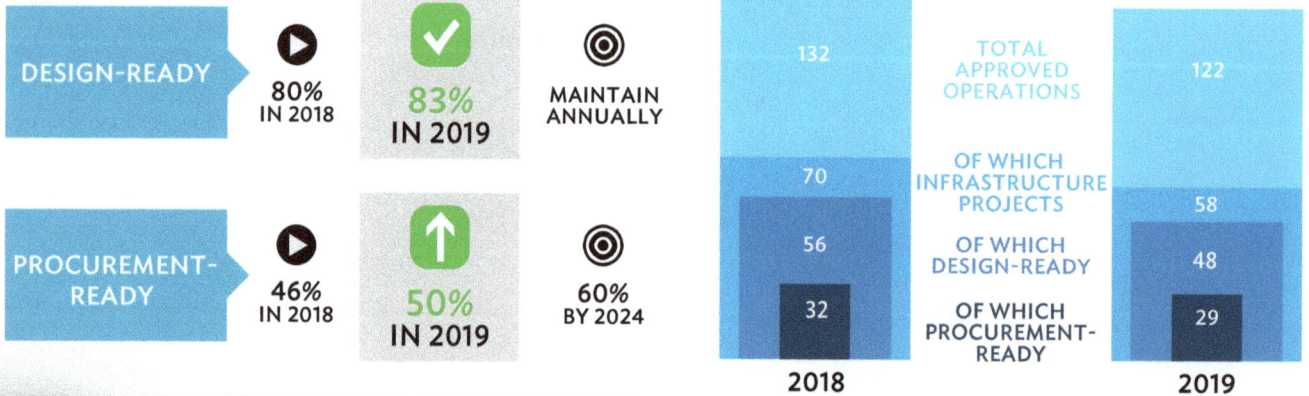

DESIGN-READY	▶ 80% IN 2018	✅ 83% IN 2019	◎ MAINTAIN ANNUALLY
PROCUREMENT-READY	▶ 46% IN 2018	⬆ 50% IN 2019	◎ 60% BY 2024

	2018	2019
TOTAL APPROVED OPERATIONS	132	122
OF WHICH INFRASTRUCTURE PROJECTS	70	58
OF WHICH DESIGN-READY	56	48
OF WHICH PROCUREMENT-READY	32	29

ENSURE SATISFACTORY IMPLEMENTATION OF PROJECTS

Provisional results from pilot of enhanced methodology

SOVEREIGN OPERATIONS AT IMPLEMENTATION RATED *SATISFACTORY*

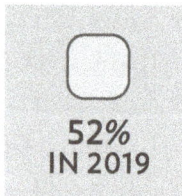

▶ NOT APPLICABLE   52% IN 2019   ◎ MONITOR

RATED *ON TRACK* BY CRITERIA

OUTPUT PROGRESS	84%
CONTRACT AWARD	75%
DISBURSEMENT	75%
FINANCIAL MANAGEMENT	65%
SAFEGUARDS	73%

DEVELOPMENT RESULTS DELIVERED TO CLIENTS AND BENEFICIARIES

SOVEREIGN OPERATIONS AT COMPLETION RATED *SUCCESSFUL*

▶ 77% IN 2016–2018   ⬇ 71% IN 2017–2019   ◎ 80% BY 2024

SUCCESS RATING

BY CRITERIA

RELEVANCE	82%
EFFICIENCY	75%
EFFECTIVENESS	68%
SUSTAINABILITY	62%

🕐 ON TIME

▶ 40% IN 2016–2018   ⬇ 36% IN 2017–2019   ◎ 45% BY 2024

BY TYPE	BY LOCATION
PBOs = 84% PROJECTS = 69%	SIDS = 42% FCAS DMCs = 54%

DMC = developing member country, FCAS = fragile and conflict-affected situation, PBO = policy-based operation, SIDS = small island developing state.

A. READINESS AT DESIGN STAGE

93. Sovereign infrastructure project readiness improved in 2019. The shares of these projects that were design- and/or procurement-ready before Board approval both grew. Of the design-ready projects, 77% had detailed engineering designs when approved, and preliminary designs and specifications had been completed for 98%.

94. ADB's regional departments made increased use of project-readiness financing facilities; 10 were committed in 2019. They also continued to use project-readiness checklists tailored to the context in individual developing member countries (DMCs). These maximized implementation readiness while recognizing the variations in domestic policies and procedures for financing preliminary or detailed designs, or launching bidding documents before project approval. ADB's continuing dialogue with DMCs on addressing barriers to readiness contributed to a notable positive development in 2019. Mongolia amended its public procurement law to allow advance procurement. The *2019 Annual Portfolio Performance Report* provides further details on implementation readiness (endnote 13).

B. IMPLEMENTATION PROGRESS

95. In 2019, ADB introduced an enhanced methodology for rating project performance during implementation. Results from the 2019 pilot demonstrate the increased rigor of the methodology; 52% of projects were rated *satisfactory*, versus 74% using the old methodology. Three of the five indicators have been improved. A new output progress indicator systematically monitors, details, and assesses the progress being achieved during implementation on each output target in the project's design and monitoring framework (DMF). The financial management indicator has been expanded to now track the timely submission of audited project and entity financial statements, the nature of the audit opinion, and compliance with financial covenants. The safeguards indicator has been made more rigorous and precise so that projects where safeguards covenants need additional attention can be more easily flagged. The enhanced methodology will be fully applied to the ongoing sovereign portfolio starting in the first quarter of 2020 and will be scored in the 2020 Development Effectiveness Review.

C. PERFORMANCE OF COMPLETED OPERATIONS

96. The share of completed sovereign operations rated *successful* in RY2017–2019 fell 6 percentage points from the RY2016–2018 baseline.[20] This was mainly because of the 2019 success rate of 68%, which was a 4-year low and down from the record high of 86% in 2016. Lowered success rates for transport sector operations, which constitute one-third of the completed sovereign portfolio, was the major sector factor weighing down the RY2017–2019 average. The 3-year average success rates dipped for both policy-based operations (from 89% to 84%) and investment projects (from 75% to 69%). The portion of investment projects rated *successful* hit a 6-year annual low of 64% in 2019.

97. As in the past, scores across the four equally weighted evaluation criteria were lowest for sustainability, followed by effectiveness, efficiency, and relevance. Despite the criteria's usual strong performance, the 3-year average rating for relevance was the lowest in 6 years. While efficiency ratings have been improving, the share of projects that closed within 1 year of the targeted date or earlier was *off track*. The 36% average was a historic low.

98. For results stories and performance summaries, and details on gender equality results, refer to Chapter 1. For details on performance in fragile and conflict-affected situations (FCAS) and small island developing states (SIDS), refer to Chapter 7.

D. IN FOCUS

1. Main Factors Lowering Sovereign Success Rates

99. **Sector factors.** The main factor pulling down the overall success rate for completed ADB operations was transport sector performance. The largest sector, it comprised one-third of all completed operations, and its success rate declined by 7 percentage points from RY2016–2018 to RY2017–2019 (Figure 3.1). The sector had a 3-year annual high success rate of 71% in RY2019, up from RY2017 (67%) and RY2018 (63%), but was still significantly weaker than the 94% achieved in 2016. Transport operations continued to suffer from low ratings on the sustainability criterion, and their effectiveness scores were also down.

100. The substantially lower success rates of the relatively small number of completed finance and education operations were another factor in the decrease in the overall sovereign success rate average. A steep decline in effectiveness criteria ratings contributed to a 13 percentage point drop in education's 3-year average success rate. Finance success rates were down 15 percentage points. In this sector, a sharp drop in the ratings for relevance and lower scores for sustainability were the most prevalent issues. The larger number and weaker performance of finance operations warrants a closer examination to shed light on challenges the sector faced (Box 3.1).

Figure 3.1: Success Rates of Completed ADB Sovereign Operations by Sector and Shares of Operations, Reporting Years 2016–2019 (%)

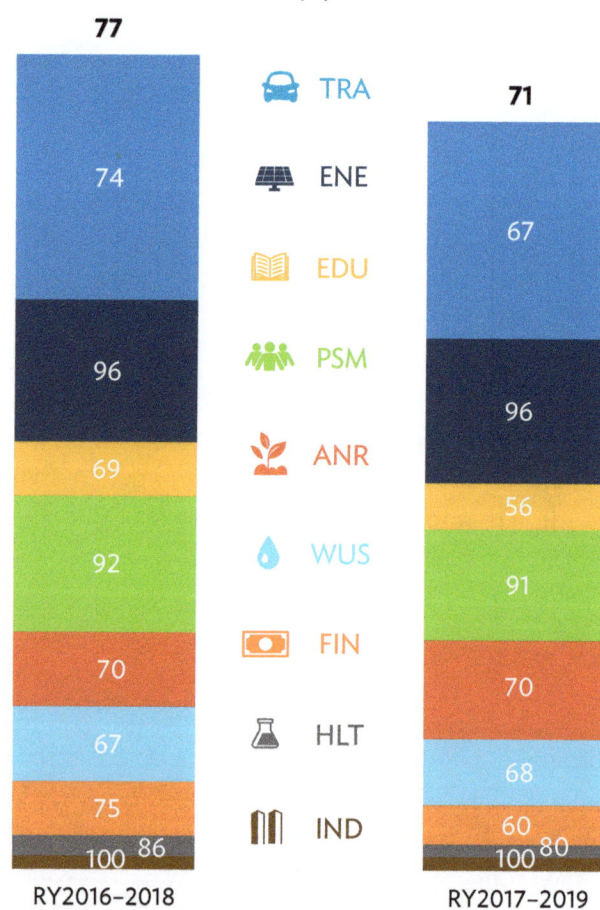

ADB = Asian Development Bank; ANR = agriculture, natural resources, and rural development; EDU = education; ENE = energy; FIN = finance; HLT = health; IND = industry and trade; PSM = public sector management; RY = reporting year; TRA = transport; WUS = water and other urban infrastructure and services.

Source: ADB Independent Evaluation Department.

58

Box 3.1: Relevance and Sustainability Challenges for Finance Sector Operations

Although finance operations again constituted a small subset of the completed portfolio, there were more of these operations in 2019 than in any recent year. Sector performance also reached a historic low with only 43% (three) of the seven operations for which completion reports were validated achieving *successful* ratings.

Based on validation reports, the four rated *less than successful* illustrated three common problems: (i) designs were not flexible enough to adjust to a changing context; (ii) the data necessary to assess whether outcome targets had been achieved were unavailable; and (iii) policy reforms lacked either the scope or adequate government-led institutional arrangements necessary to mobilize domestic resources to sustain medium-term lending to micro, small, and medium-sized enterprises.

Source: ADB Independent Evaluation Department.

101. **Modality factors.** The 3-year average success rate for investment projects declined because the share of projects rated *successful* hit a 6-year annual low in 2019, replacing the record-high 2016 success rate in the 3-year rolling average (Figure 3.2). Policy-based operations, which accounted for one-fifth of the portfolio of sovereign operations, also recorded a 2019 success rate that was lower than that of 2016, but higher than 2017. A sector development program to improve the enabling environment for women entrepreneurs was the only policy-based operation rated *less than successful* in 2019. It received low scores for efficiency and sustainability. Independent Evaluation Department (IED) validation reports indicated that capacity constraints of participating financial institutions meant that the financial intermediation loans could not be disbursed in full, and no documented evidence was available to show that policy reforms intended to benefit micro, small, and medium-sized enterprises led by women would be sustained.

Figure 3.2: Success Rates of Completed ADB Sovereign Investment Projects and Policy-Based Operations, Reporting Years 2016–2019

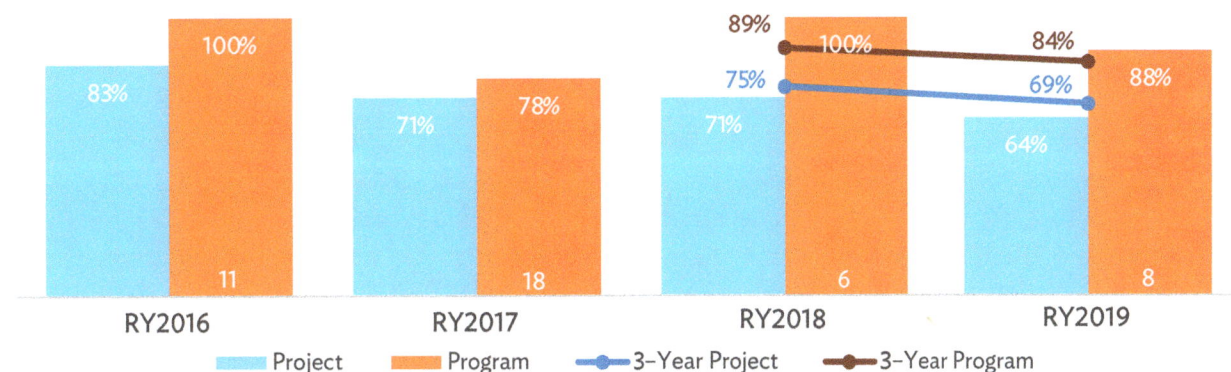

Note: Numbers at the bottom of data bars indicate the total number of successful projects and programs.
ADB = Asian Development Bank, RY = reporting year.
Source: ADB Independent Evaluation Department.

2. Learning from Completed Operations

Delivering Relevant Results

102. **Strong but declining relevance ratings.** Scores for relevance, historically the highest performer among the four evaluation criteria, have been declining since 2016 (Figure 3.3). Industry and trade was the only sector where scores were not lower. The share of completed operations rated *relevant* during RY2017–2019 was lowest in the information and communication technology (ICT) (50%) and education (60%) sectors. While still comparatively strong, the relevance of transport (92%) and energy (89%) also declined.

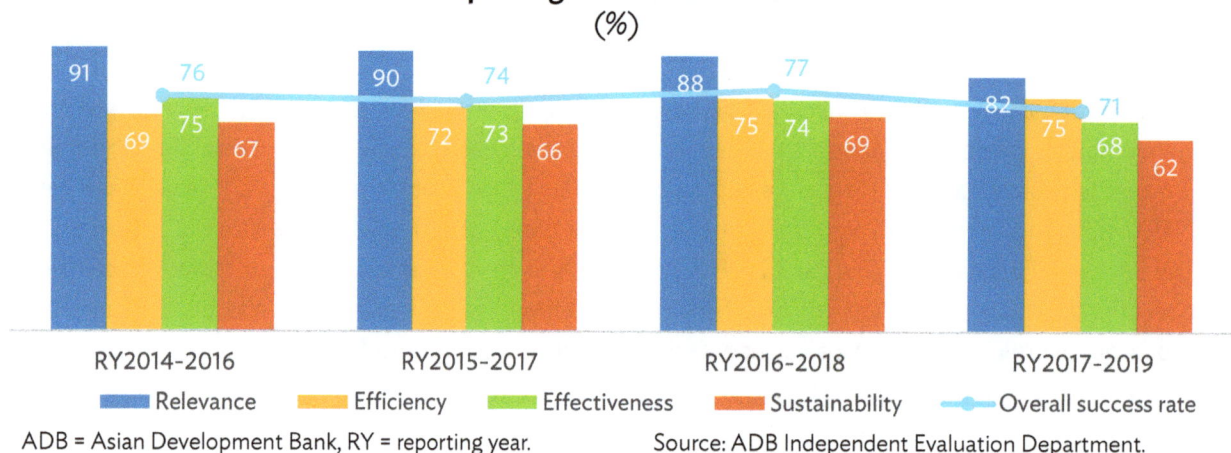

Figure 3.3: Success Rate of Completed ADB Sovereign Operations by Evaluation Criteria, Reporting Years 2014–2019
(%)

ADB = Asian Development Bank, RY = reporting year.
Source: ADB Independent Evaluation Department.

103. **Factors affecting relevance ratings.** Sovereign operations rated *less than relevant* in 2019 were aligned with DMC and ADB objectives and priorities, but IED validations identified other shortcomings. Many designs were assessed as generally overambitious. Of these, some were found to be insufficiently tailored to the needs of intended beneficiaries or not flexible enough to cope with changing conditions. Some were assessed to have insufficiently recognized and addressed institutional weaknesses. Such deficiencies led to safeguard issues, and in some cases outputs were reported as not being used by or to the benefit of the intended beneficiaries. Relevance was diminished in a few operations because their DMFs lacked the quality indicators required to fully measure the intended outcome.

104. **Actions taken in 2019 to improve relevance.** Among the steps taken in 2019 to boost relevance was the increased use by ADB project teams of project readiness financing facilities and technical assistance. This financing can be used during the project identification and design phases to more thoroughly assess and build institutional capacity, and develop detailed designs suited to the context and intended beneficiaries to help identify objectives that are ambitious yet realistic.

Effectively and efficiently achieving development results

105. **Decline in effectiveness ratings.** Only 68% of completed sovereign operations were rated *effective* in RY2017–2019, down from 74% in RY2016–2018 and making effectiveness the second-lowest ranking criterion. The biggest sector declines were in education (from 83% to 60%) and water and other urban infrastructure and services (from 76% to 67%), but the lowest-performing sectors were ICT at 0% and finance at 57%.

106. **Factors affecting effectiveness ratings.** Overambitious targets that led to underachievement was a principal factor found in education projects rated *less than effective* by IED validations. In some cases, designs or implementation arrangements were reported to have been adjusted during implementation, but by then it was too late. A few education projects simply lacked any evidence to establish whether the results targets they set had been met. Weak formulation and other issues in the DMF are not unique to education projects. In some *less than effective* operations in various sectors, adjustments were made during implementation to reflect changes in the project environment, but targets and indicators in the DMF were not updated accordingly.

107. **Consistent efficiency ratings**. The share of completed operations rated *efficient* remained constant at 75%. The 3-year averages for RY2017–2019 were highest in industry and trade (100%), ICT (100%), and energy (89%); and lowest in health (60%), water and other urban infrastructure and services (63%), and education (67%). The health and water and other urban infrastructure and services projects rated *less than efficient* most commonly did not achieve their originally targeted economic internal rate of return and, in a few cases, lacked the outcome-level data necessary to verify the rate of return. Many also experienced significant delays.

108. **Fewer projects completed on time.** Completing on time is among the measures of a project's efficiency. The share of projects that closed on time—within 1 year of the targeted date or earlier—hit an all-time low of 36% during the calendar years 2017–2019, putting sovereign operations *off track* on this indicator. Projects that were not completed on time were delayed by an average of 2.7 years, compared with 2.8 years in RY2016–2018. Issues related to land acquisition, performance of contractors and consultants, and lack of counterpart funding contributed to the delays. These remain perennial issues; however, earthquakes and severe weather events affected more projects than previously. The *2019 Annual Portfolio Performance Report* provides further details about implementation timelines (endnote 13).

109. **Actions in 2019 to improve efficiency and effectiveness.** Among the steps taken in 2019 to boost efficiency and effectiveness was increasing the share of infrastructure projects that were design-ready and procurement-ready, and increasing the use of project readiness financing facilities. Of the 10 facilities committed in 2019, all but one in concessional assistance DMCs, six will focus on institutional capacity development and eight on preparing detailed engineering designs. Focusing on these issues before project approval is expected to help inform performance targets and implementation timelines and arrangements that are realistic and ready to be carried out effectively and efficiently. In addition, the enhanced project performance rating methodology ADB piloted in 2019 is designed to detect and flag issues with output delivery, and compliance with safeguards and financial management covenants more accurately. Taking early action on any issues flagged should in turn help improve the performance of ADB operations in fully delivering the intended benefits within the intended timeline.

Ensuring development results are sustained

110. **Establishing conditions for sustainability an ongoing challenge.** Sustainability is a long-standing and ongoing challenge for ADB operations and the worst performer among the four evaluation criteria. The reason most commonly cited for IED downgrades of operations success ratings is a lack of evidence that the government policies and financial commitments required to sustain the development outcome achieved by an operation are or will be in place. The share of sovereign operations rated *likely sustainable* declined to 62% in RY2017–2019. Among ADB's main sectors, transport (51% in RY2017–2019); agriculture, natural resources, and rural development (53%); and water and other urban infrastructure and services (57%) consistently had the lowest sustainability ratings. The share of transport operations rated *likely sustainable* dropped by 6 percentage points in RY2017–2019, which in turn brought down the sector's average success rate.

111. **Learning and taking action to improve sustainability.** To learn more about the causes of poor sustainability and derive lessons for improvement, ADB studied 86 infrastructure projects in the road transport and water sectors. The main findings and lessons are summarized on the opposite page. ADB responded to one of these lessons in 2019 by adding a new section to the approval documents of investment projects that identifies major barriers to sustainability and the actions to be taken to address them. ADB also developed and piloted a new methodology for screening the quality of infrastructure projects at the design stage that includes sustainability as a criterion, alongside green, inclusive, and resilient attributes. Refer to Chapter 2 for further details.

3. Performance of Completed Concessional Assistance Operations

112. The share of completed concessional assistance operations rated *successful* was *off track* in RY2017–2019, declining to 70% from 77% in RY2016–2018. This portfolio was impacted by the same negative sector and modality factors that lowered the performance of ADB operations overall. Its evaluation criteria ratings for relevance, efficiency, effectiveness, and sustainability were similar as well.

113. In terms of on-time performance, concessional assistance projects recorded an even steeper decline (10 percentage points) than did ADB operations overall (4 percentage points). They were also rated *off track*, with only 30% closing on time in calendar years 2017–2019. On-time implementation is more difficult to achieve in concessional assistance DMCs, given the heightened challenges of institutional capacity and other operational issues projects face in those countries.

IMPROVING THE
SUSTAINABILITY OF RESULTS
IN ADB-FINANCED OPERATIONS

Post-completion sustainability remains a challenge in one in three operations.
ADB studied 86 infrastructure projects in the road transport and water sectors
to learn more about the causes of poor sustainability and derive lessons for improvement.[a]

WHAT ADB OPERATIONS ALREADY DO

1. Assess full life cycle sustainability costs
2. Require developing member countries to commit to maintenance funding
3. Tailor activities to whole-of-life maintenance needs
4. Focus on financial sustainability in operational plans
5. Build vital capacity and systems
6. Establish sector financing partnership facilities

SUMMARY FINDINGS

ADB is learning from its completed operations, adjusting its preparation and implementation practices, and making it more probable that the benefits delivered will last.

The sustainability situation in operations was better than might have been expected given the prospects for sustainability reported by project evaluations several years earlier.

Sustainability is a shared responsibility; ADB and its developing member countries must work hand in hand to do better.

MAIN OBSTACLE TO SUSTAINABILITY

POOR OPERATION AND MAINTENANCE (O&M) ▸ DETERIORATION OF ASSETS

▸ INCREASED COSTS

▸ REDUCED SOCIOECONOMIC BENEFITS

KEY CHALLENGES IN O&M

Unsustained finance and funding	Weak institutions and governance	Capital cost focus in decision-making	Insufficient expertise	Limited awareness and commitment

SUGGESTIONS FOR FURTHER EXPLORATION

Examine sustainability across entire organizations and O&M support beyond ADB project assets. Explore setting aside a portion of loans for O&M. Focus on the reliability and good planning of maintenance funding, rather than its source. Be patient and pragmatic when pursuing higher user charges and tariffs.	Factor institutional and capacity assessments into all infrastructure operation preparation. Support reforms and institutional capacity for sector-wide O&M through multitranche financing facility and policy-based lending.	Reflect realistic assessments of an operator's technical capabilities, the availability of parts, and how much maintenance to expect in designs and specifications. Expand technology transfer in the transport sector. Base value-for-money decisions on life-cycle cost analysis.	Systematically ensure all infrastructure project teams include the special institutional and capacity-building expertise needed to establish the conditions necessary for outcome sustainability.	Formulate loan covenants to help underpin sustainability in a manner that realistically reflects what is feasible.

KEY LESSONS

Strengthen the focus on sustainability in project design documents.

Shape sustainability approaches to a project's context, circumstances, and conditions.

Base sustainability evaluations on the issue of whether sound O&M systems and funding, as designed or otherwise, are likely to be available or are already in place.

---

[a] ADB Strategy, Policy and Partnerships Department. Improving the Sustainability of Results in ADB Financed Operations: Operations Research Study. Unpublished.

A **prosperous future.** Loans from Access Bank in Azerbaijan have given small businesses a chance to develop and grow (photo by Daro Sulakauri).

CHAPTER 4
PRIVATE SECTOR OPERATIONS

Lessons from **ongoing and completed** operations inform improved selection and design of new ones, in a continuous cycle of **learning and adaptation**.

ASSESS OPERATIONS COMMITTED IN 2019

AT COMMITMENT

SCALE UP NONSOVEREIGN OPERATIONS AND ENSURE THEIR STRATEGIC RELEVANCE

LESSONS LEARNED

DEVELOPMENT RESULTS DELIVERED TO CLIENTS AND BENEFICIARIES

PRIVATE SECTOR OPERATIONS

SCALING UP WHILE ENSURING GOOD PORTFOLIO QUALITY AND RESULTS DELIVERY

LESSONS CAPTURED

AT COMPLETION

AT IMPLEMENTATION

ENSURE PORTFOLIO IS FINANCIALLY HEALTHY AND DELIVERING RESULTS

ASSESS AND LEARN FROM COMPLETED OPERATIONS VALIDATED IN 2017–2019

MEASURE AND MONITOR PERFORMANCE OF OPERATIONS UNDER IMPLEMENTATION IN 2019

Strategy 2030 recognizes the important role that private sector operations play in delivering strong development results. It sets ambitious goals for scaling up ADB's nonsovereign operations to account for one-third of all ADB operations by number in 2024. Nonsovereign operations should help accomplish all seven Strategy 2030 operational priorities, but this growth should not come at the expense of portfolio quality. ADB must ensure that private sector operations are financially sustainable and deliver development results. The indicators in the new corporate results framework reflect these aims.

NONSOVEREIGN OPERATIONS COMMITTED IN 2019

SCALE UP NONSOVEREIGN OPERATIONS AND ENSURE THEIR STRATEGIC RELEVANCE

TOTAL OPERATIONS AT COMMITMENT THAT ARE NSOs

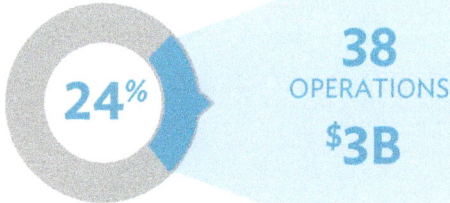

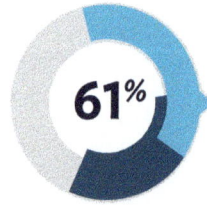

24%

38 OPERATIONS

$3B

20% IN 2018

↑ 24% IN 2019

33% BY 2024

NSO PROJECTS IN FRONTIER ECONOMIES OR NEW SECTORS

61%

FRONTIER ECONOMIES 39%

NEW SECTORS 34%

48% IN 2018

✓ 61% IN 2019

55% BY 2024

82% OF NSOs PROMOTE GENDER EQUALITY

$724M NSO FINANCING FOR CLIMATE CHANGE

8 NSOs SUPPORTING INCLUSIVE BUSINESS

OPERATIONS UNDER IMPLEMENTATION IN 2019

ENSURE PORTFOLIO IS HEALTHY AND DELIVERING RESULTS

Results from pilot based on sample of operations

NSOs AT RISK OF NOT ACHIEVING DEVELOPMENT RESULTS

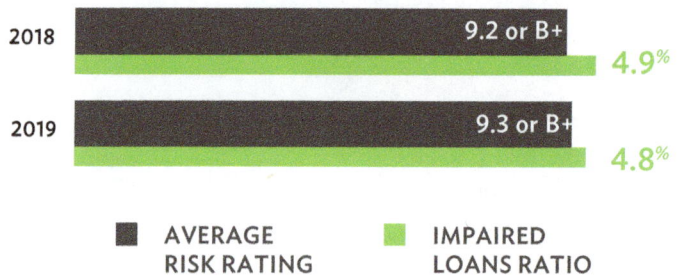

NOT APPLICABLE

23% IN 2019

MONITOR

2018 — 9.2 or B+ — 4.9%

2019 — 9.3 or B+ — 4.8%

■ AVERAGE RISK RATING   ■ IMPAIRED LOANS RATIO

COMPLETED OPERATIONS VALIDATED 2017–2019

DEVELOPMENT RESULTS DELIVERED TO CLIENTS AND BENEFICIARIES

NSOs AT COMPLETION RATED *SUCCESSFUL*

54% IN 2016–2018

↓ 52% IN 2017–2019

70% BY 2024

SUCCESS RATING BY CRITERIA

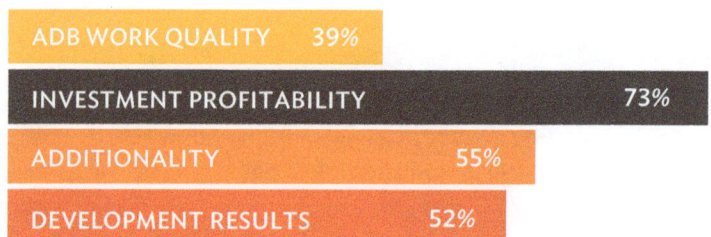

ADB WORK QUALITY — 39%

INVESTMENT PROFITABILITY — 73%

ADDITIONALITY — 55%

DEVELOPMENT RESULTS — 52%

ADB = Asian Development Bank, B = billion, M = million, NSO = nonsovereign operation.

A. SCALING UP AND STRATEGIC FIT

114. The first full year of Strategy 2030 implementation saw a good start made on scaling up the annual number of nonsovereign operations to one-third of all ADB operations by 2024. The percentage of newly committed nonsovereign operations in the total number of operations grew substantially in 2019. Volume growth of nonsovereign operation financing was also strong.

115. Equally important, these operations played a key role in strategic areas. Almost two-thirds of all committed nonsovereign operations support frontier economies or new sectors. More than 80% promote gender equality, up substantially from 69% in 2018. Almost a quarter of

nonsovereign operation financing supported climate change in 2019, highlighting these operations' important role in achieving ADB's overall target for climate mitigation and adaptation. The number of nonsovereign operations supporting ADB's agenda to promote inclusive business also grew from 2018.

116. ADB is *on track* to achieve its 2024 nonsovereign cofinancing ratio target of 200%. During 2017–2019, a total of $10.1 billion was mobilized against $7.1 billion in net ordinary capital resources (less risk transfers), with every $1 in financing ADB committed for its nonsovereign operations matched by $1.43 in long-term cofinancing.

B. PERFORMANCE AT IMPLEMENTATION

117. As with sovereign operations, flagging implementation issues as early as possible is important if nonsovereign operations are to deliver the best possible outcomes at completion. ADB piloted a new indicator in 2019 to measure the risk that ongoing nonsovereign operations will not achieve the targeted development results. About 20% of the nonsovereign portfolio was assessed on a provisional basis. Almost a quarter of the portfolio was determined to be "at risk" of not achieving outcomes. However, the small sample size and emergent methodology makes it too early to draw conclusions. More detailed analysis

will follow once the methodology is finalized and the entire portfolio is assessed in 2020.

118. Sound financial performance by ongoing projects is integral to the long-term sustainability of ADB's nonsovereign lending activities. ADB has a robust risk management framework and closely monitors the health of its nonsovereign portfolio. Credit quality in 2019 remained largely unchanged from the year before as nonsovereign operations continued to operate in more challenging markets. The risk issues were deal-specific and did not reflect systemic factors.

C. PERFORMANCE AT COMPLETION

119. The share of completed nonsovereign operations rated *successful* declined for the third consecutive 3-year period and, at 52% during reporting years (RY) 2017–2019, was *off-track* to meet the 2024 target of 70%.

120. The share of operations in infrastructure, generally the best-performing sector in the nonsovereign portfolio, dropped from 34% in RY2016–2018 to 18% in RY2017–2019. The poorest performers were the private equity fund operations (21% of the total), where one of

the seven completed transactions was rated *successful*.

121. The rating for the development results criterion mirrors the overall success rate and remained low, reflecting underachievement against ambitious project targets and ongoing challenges with data availability and design and monitoring framework quality. On the other criteria, performance continued to be strongest on investment profitability and weakest on ADB work quality.

D. IN FOCUS
1. Newly Committed Nonsovereign Operations

122. **New high in 2019.** The nonsovereign operation share of total ADB commitments reached an all-time high of 24% in 2019, putting ADB firmly *on track* to achieve the 2024 target (Figure 4.1). During the year, 38 nonsovereign operations were committed, compared with 32 in 2018.

123. **Smaller deals, in line with operational directions.** Reflecting the directions of Strategy 2030, the operational plan for private sector operations for 2019–2024 prioritizes smaller and riskier transactions across a larger number of countries. The average deal size decreased to $79 million in 2019 from $98 million in 2018. As well as being in line with the directions in the operational plan, this is expected to help diversify portfolio risk. While the nonsovereign operation share in overall ADB financing decreased in 2019, the volume did not change substantially and almost matched the record high of $3.1 billion in 2018 (Figure 4.2).

Figure 4.1: Share of Nonsovereign Operation Commitments in Total ADB Lending, 2016–2019
(%)

2024 Target for ADB = 33

ADB = Asian Development Bank.

Figure 4.2: Nonsovereign Operation Commitments in Number and Financing, 2010–2019

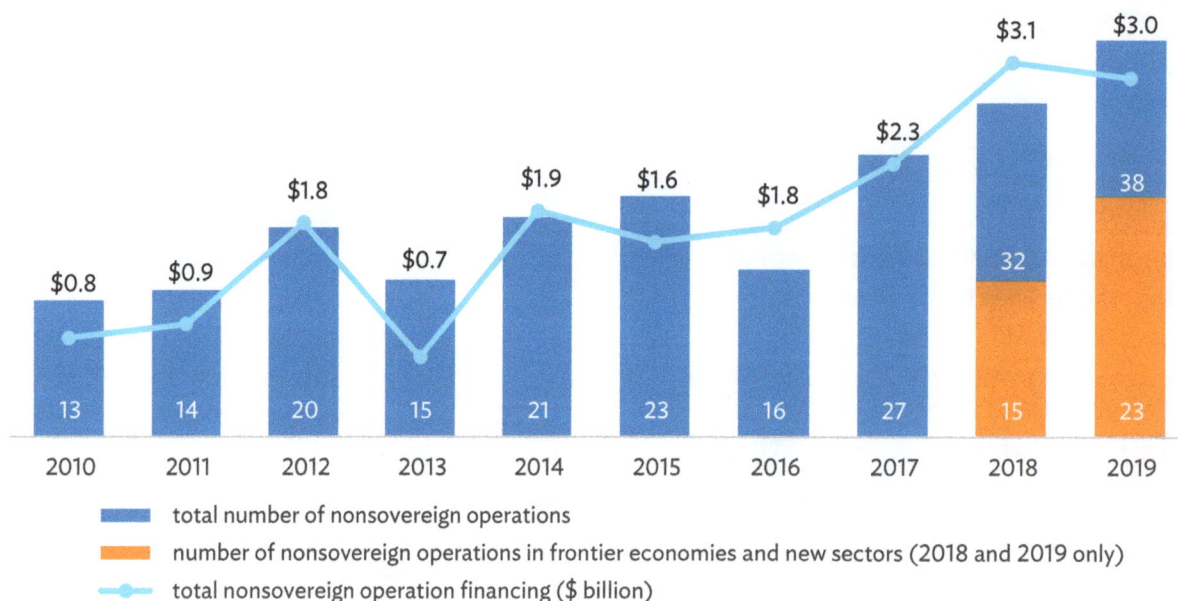

- total number of nonsovereign operations
- number of nonsovereign operations in frontier economies and new sectors (2018 and 2019 only)
- total nonsovereign operation financing ($ billion)

124. **Large majority of new transactions in more challenging segments.** Of the projects committed in 2019, 23 (61%) will be implemented in frontier economies and/or new sectors. This was up from 16 in 2018 (48%) and above the 2024 target of 55%. Sustaining these numbers throughout the 6-year results framework period will nonetheless require continuing efforts.

125. **Substantial rise in operations in group A countries.** Growth in nonsovereign operation commitments occurred in frontier economies and new sectors but was particularly strong in the group A countries. Commitments in these most operationally challenging developing member countries (DMCs) more than doubled from three projects in 2018

to seven in 2019. These operations are playing an important role in supporting private sector-led growth in countries such as Afghanistan and Myanmar where ADB is working with private clients in areas such as telecommunications and renewable energy.

126. **Strong demonstration effects through transactions in new sectors.** Engaging private sector operators to run infrastructure services is still at a nascent stage even in the more advanced DMCs. ADB's nonsovereign lending is a more sustainable way to finance infrastructure projects, and it also demonstrates the viability of such investments to other private players. Transport is one sector where ADB has been making headway in applying this approach (Box 4.1).

Box 4.1: ADB Private Sector Financing Supports Railway Projects in India and Thailand

Building on past and ongoing sovereign projects in the railway sector in India, the Asian Development Bank (ADB) is involved in the electrification of 3,378 route kilometers of existing railway track in 13 states in India. A central aim of the 2019 nonsovereign loan of $746 million, ADB's largest ever, is to increase the volume of passengers and cargo being moved by more environmentally friendly electric power rather than diesel on the country's railways. The example of ADB's participation is expected to crowd in insurance companies and other private institutions to help the Indian Railway Finance Corporation finance, through unfunded risk transfers, the projects in its railway development pipeline.

ADB is also providing the equivalent of $311 million to help finance the private sector construction and operation of the Pink and Yellow lines of Bangkok's mass rapid transit system. ADB's involvement as a lender enhanced the overall bankability of the project by providing a long tenor repayment profile. ADB's terms will add flexibility to the project's cash flow management and help it through any low-ridership period when the lines begin operations. The new lines will help provide a wider choice of affordable, efficient, and more environmentally friendly public transport for Bangkok's rapidly growing population.

Sources: ADB. 2019. *Report and Recommendation of the President to the Board of Directors: Proposed Loan to the Indian Railway Finance Corporation for the Railways Track Electrification Project.* Manila; and ADB. 2019. *Report and Recommendation of the President to the Board of Directors: Proposed Loans to the Northern Bangkok Monorail Company Limited, Eastern Bangkok Monorail Company Limited for the Bangkok Mass Rapid Transit Project (Pink and Yellow Lines).* Manila.

127. **Inclusive business support on rise.** Eight nonsovereign operations committed in 2019 will support inclusive business, two more than in 2018. Four will enable more lending to low-income households and micro, small, and medium-sized enterprises. The other four are in the agribusiness sector and are expected to help create jobs, improve livelihood opportunities for smallholder farmers, and strengthen food security.

2. Main Factors Lowering Success Rates

128. **Continuing deterioration.** Only 52% (17 of 33) of completed nonsovereign operations in RY2017–2019 were rated *successful*, 2 percentage points down from the previous reporting period. Most of the successful projects were investments in financial market operations (11 projects) and private sector support for renewable energy generation (5 projects).

129. **Uneven performance by types of investment.** The overall decline in the completed nonsovereign operations success rate highlighted continuing uneven performance by different types of investments (Figure 4.3). A lower of share of better-performing investments in infrastructure was partially tempered by the improved success rate of investments in financial institutions, which made up the majority of completed nonsovereign operations in RY2017–2019.

Figure 4.3: Performance at Completion by Type of Investment, 2014–2019
(%)

FIN = direct equity and loans to financial institutions, INF = direct equity and loans in infrastructure, PEF = private equity fund, RY = reporting year, XARR = extended annual review report.
Source: ADB Independent Evaluation Department.

130. **Private equity funds challenging.** Although private equity funds made up just one-fifth of completed nonsovereign operations, their very low success rate (14% in RY2017–2019, down from 43% in RY2016–2018) had a sizable downside impact on the overall success rate. The six *unsuccessful* private equity funds posted negative or very low financial returns and thus failed to demonstrate the viability of private equity investments in the target markets. ADB support for these funds was aimed at creating jobs and catalyzing additional investments into nascent fund management markets, but there was a lack of good investment opportunities in the challenging macroeconomic environment during their active life span. The performance of investee companies was also affected, exacerbated by shortcomings in the operational background and industry expertise of the fund managers.

131. **Performance upturn in 2019.** ADB's more recently completed nonsovereign operations showed improving performance, with the average success rate up 13 percentage points to 55% in RY2019 from the previous reporting year. The biggest impact came from investments in financial institutions, where six of seven were rated *successful* at completion.

132. **Delivery of development results affected by data issues.** The overall success of a nonsovereign operation rests on the assessment of its development results rating (Figure 4.4). If this is found to be *less than satisfactory*, a nonsovereign operation cannot be evaluated as *successful*. As in the previous reporting period, almost half of completed nonsovereign operations fell short on this critical measure. Among

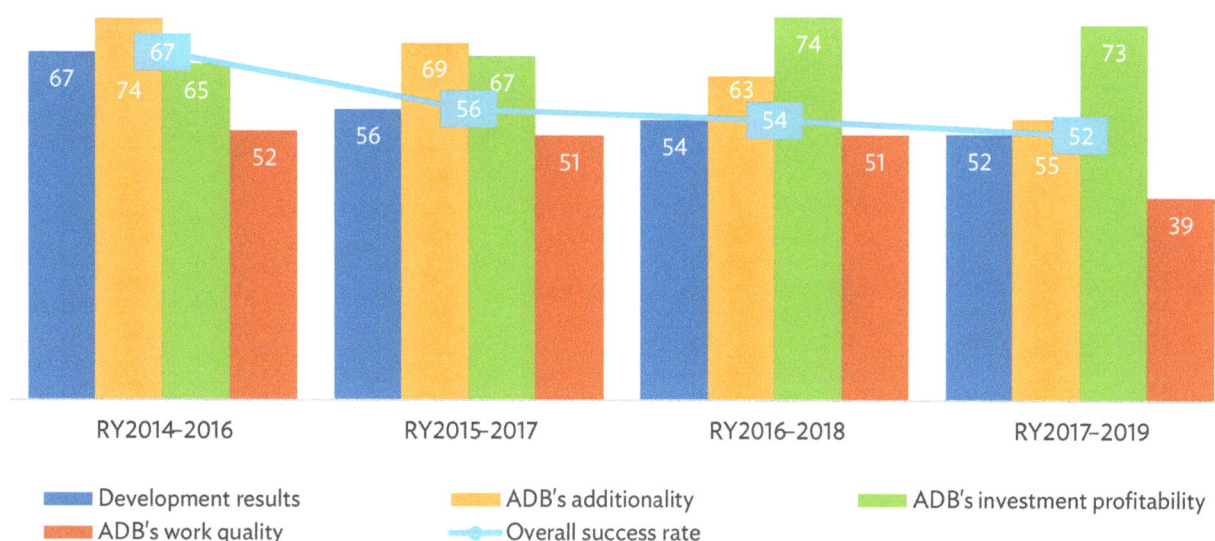

Figure 4.4: Performance at Completion by Criteria, 2014–2019
(%)

	RY2014–2016	RY2015–2017	RY2016–2018	RY2017–2019
Development results	67	56	54	52
ADB's additionality	74	69	63	55
ADB's investment profitability	65	67	74	73
ADB's work quality	52	51	51	39
Overall success rate	67	56	54	52

- Development results
- ADB's additionality
- ADB's investment profitability
- ADB's work quality
- Overall success rate

ADB = Asian Development Bank, RY = reporting year.
Source: ADB Independent Evaluation Department.

the most common reasons for downgrades were poorly conceived design and monitoring frameworks (DMFs) or insufficient data collection and monitoring that made it impossible to ascertain the operations' actual contributions to delivering development results. Some operations also underachieved relative to ambitious targets, in particular for expanding financial products to targeted groups. Challenging market conditions, which undermined the delivery of expected development results, were also cited as a reason for giving a *less than satisfactory* rating to several completed nonsovereign operations.

133. **Solid profitability amid declining ADB work quality.** Other evaluation criteria have lesser effect on nonsovereign operations' overall success ratings but do provide important insights into their performance. Investment profitability was the strongest criterion in RY2017–2019, with almost three-quarters of nonsovereign operations rated at least *satisfactory* (about the same level as in the previous reporting period). At the low end of the spectrum, however, was ADB's work quality. The share of projects assessed as *satisfactory* dropped significantly to 39%. Weaknesses in client appraisals during project design was among the main factors, along with shortcomings in progress monitoring and compliance.

3. Learning from Completed Operations

134. **Actions underway to improve quality at completion.** ADB recognizes the need to address the persisting challenges to success in nonsovereign operations, particularly as it shifts investments into more challenging markets and activities. Among the steps underway are actions to enhance the process for data collection and early flagging of problems, and the development of a tool to better identify and target development results at the outset.

135. **Identifying risks to development results during implementation.** A new indicator in the corporate results framework for ongoing nonsovereign operations aims at establishing an early warning system on risks to the delivery of targeted development results, which is intended to improve quality at completion. While some issues flagged during the implementation of a nonsovereign operation may be beyond ADB's control, the new system will allow operations teams to consider them and perform corrective actions that ADB can guide or manage, such as timely delivery of outputs and adherence to standards. This new system will facilitate systematic collection of development results data and regular update of DMFs to reflect any post-commitment changes.

136. **Ex ante development impact assessment tool.** ADB is working to improve its ability to assess the anticipated development results of each nonsovereign operation. A new ex ante assessment tool to be introduced in 2020 will make appraisals of proposed nonsovereign operations objective and will help set targets for development results that are measurable and realistic. This will enable ADB to select projects with the highest potential for development impact and gain a clearer picture of the nonsovereign operation portfolio, strengthening analysis of whether and how it is achieving its dual mandate of delivering financial sustainability and development impact.

Learning for everyone. Student Taslima Akter at the Faliapara Alimuddi Government Primary School, Ukhiya, Cox's Bazar, Bangladesh (photo by Abir Abdullah).

CHAPTER 5
ADB AS A KNOWLEDGE ORGANIZATION

KNOWLEDGE BENEFITED

KNOWLEDGE USED

KNOWLEDGE DELIVERED

ADB AS A KNOWLEDGE ORGANIZATION

ADB is working to expand its role, reach, and quality as a knowledge institution. Based on new and long-standing performance indicators in the corporate results framework, this chapter assesses how well it is doing in these efforts, along with how well it is perceived to be doing. ADB's work as a provider of practical development knowledge is examined, as are the factors affecting performance in 2019 and the key actions ADB took during the year to make itself a stronger knowledge and learning organization both internally and for the benefit of its developing member countries.

BENEFITS			
	CLIENTS SATISFIED WITH THE USE OF ADB KNOWLEDGE PRODUCTS	78% IN 2018	Data to be collected in 2020	80% BIENNIAL
	EVENT PARTICIPANTS REPORTING INCREASED KNOWLEDGE AND/OR SKILLS	Data to be collected in 2020	
	TECHNICAL ASSISTANCE PROJECTS RATED *SUCCESSFUL*	86% IN 2017–2019	

A. BENEFITS

Clients' Feedback to Deliver Quality Knowledge Solutions

137. **Baseline client satisfaction rate at 78%.** ADB conducted a survey in 2019 to determine a baseline against which it can gauge the future reach, quality, use, and ultimately the benefits to its developing member country (DMC) clients of the knowledge products and services (KPS) it delivers. A total of 338 respondents answered 15 questions, including about the benefits of using key ADB KPS.[21] Based on the overall 78% baseline satisfaction rate, ADB has set an 80% satisfaction rate as its minimum target for future surveys to be conducted every 2 years.

138. **Tangible benefits reported by majority surveyed.** Almost three-quarters of the respondents (73%) reported having improved their work quality and output through the use and application of ADB KPS. Nine of every ten of these participants indicated they had amplified the impact by sharing or discussing this new knowledge with others. The examples of KPS benefits reported included better decision-making; improved work efficiency; clearer understanding of policy issues and implications; help in policy formulation; and a deeper knowledge of how to implement climate actions, carry out procurement, and use monitoring tools. The survey indicated room for improvement—while 48% of respondents considered ADB an "essential" source of knowledge, another 48% rated it "useful," and the remaining 4% "not useful."

139. **Event participant feedback to be collected and reported.** ADB provides many knowledge-related events each year on a variety of topics and projects across all its sectors and themes.[22] The new corporate results framework (CRF) added a tracking indicator to measure the share of participants who report gaining knowledge and/or skills from such events. Provisional survey results of 271 participants in 54 of these events and training courses since the CRF was approved in September 2019 showed 93% reporting knowledge and/or skills gains. The first data for the CRF cycle will be reported in 2020.

140. **Technical assistance success rates largely stable.** Technical assistance (TA) can create knowledge solutions that are tailored to the needs of individual DMCs. Of the 486 sovereign and nonsovereign TA projects completed in RY2017–2019, 86% were rated *successful* in the completion reports of the regional departments, a change of 2 percentage points from the ratio for RY2016–2018. ADB's Independent Evaluation Department has been piloting the validation of selected TA completion reports and, based on the findings, introduced TA completion report validation guidelines in 2019.

USED		WEB-DISTRIBUTED KNOWLEDGE SOLUTIONS	834,900 IN 2019
		ACTIVE ENGAGEMENT ON SOCIAL MEDIA	391,830 IN 2019

B. USED

Clients' Use of ADB Knowledge Solutions and Engagement via Social Media

141. **Downloads of knowledge products and services increased.** The volume of client interactions with ADB websites and social media is a leading indicator of the use of ADB KPS. Knowledge solution downloads increased 15% from 725,000 to 834,900 year-on-year. An upward trend in the share of ADB. org connections made through mobile phones and tablets continued. They accounted for almost 35% of usage in 2019. The five publications with the most downloads are shown below.

142. **Broader social media audience but lower engagement.** Social media is proactive and enables ADB to reach and disseminate KPS to a broader audience. The overall number of followers and subscribers to the social media platforms ADB uses increased from 653,788 in 2018 to 774,792.[23] However, a change in the platforms' algorithms in early 2019 reduced social media engagement to 391,830 shares and likes in 2019 from 1,157,259 in 2018.[24]

DELIVERED		
	KNOWLEDGE PRODUCTS AND SERVICES DRAWN FROM K-NEXUS	**301** IN 2019
	KNOWLEDGE PRODUCTS AND SERVICES DELIVERED	**106%** IN 2019
	IMPACT EVALUATIONS COMPLETED	**2** IN 2019
	INNOVATIVE OPERATIONS AND TECHNICAL ASSISTANCE PROJECTS	Data to be collected in 2020

C. DELIVERED

More ADB Knowledge Products and Services Delivered

143. **Increasing needs for internal communication and use of k-Nexus.** ADB developed an online platform, k-Nexus, to better manage and share its knowledge internally, along with data and information on what KPS are currently in or planned for operations pipelines. A new tracking indicator measures the use of this database through the number of KPS drawn from k-Nexus to support development of ADB's country operations business plan (COBPs). About 45% (301 of 664) of the planned KPS titles in the 30 COBPs approved in 2019 were accessed from k-Nexus. The migration of k-Nexus from FileNet to SharePoint that began in the second quarter presented challenges for departments to input their KPS into the database, and discouraged those preparing many of the COBPs from using it.

144. **More knowledge products and services delivered.** In line with Strategy 2030's vision for ADB as a knowledge bank, explicit knowledge sharing is delivered through KPS, making it important to know how effectively this is being done. Slightly more ADB KPS were delivered during the year than planned in the annual work program and budget framework. The KPS delivery rate increased steadily from 62% in 2017, to 84% in 2018, and to 106% in 2019.

145. **Two impact studies completed.** ADB conducts impact studies to gather empirical evidence for planning future operations on what has worked well in previous interventions and what has not. Two impact studies were completed in 2019: a completed ADB operation on a lower secondary education in the Lao People's Democratic Republic (Box 5.1) and a program supporting social protection in the Philippines (Box 5.2).

> **Box 5.1: Impact Study 1—Secondary Education Sector Development**
>
> An impact study found that an Asian Development Bank (ADB) operation had helped lift the gross enrollment rates for girls and the secondary–primary school ratio in 30 of the poorest and most educationally disadvantaged districts in the Lao People's Democratic Republic. The Secondary Education Sector Development Program, implemented during 2012–2018, aimed to enhance equity, quality, and efficiency in secondary education. The study rated the program's development impact *satisfactory* and found that its support for improving education policy, curriculum, stipends, and associated facilities also produced sustained results in terms of overall enrollment numbers in the targeted districts and gender parity in the classroom.
>
> Source: ADB Southeast Asia Department.

> **Box 5.2: Impact Study 2—Social Protection Support Project**
>
> The ongoing Asian Development Bank (ADB) Social Protection Support Program in the Philippines achieved its planned results of improving access to health and education for children from poor households. An ADB impact study found that more of the children the project has targeted were attending school, and more of these children and pregnant mothers were using and receiving health care services. The study reaffirmed earlier findings that the conditional cash transfers under the program had not encouraged dependency or increased expenditures on tobacco, alcohol, or gambling.
>
> Source: ADB Southeast Asia Department.

System, Process, and Capacity Promoting Innovation at ADB

146. **Innovation task force formed.** ADB will increase its sharing of experience, best practices, and innovation with its DMCs under Strategy 2030. As an initial step, ADB established a bank-wide innovation task force to discuss how it can best enhance innovation. The task force, comprising more than 150 staff members from across all departments, including resident missions, has identified three drivers of change: an enabling culture for people, the right skills and knowledge, and enabling processes and structures. Measures for promoting innovation initiatives have been included in the 2019–2020 operational performance metrics.

147. **Innovation indicator and framework under development.** An assessment methodology for the innovation indicator included in the new CRF is under development. The indicator will track the innovative components, the scaling up of previously tested innovations, and/or the innovative financing structures in sovereign and nonsovereign operations and TA projects. Also being prepared are an innovation framework and guidance note that will provide a structured approach and road map to enhancing innovation at ADB, enable reporting on the three identified drivers of innovation, and serve as a basis for validating actual innovation in project components. The framework and indicator methodology will be finalized in 2020. Innovation-related elements will then become part of staff work plans.

148. **Innovation initiatives piloted.** ADB has developed innovation piloting tools for the energy sector, such as the Technology Innovation Challenge.[25] It has piloted innovations in operations in Armenia, Cambodia, Mongolia, the Philippines, and Timor-Leste. A repository of ADB innovation initiatives was established to enhance communication and knowledge flow throughout the organization on innovation ideas, efforts, and projects.

ADB

AS A KNOWLEDGE ORGANIZATION

STAFF RATING ADB AS AN EFFECTIVE KNOWLEDGE AND LEARNING ORGANIZATION

63% IN 2018

65% IN 2019

75% BY 2024

D. KNOWLEDGE ORGANIZATION
Transformation into a Knowledge and Learning Institution

149. **Gradual transformation into knowledge and learning institution taking place.** ADB's transformation into a knowledge and learning institution requires the right culture, processes, and capacity. In 2019, ADB's performance on the eight key drivers of a knowledge-driven enterprise, based on its latest globally benchmarked Most Admired Knowledge Enterprise (MAKE) survey, rose 2 percentage points from 2018 to 65% (51.97 points [Figure 5.1]). This puts ADB *on track but watch* on the CRF indicator.

Figure 5.1: Dimensions of the Most Admired Knowledge Enterprise Survey Scores

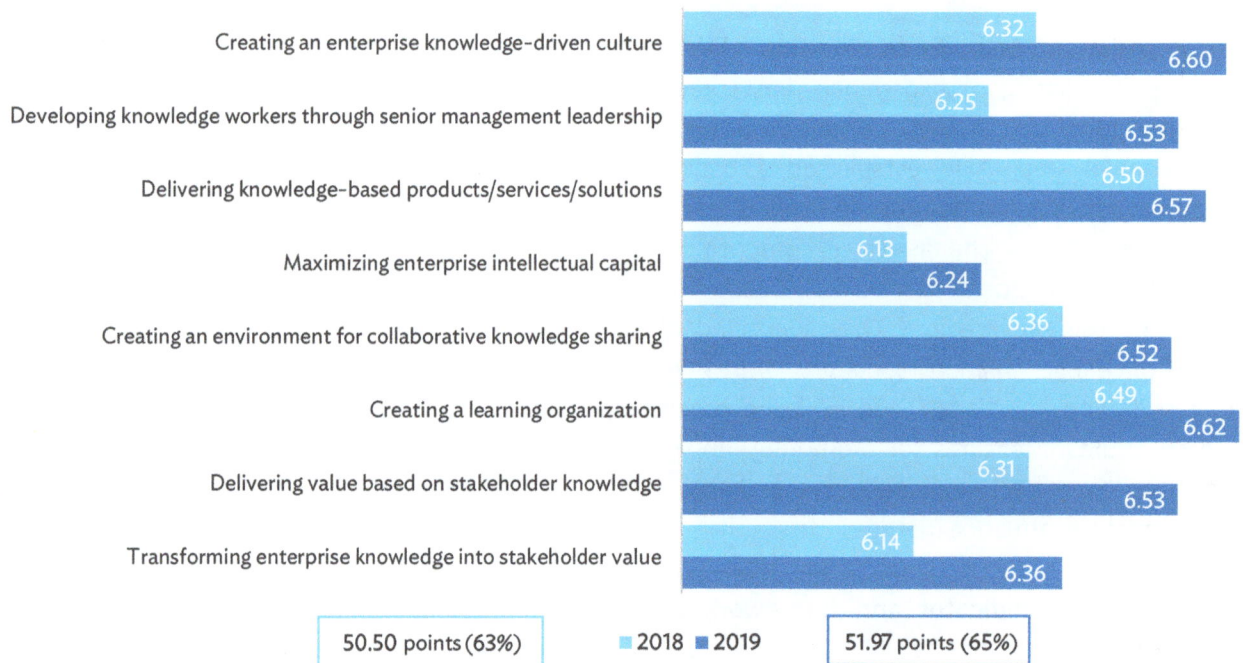

Dimension	2018	2019
Creating an enterprise knowledge-driven culture	6.32	6.60
Developing knowledge workers through senior management leadership	6.25	6.53
Delivering knowledge-based products/services/solutions	6.50	6.57
Maximizing enterprise intellectual capital	6.13	6.24
Creating an environment for collaborative knowledge sharing	6.36	6.52
Creating a learning organization	6.49	6.62
Delivering value based on stakeholder knowledge	6.31	6.53
Transforming enterprise knowledge into stakeholder value	6.14	6.36

50.50 points (63%) ■2018 ■2019 51.97 points (65%)

Note: Each dimension has a 10-point score and the total is 80.
Source: ADB Sustainable Development and Climate Change Department.

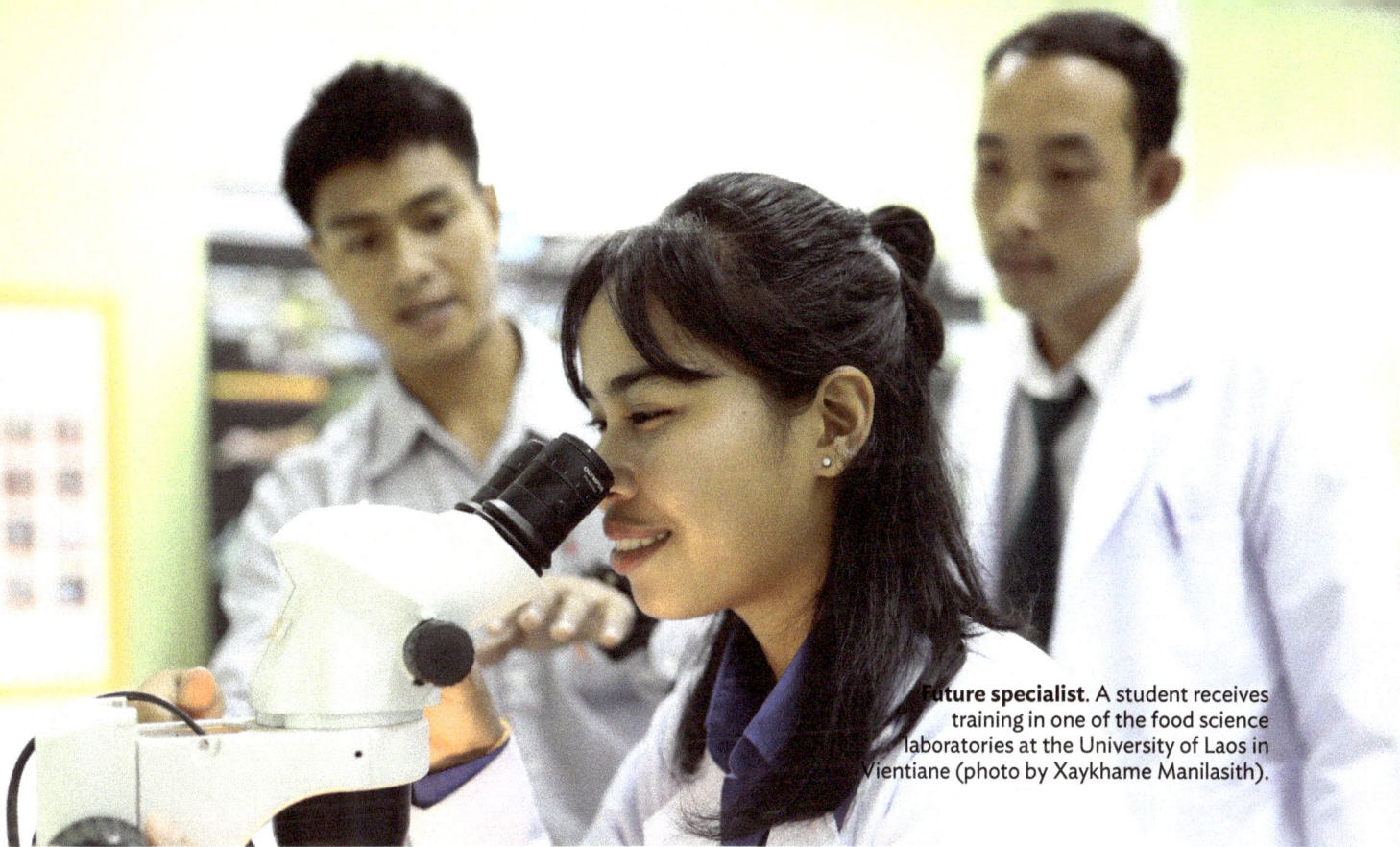

Future specialist. A student receives training in one of the food science laboratories at the University of Laos in Vientiane (photo by Xaykhame Manilasith).

150. **Midway to reaching knowledge enterprise maturity.** ADB is in stage three of the five stages in the MAKE knowledge management implementation model. MAKE researchers identified these stages as pre-implementation (up to 1 year), implementation (1–3 years), reinvigoration (4–6 years), inculcation (7–9 years), and holistic (10+ years). Based on the latest MAKE survey results, to move up from reinvigoration (stage 3) to inculcation (stage 4), ADB needs to take several steps. These include a review of its knowledge culture and capacity development, improvement of overall leadership in knowledge work, and the establishment of greater buy-in and stronger ownership from all the key stakeholders.

151. **High and low dimension scores.** The two of the eight MAKE dimensions in which ADB achieved its highest score in 2019 were "creating a learning organization" and "creating an enterprise knowledge-driven culture." For the second year in a row, ADB scored lowest on "maximizing enterprise intellectual capital." The 1,115 ADB staff members who answered the survey's 21 questions included more women (59.46%) than men. Figure 5.1 provides ADB dimension and total scores from the 2018 and 2019 surveys.

Learning How to Deliver Successful Demonstration Projects

152. **Demonstration and replication.** Strategy 2030 calls for ADB to use its resources to pilot innovative approaches and solutions that, when successful, can be replicated more widely and/or on a larger scale. It also commits ADB to developing demonstration projects in the region's growing number of upper middle-income countries. Successful replication can amplify the value added by such projects in these DMCs, where the scale and complexity of development challenges is often orders of magnitude larger than ADB's available resources. A recent study on demonstration and replication in the People's Republic of China is ADB's first attempt to determine what part replication has played in its operations to date, what drives or stands in the way of success in this activity, and what refinements and improvements might make replication a more effective part of ADB's growing catalytic role under Strategy 2030. The main findings are summarized in Box 5.3 and on p. 83.

Box 5.3: Bus Rapid Transit—A Long Chain of Replication

The development of bus rapid transit (BRT) systems in the People's Republic of China (PRC) illustrates the full process of demonstration and replication of Asian Development Bank (ADB) project designs and features. The 2009 Lanzhou Sustainable Urban Transport Project was ADB's first BRT project in the country. The operation drew on the successful designs and construction practices of BRT systems in the PRC and around the world. Although it reduced traffic congestion, the project encountered obstacles during implementation. It lacked the full backing of the governments of the municipalities the BRT route traversed and encountered resettlement challenges in densely populated areas. Because the BRT system was designed to connect newly developed areas, initial passenger uptake was also slow.

The ADB-financed 2013 Hubei–Yichang Sustainable Urban Transport Project applied the lessons learned from the Lanzhou project and built on its accomplishments. The Yichang project's BRT component was a clear success. Yichang's municipal government exercised strong ownership as the executing agency. It had toured the Lanzhou project and other BRT systems in the country looking for answers to its own urban transit problems. It improved on the Lanzhou project's route selection and devoted more time at the design stage to planning and coordinating the resettlement required. An extensive information campaign promoted the new system's benefits and addressed public uncertainties. The project was successfully implemented, solved the city's traffic problems, and increased public transportation ridership. The new BRT system won design awards and became widely known in the PRC. Other cities became interested in building similar systems. Further replication followed.

Nanning municipal government officials visited the Yichang BRT system after learning of its success. Nanning's replication of the Yichang BRT design added such features as solar panels and wheelchair access. The Nanning project was also ADB's first public–private partnership BRT operation in the PRC—an example of replication's potential for catalyzing additional development finance. The private sector designed, built, and operates the system. Although fare levels are still regulated, and the government will fill the financial gap if fare revenue cannot cover costs, this has been a step toward full privatization.

The Yichang BRT model has also been replicated in an ADB project under construction in Peshawar; and in planned projects in Jiangxi Ji'an, Jiangxi Fuzhou, Ulaanbaatar, Vientiane, and Yangon.

Source: ADB Strategy, Policy and Partnerships Department. Replication in ADB Operations, A Case in the People's Republic of China: Operations Research Study. Unpublished.

REPLICATION OF ADB OPERATIONS: A CASE STUDY IN THE PEOPLE'S REPUBLIC OF CHINA

What is demonstration?

A demonstration project is designed with the intent to showcase and make potential future implementers aware of one or more unique components, features, or approaches for use in future projects.

What is replication?

Replication is when the design of a project or one of its unique features is adopted in whole or in part for use in a separate project.

55%

of the 22 sampled projects[d] had verified replication

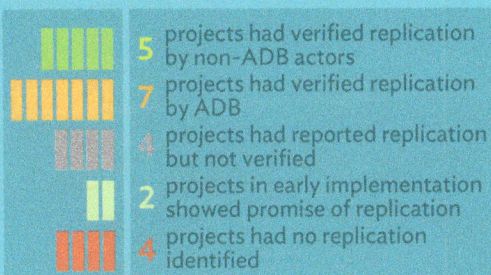

- **5** projects had verified replication by non-ADB actors
- **7** projects had verified replication by ADB
- **4** projects had reported replication but not verified
- **2** projects in early implementation showed promise of replication
- **4** projects had no replication identified

Summary Findings[b]

ADB is increasing its efforts to demonstrate distinctive design and implementation features in projects and programs for potential replication within and across its developing member countries.

Although there is no single formula for successful replication, the study findings suggest how ADB can begin to systemize and operationalize its replication goals and achieve better results. The study has underlined the key elements and factors that promote or hinder successful demonstration and replication.

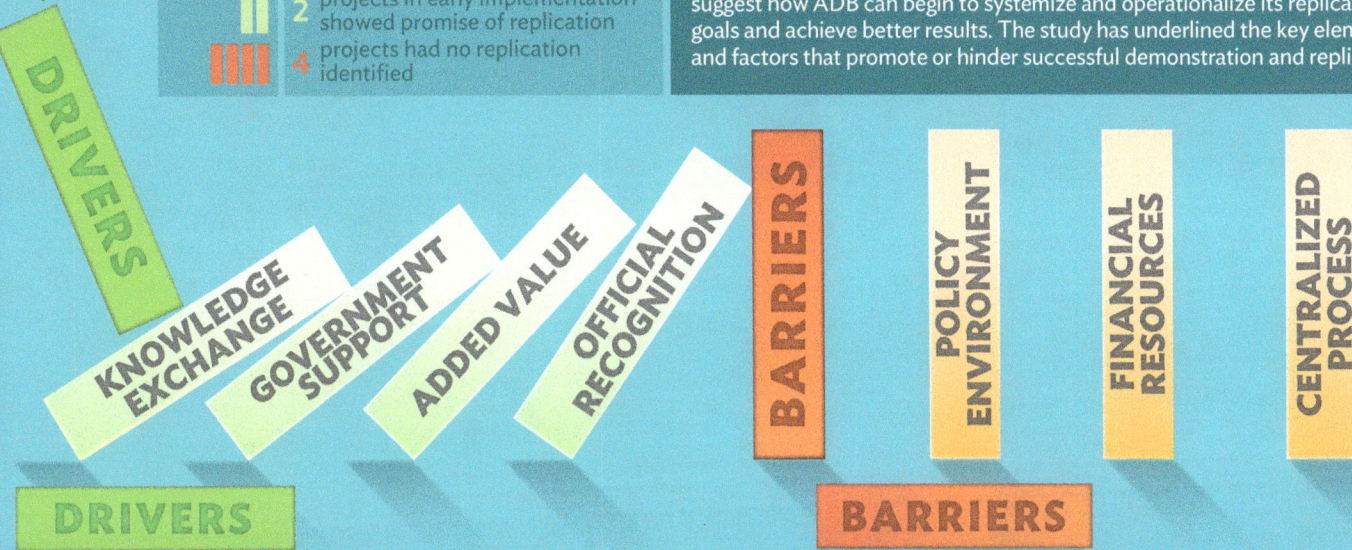

DRIVERS

KNOWLEDGE EXCHANGE · GOVERNMENT SUPPORT · ADDED VALUE · OFFICIAL RECOGNITION

BARRIERS

POLICY ENVIRONMENT · FINANCIAL RESOURCES · CENTRALIZED PROCESS

DRIVERS

Four important drivers of the intended or unintended replication of unique features of ADB projects:

1. Active knowledge exchange. Two-way knowledge sharing between demonstration project implementers and officials and planners during site visits and road shows can lead to replication.

2. Strong government support. Strong government support and championing at the subnational level can power replication.

3. Significant added value. Financial viability and profitability strengthen the replication argument for both governments and the private sector.

4. Official recognition. An award from ADB or another reputable international organization can raise a project's profile, spotlight its features, and sometimes draw the attention of the niche development market in which the most likely replicators will be found.

BARRIERS

Three main barriers to replication success:

1. Shifts in government priorities or unfavorable policy environment. Government policy that replication is aligned with changes or is no longer a priority.

2. Inadequate financial resources. Projects or components that are socially or environmentally beneficial but expensive and unprofitable are less likely to generate financing for replication.

3. Inability to link with centralized decision-making processes. Top-down support for concepts can drive replication but reversing the information flow is difficult. Limited lateral communication between subnational institutions hinders the sharing of replicable solutions.

KEY ELEMENTS

Elements conducive to one-time or broader replication

To generate a reasonable expectation of replication, a demonstration project should at a minimum

- display features applicable to other contexts,
- align with government priorities, and
- implement and monitor a targeted outreach strategy.

1. Sufficient demand
- Similar development challenge
- Comparable context

2. Conducive environment
- Policies and plans
- Mandate or green light

NECESSARY FACTORS

3. Sufficient Resources
- Financial
- Technical

4. Enablers
- Ambassador
- Intermediary organizations
- Platform
- Demonstration tool

LEVERS

ADB can help leverage replication by

- ensuring demonstration and replication are considered in project design;
- bridging knowledge silos within different levels in developing member countries and internally in ADB;
- encouraging strong planning directives from central government;
- promoting horizontal communication between provinces or subnational governments;
- instituting comprehensive and systematic tracking, monitoring, and reporting on demonstration activities and replication results;
- strategically supporting priority areas by financing replication itself or providing incentives to government or third party; and
- allocating technical assistance or other ADB funds to promoting replication and monitoring demonstration outcomes.

a The sample included operations that included statements of a demonstration intent in their reports and recommendations of the President, and other projects that ADB's East Asia Department identified as having demonstration components and the possibility of replication.

b ADB Strategy, Policy and Partnerships Department. Replication in ADB Operations, A Case in the Peoples' Republic of China: Operations Research Study. Unpublished.

CHAPTER 6
ADB'S SYSTEMS, PROCESSES, AND CAPACITY

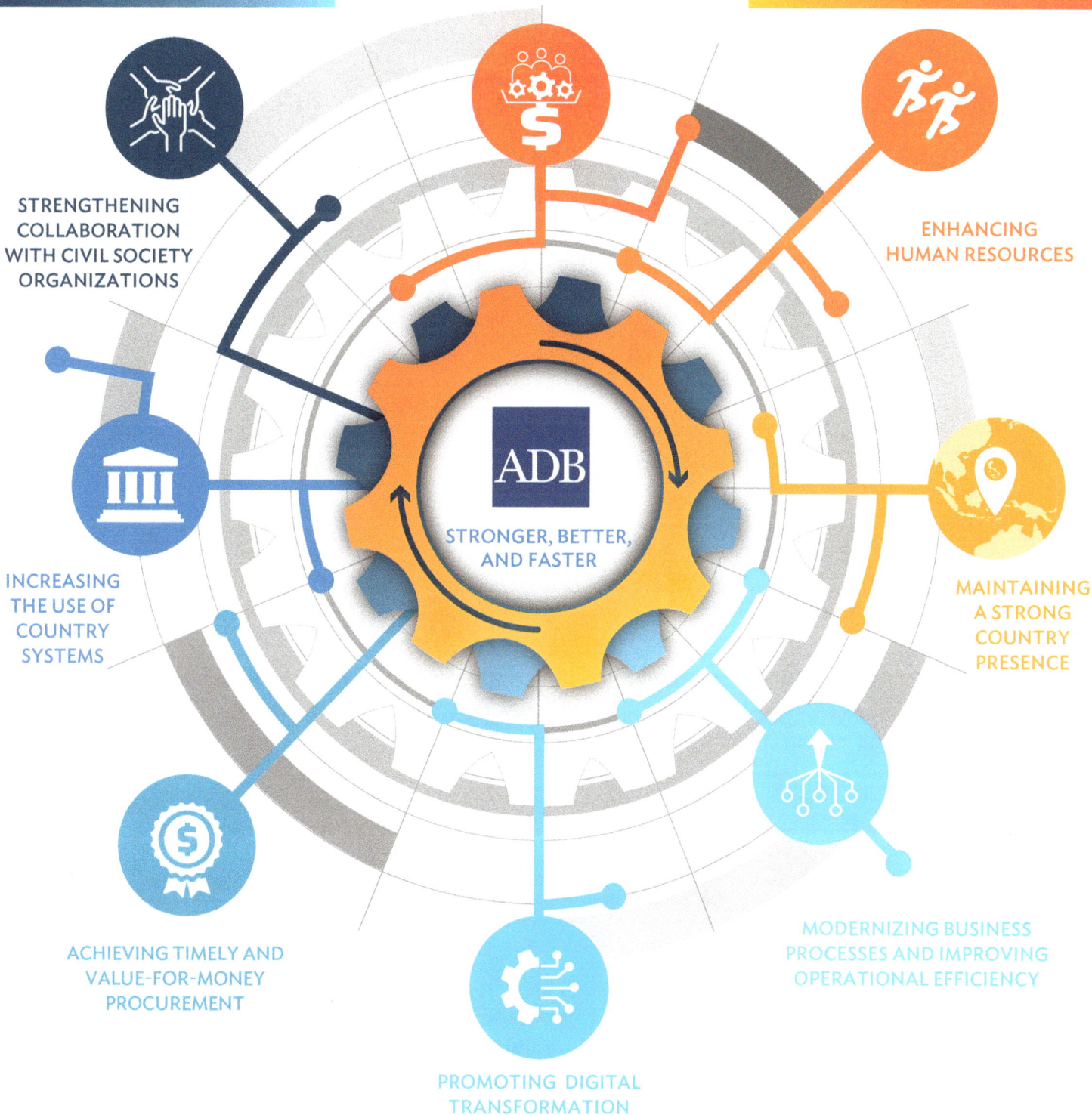

ORGANIZATIONAL
SYSTEMS AND PROCESSES

ENSURING A ROBUST
RESOURCE BASE

ORGANIZATIONAL
CAPACITY

STRENGTHENING
COLLABORATION
WITH CIVIL SOCIETY
ORGANIZATIONS

ENHANCING
HUMAN RESOURCES

ADB
STRONGER, BETTER,
AND FASTER

MAINTAINING
A STRONG
COUNTRY
PRESENCE

INCREASING
THE USE OF
COUNTRY
SYSTEMS

MODERNIZING BUSINESS
PROCESSES AND IMPROVING
OPERATIONAL EFFICIENCY

ACHIEVING TIMELY AND
VALUE-FOR-MONEY
PROCUREMENT

PROMOTING DIGITAL
TRANSFORMATION

Strategy 2030 calls on ADB to be stronger, better, and faster in its work to enhance development results in Asia and the Pacific. A stronger ADB requires a robust resource base, enhanced human resources, and the presence on the ground needed to be more attentive to the needs of its developing member countries. A better ADB demands more modern business processes, more efficient operations, and more use of country systems. A faster ADB will be achieved by ensuring that procurement is timely and providing value for money. To achieve greater operational effectiveness and efficiency, ADB must also have the right skill sets in place. This chapter assesses ADB's effectiveness in key performance areas, including operational systems and processes and organizational capacity. It also examines factors that affected performance in these areas during 2019 and highlights ADB's main advances in better managing its internal resources and processes.

ENSURING A ROBUST RESOURCE BASE

EQUITY–LOAN RATIO (SOV AND NSO)	WEIGHTED AVERAGE RISK RATING (NSO)	IMPAIRED LOANS RATIO (NSO)
45.32% IN 2019	**9.3 or B+** IN 2019	**4.8%** IN 2019

ENHANCING HUMAN RESOURCES

REPRESENTATION OF WOMEN

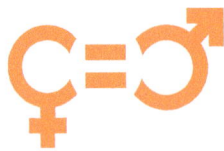

REPRESENTATION OF WOMEN IN THE INTERNATIONAL STAFF CATEGORY

▶ **36.3%** IN 2018   **36.7%** IN 2019   ◎ **40%** BY 2024

PER CATEGORY
■ WOMEN ■ MEN

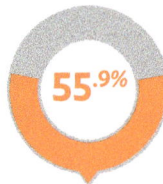 **55.9%** LEVELS 1–3

 **36.7%** LEVELS 4–6

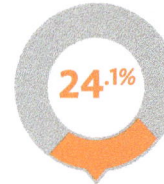 **24.1%** LEVELS 7–8

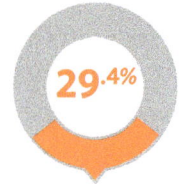 **29.4%** LEVELS 9–10

INTERNAL TRAINING BUDGET	**$887** IN 2019	AVG $ PER STAFF PARTICIPANT	

MAINTAINING A STRONG COUNTRY PRESENCE

BUDGETED INTERNATIONAL AND NATIONAL STAFF POSITIONS IN FIELD OFFICES

▶ **48%** IN 2018   ↓ **45%** IN 2019   ◎ MONITOR

SHARE OF TOTAL OPERATIONS DEPARTMENTS

FIELD OFFICES

53% IN 2019

84 IN 2019

OPERATIONS ADMINISTERED (SOV)

BUDGETED INTERNATIONAL AND NATIONAL STAFF POSITIONS IN FCAS DMCs AND SIDS

AVG = average, DMC = developing member country, FCAS = fragile and conflict-affected situations, NSO = nonsovereign operation, SIDS = small island developing state, SOV = sovereign operation.

A. ORGANIZATIONAL CAPACITY

153. **Robust capitalization.** The loan portfolio continued to grow in 2019, utilizing more cofinancing to optimize growth. Loan portfolio growth outpaced capital formation, reducing the equity–loan ratio to 45.32% in 2019 from 47.48% in 2018. Both the impaired loans ratio (4.8%) and the weighted average risk rating of nonsovereign operations (9.3 or B+) remained almost unchanged in 2019.

154. **Representation of women *on track but watch.*** Women's share of ADB's international staff positions grew to 36.7% year-on-year from 36.3% in 2018, although their representation in leadership roles (levels 7–8) declined to 24.1% from 26.1%.

155. **Staff capacity enhanced.** An average of $887 was spent on training per staff member trained in 2019, with 2,090 individual staff attending at least one training program provided by ADB's Budget, Personnel, and Management Services Department (BPMSD).[26] This equates to 59% of ADB staff attending at least one BPMSD training program.

156. **Field office staffing ratio reduced slightly.** The share of all ADB staff assigned to field offices declined by 3 percentage points to 45% in 2019.[27] Additions raised the number of field office positions to 452 from 444, but a decline in outposted positions to 87 from 100 reduced ADB's overall field office presence to 539 staff members from 544. Reasons included the expiration of outposting arrangements and the departure from ADB of outposted personnel. Positions at four new Pacific country offices were recategorized as field-office-owned from outposted. The addition of 28 positions in the Private Sector Operations Department (PSOD) helped raise the number of operations department staff positions by 54 to 1,191.

157. **Field staff numbers up in fragile, conflict-affected, and small island countries.** Two budgeted international and national staff positions were added in the field offices in countries with fragile and conflict-affected situations (FCAS) and in small island developing states (SIDS). The new total of 84 was about 16% of the 539 such positions in all field offices in 2019 and equated to 7% of the 1,191 overall staff of ADB's operations departments. ADB's efforts to expand its field presence in response to Strategy 2030 calls for strengthening resident mission capacity and improving business processes in the field.

158. **More than half of operations administered by field offices.** About 53% (327) of the 613 active sovereign operations in 2019 were administered in the field—47.8% (293) by field-office-based staff, and 5.5% (34) by staff posted from ADB headquarters. The share was slightly higher in concessional assistance operations, where 55% (184 of 335) of active sovereign operations were administered in field offices, 50% (166) of them by field office staff and 5% (18) by outposted headquarters staff.

MODERNIZING BUSINESS PROCESS AND IMPROVING OPERATIONAL EFFICIENCY

TIME FROM CONCEPT APPROVAL OR CLEARANCE TO FIRST DISBURSEMENT (MONTHS)

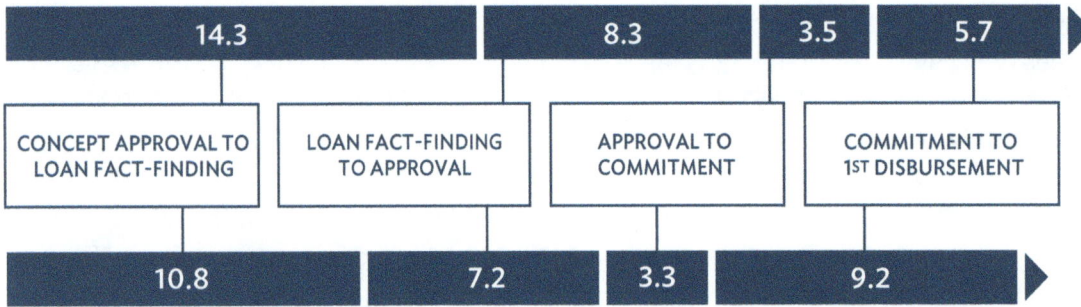

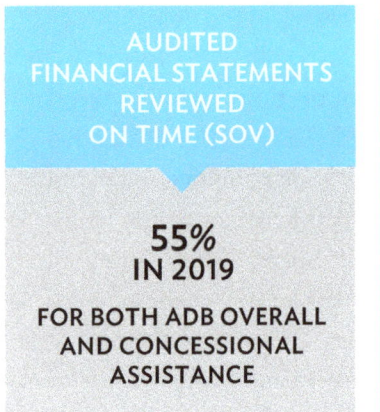

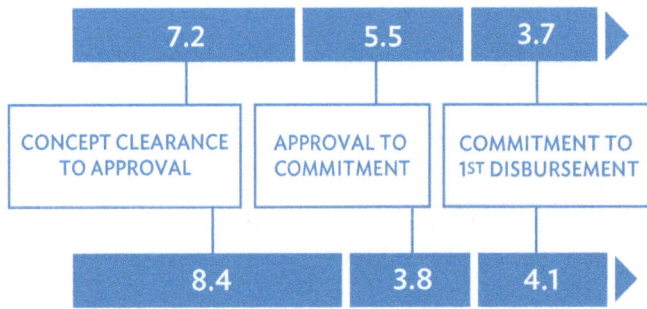

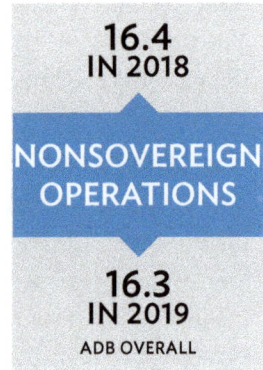

14.3	8.3	3.5	5.7
CONCEPT APPROVAL TO LOAN FACT-FINDING	LOAN FACT-FINDING TO APPROVAL	APPROVAL TO COMMITMENT	COMMITMENT TO 1ST DISBURSEMENT
10.8	7.2	3.3	9.2

SOVEREIGN OPERATIONS
31.8 IN 2018

30.5 IN 2019
ADB OVERALL

AUDITED FINANCIAL STATEMENTS REVIEWED ON TIME (SOV)

55% IN 2019

FOR BOTH ADB OVERALL AND CONCESSIONAL ASSISTANCE

7.2	5.5	3.7
CONCEPT CLEARANCE TO APPROVAL	APPROVAL TO COMMITMENT	COMMITMENT TO 1ST DISBURSEMENT
8.4	3.8	4.1

NONSOVEREIGN OPERATIONS
16.4 IN 2018

16.3 IN 2019
ADB OVERALL

QUALITY OF BUDGET MANAGEMENT (%, UNUTILIZED IAE)

5.4% IN 2018

0% IN 2019
(including 1.8% carryover)

5% OR LESS ANNUAL

DEPARTMENTS WITH DOCUMENTED AND TESTED BUSINESS CONTINUITY PLANS IN PLACE

7 IN 2019

INTERNAL ADMINISTRATIVE EXPENSES ($'000)

49 IN 2019	795 IN 2019	4,865 IN 2019
PER $1 MILLION DISBURSEMENT	PER PROJECT UNDER ADMINISTRATION	PER PROJECT APPROVED

ADB = Asian Development Bank, IAE = internal administrative expenses, SOV = sovereign operations.

B. ORGANIZATIONAL SYSTEMS AND PROCESSES

159. **Sovereign processing time shorter overall.** Sovereign operations were processed over an average of 30.5 months in 2019, 1.3 months faster than in 2018. The disbursement time for the concessional assistance subset was also shortened by 3.6 months to 29.6 months.[28] Concept approval to fact-finding was the longest stage in both cases—10.8 months for sovereign operations overall, and 10.6 months for those receiving concessional assistance. While the time to complete the first three stages shortened in 2019, the average time for the final phase—commitment to first disbursement—lengthened to 9.2 months from 5.7 months in 2018. One energy project in Myanmar and two industry and trade sector projects in Bhutan and Viet Nam took between 30 and 39 months to complete this stage, lengthening the average time for ADB overall. First disbursement was delayed because these projects needed to revise their detailed designs or experienced contracting issues.

160. **Nonsovereign operations start-up time steady.** The average time from concept clearance to first disbursement was about 16.3 months for nonsovereign operations in 2019, about the same as in 2018.[29] The period from concept clearance to project approval, the longest processing stage, averaged 8.4 months. The *2019 Annual Portfolio Performance Report* provides further details on procurement processing time for sovereign and nonsovereign operations, including the use of FAST (Faster Approach to Small Nonsovereign Transactions) to shorten processing time (endnote 13).

161. **Most audit result reviews timely.** ADB reviewed 55% of the audited project financial statements for sovereign operations submitted in 2019 on time—i.e., 466 of 847 within 8.0 weeks of receiving them from the executing or implementing agency. The reviews took an average of 9.0 weeks.

162. **Budget utilization *on target*.** ADB's budget utilization rate in 2019 was 100.0%, including a 1.8% carryover to 2020. Internal administrative expenses (IAE) per $1 million in disbursements stood at $49,000 in 2019, down a little from $49,700 in 2018. IAE per project under administration rose from $751,000 in 2018 to $795,000, and IAE per project approved increased from $4,537,000 to $4,865,000.

163. **More departments with continuity plans.** To help ensure organizational resilience, seven departments and divisions prepared and tested business continuity plans. These map out the steps required to reestablish critical business processes in the event of a business disruption. ADB's Office of Administrative Services conducts an annual business impact analysis and risk assessment for financial and supporting departments that are responsible for critical, time-sensitive deliverables that need to be recovered within a 7-day period. ADB approved and tested business continuity plans for 16 divisions across seven departments and offices in 2019.[30]

PROMOTING DIGITAL TRANSFORMATION

| DIGITAL PRODUCTS COMPLETED | 27 IN 2019 |

ACHIEVING TIMELY AND VALUE–FOR–MONEY PROCUREMENT

PROCUREMENT CONTRACT TRANSACTIONS OF $10 MILLION OR MORE WITH PROCESSING TIME OF 40 DAYS OR LESS (SOV)

ADB OVERALL
- 67% IN 2018
- 67% IN 2019
- 80% BY 2024

CONCESSIONAL ASSISTANCE
- 60% IN 2018
- 71% IN 2019
- 80% BY 2024

PROCUREMENT TIME FOR $10 MILLION OR MORE IN 2019 (SOV)

ADVERTISEMENT — CONCESSIONAL ASSISTANCE — 322 DAYS — CONTRACT SIGNING

ADVERTISEMENT — ADB OVERALL — 265 DAYS — CONTRACT SIGNING

CONSULTING SERVICES RECRUITMENT TIME FOR ADB-ADMINISTERED CONTRACTS IN 2019 (SOV)

RECRUITMENT NOTICE — ADB OVERALL — 163 DAYS — CONTRACT SIGNING

INCREASING THE USE OF COUNTRY SYSTEMS

CONTRACTS USING GOVERNMENT E-PROCUREMENT SYSTEMS (SOV)	OPERATIONS USING COUNTRY PROCUREMENT SYSTEMS (SOV)
$4.5B IN 2019	60% IN 2019

ADB = Asian Development Bank, B = billion, SOV = sovereign operation.

164. **Digital transformation in progress.** The IT investments being delivered under Real-Time ADB and Digital Agenda 2030 Stage 1 will automate, simplify, and integrate key systems; improve collaboration; strengthen data quality; replace manual processes; increase resilience; and enable greater agility and mobility. A total of 27 digital products were completed in 2019, including the Partner Fund Management System, the e-Procurement System, and the Treasury System Improvement for Pricing.

165. **Procurement time steady.** ADB's new procurement framework is intended to ensure project quality, optimize processing times, and strengthen procurement delivery.[31] The framework increased the Procurement Committee threshold from $40 million to $50 million in 2018 and raised the Consulting Selection Committee threshold from $600,000 to $750,000. The effect of these reforms is gradually materializing. While the share of sovereign operation procurement transactions that were processed within the target time of 40 days remained unchanged at 67% (*on track but watch*), an 11 percentage point improvement in on-time procurement in concessional assistance operations resulted in an *on track* rating for this indicator. ADB will continue to monitor and address issues affecting processing times.

166. **End-to-end procurement time shortened.** The average procurement time from the date that an invitation for bids was advertised on the ADB website to the date a contract of $10 million or more was signed shortened by 4 days in 2019 to 265 days.

167. **Faster onboarding of consulting firms and individuals.** Recruitment of consultants was also faster. It took an average of 163 days, 15 fewer than in 2018, to engage consulting firms and individuals for technical assistance projects through quality- and cost-based selection.

168. **Promoting use of country systems.** ADB continues to help developing member countries establish and strengthen their procurement systems. The share of disbursements made through open competitive bidding processes with national advertisement, results- and policy-based lending, and onlending by financial intermediaries was 60% overall and 58% for concessional assistance operations. ADB encourages the use of electronic procurement (e-procurement) at different stages of the procurement process because it promotes good governance, transparency, value for money, audit trails, and the broadest possible access to suppliers. The volume of sovereign contracts that used government e-procurement systems reached $4.5 billion in 2019 of a total of $14.4 billion.

STRENGTHENING COLLABORATION

SOVEREIGN–NONSOVEREIGN COLLABORATION

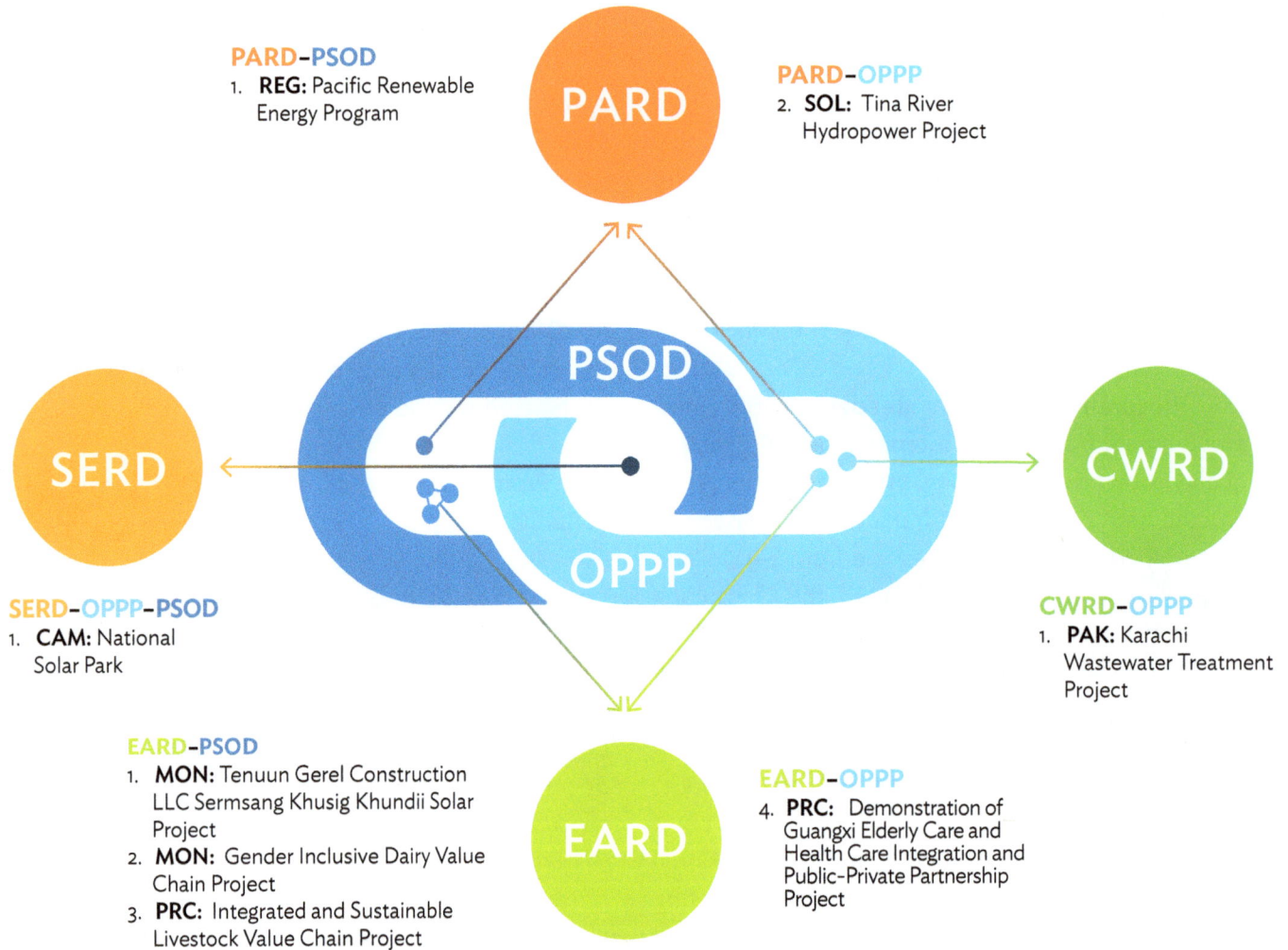

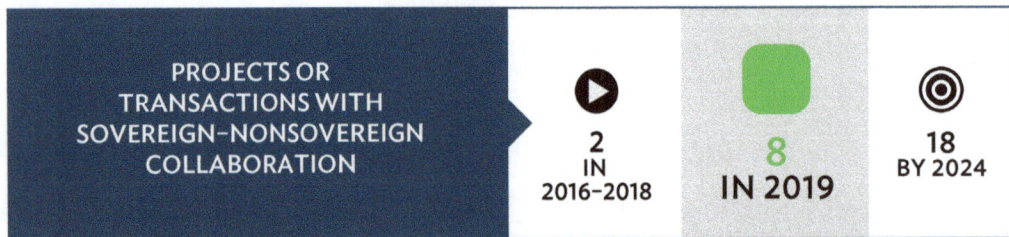

PARD

PARD-PSOD
1. **REG:** Pacific Renewable Energy Program

PARD-OPPP
2. **SOL:** Tina River Hydropower Project

PSOD

OPPP

SERD

SERD-OPPP-PSOD
1. **CAM:** National Solar Park

CWRD

CWRD-OPPP
1. **PAK:** Karachi Wastewater Treatment Project

EARD-PSOD
1. **MON:** Tenuun Gerel Construction LLC Sermsang Khusig Khundii Solar Project
2. **MON:** Gender Inclusive Dairy Value Chain Project
3. **PRC:** Integrated and Sustainable Livestock Value Chain Project

EARD

EARD-OPPP
4. **PRC:** Demonstration of Guangxi Elderly Care and Health Care Integration and Public-Private Partnership Project

---

PROJECTS OR TRANSACTIONS WITH SOVEREIGN-NONSOVEREIGN COLLABORATION

| 2 IN 2016–2018 | 8 IN 2019 | 18 BY 2024 |

PARTICIPATION BY CIVIL SOCIETY ORGANIZATIONS

90%
IN 2019
% OF COMMITTED OPERATIONS (SOV)

ADB = Asian Development Bank, CAM = Cambodia, CWRD = Central and West Asia Department, DMC = developing member country, EARD = East Asia Department, MON = Mongolia, OPPP = Office of Public–Private Partnership, PARD = Pacific Department, PAK = Pakistan, PRC = People's Republic of China, PSOD = Private Sector Operations Department, REG = regional, SERD = Southeast Asia Department, SOL = Solomon Islands, SOV = sovereign operation.

169. **One ADB collaboration increased.** ADB needs to bring knowledge and expertise together from across the organization to implement Strategy 2030 effectively. The "One ADB" approach involves cooperation of many different types between many different operational and support departments and offices. In the CRF, collaboration between ADB's sovereign and nonsovereign operations departments is measured through a new performance indicator. Operations departments responded strongly to the One ADB imperative in 2019, with eight projects bringing together private sector and sovereign operations expertise and knowledge—a good start toward the 2024 cumulative target of 18 such projects or transactions each year. Boxes 6.1 and 6.2. provide two examples of One ADB collaboration.

Box 6.1: National Solar Park Project in Cambodia

The Asian Development Bank (ADB) is providing collaborative end-to-end "One ADB" support for the construction of solar photovoltaic power plants by Cambodia's national electricity utility, Electricite du Cambodge. Sovereign financing from ADB's Southeast Asia Department will be provided to help reduce the private investment risk associated with solar generation projects in Cambodia by building the solar park and transmission infrastructure.

Technical assistance provided by ADB's Office of Public–Private Partnership is helping the electricity authority design and conduct a competitive tender for procuring a private sector entity to build the first power plant (60 megawatts) in the park. ADB's Private Sector Operations Department provided inputs for the tender's design.

Source: ADB. 2019. *Report and Recommendation of the President to the Board of Directors for the Proposed Loan and Administration of Loan, Grant, and Technical Assistance Grant for the Kingdom of Cambodia: National Solar Park Project*. Manila.

Box 6.2: Pacific Renewable Energy Program

"One ADB" collaboration by the Asian Development Bank (ADB) in the Pacific used blended finance to address some of the fundamental bankability issues and barriers to private sector development in remote small islands where scale is always a challenge. ADB's Private Sector Operations Department and Pacific Department will provide a credit enhancement structure to support the creditworthiness of Pacific power utilities when governments are unable or unwilling to provide guarantees. The program is designed to encourage private sector investments by backstopping the utilities' power payment obligations using development partner funds. The two ADB departments will implement the program and identify pipeline transactions together. The Private Sector Operations Department will be responsible for processing guarantees and project financing for individual private sector projects.

Source: ADB. 2019. *Report and Recommendation of the President to the Board of Directors for the Proposed Pacific Renewable Energy Program*. Manila.

170. **More collaboration with civil society organizations.** ADB continues to track its important collaboration with civil society organizations (CSOs) and recognizes their unique strengths and extensive local presence.[32] Measurement through a tracking indicator shows that CSOs played a role in 90% of the sovereign operations committed in 2019. ADB considers a project to have civil society engagement if its approval documents indicate intent to engage with citizens and CSOs in a formal way during project implementation. CSO participation ranges in extent from information sharing to formal partnership.

Energy savings. A resident switches to a more energy-efficient bulb for his house in Kabul, Afghanistan (photo by Jawad Jalali).

CHAPTER 7
APPLYING DIFFERENTIATED APPROACHES

FRAGILE AND CONFLICT-AFFECTED SITUATIONS, AND SMALL ISLAND DEVELOPING STATES

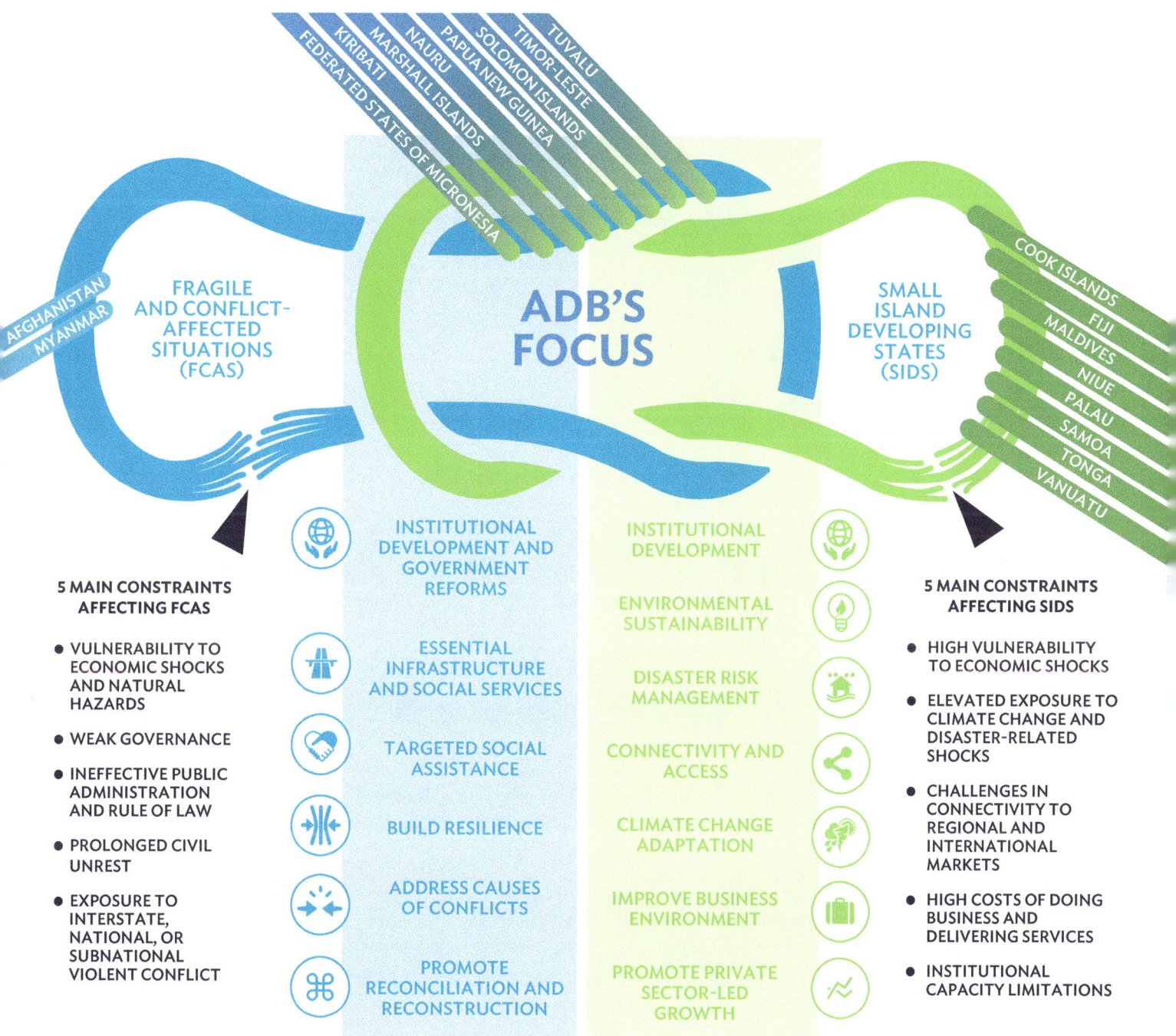

AFGHANISTAN
MYANMAR

FEDERATED STATES OF MICRONESIA
KIRIBATI
MARSHALL ISLANDS
NAURU
PAPUA NEW GUINEA
SOLOMON ISLANDS
TIMOR-LESTE
TUVALU

COOK ISLANDS
FIJI
MALDIVES
NIUE
PALAU
SAMOA
TONGA
VANUATU

FRAGILE AND CONFLICT-AFFECTED SITUATIONS (FCAS)

ADB'S FOCUS

SMALL ISLAND DEVELOPING STATES (SIDS)

5 MAIN CONSTRAINTS AFFECTING FCAS

- VULNERABILITY TO ECONOMIC SHOCKS AND NATURAL HAZARDS
- WEAK GOVERNANCE
- INEFFECTIVE PUBLIC ADMINISTRATION AND RULE OF LAW
- PROLONGED CIVIL UNREST
- EXPOSURE TO INTERSTATE, NATIONAL, OR SUBNATIONAL VIOLENT CONFLICT

INSTITUTIONAL DEVELOPMENT AND GOVERNMENT REFORMS

ESSENTIAL INFRASTRUCTURE AND SOCIAL SERVICES

TARGETED SOCIAL ASSISTANCE

BUILD RESILIENCE

ADDRESS CAUSES OF CONFLICTS

PROMOTE RECONCILIATION AND RECONSTRUCTION

INSTITUTIONAL DEVELOPMENT

ENVIRONMENTAL SUSTAINABILITY

DISASTER RISK MANAGEMENT

CONNECTIVITY AND ACCESS

CLIMATE CHANGE ADAPTATION

IMPROVE BUSINESS ENVIRONMENT

PROMOTE PRIVATE SECTOR-LED GROWTH

5 MAIN CONSTRAINTS AFFECTING SIDS

- HIGH VULNERABILITY TO ECONOMIC SHOCKS
- ELEVATED EXPOSURE TO CLIMATE CHANGE AND DISASTER-RELATED SHOCKS
- CHALLENGES IN CONNECTIVITY TO REGIONAL AND INTERNATIONAL MARKETS
- HIGH COSTS OF DOING BUSINESS AND DELIVERING SERVICES
- INSTITUTIONAL CAPACITY LIMITATIONS

Strategy 2030 specifies the differentiated approaches ADB must take to meet the distinct needs and conditions of the diverse groups within its developing country membership. These include the low-income and lower middle-income developing member countries, as well as upper middle-income countries.[a] Strategy 2030 calls for prioritized support and tailored attention to the poorest and most vulnerable developing member countries, including those dealing with fragile and conflict-affected situations and the difficult challenges of small island developing states.

[a] Refer to the feature on replication of ADB-financed operations in the People's Republic of China in Chapter 5 as an example of how ADB is providing selective support to upper middle-income countries in areas where it can add value.

FOCUSING OPERATIONS ON FCAS AND SIDS

SHARE OF COMMITMENTS IN FCAS DMCS AND SIDS

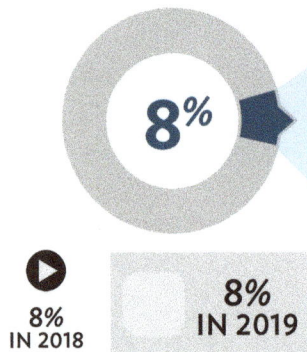

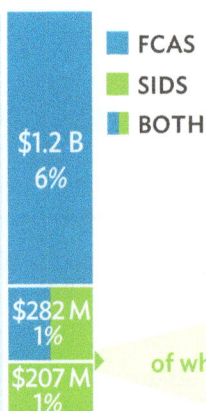

8%

8% IN 2018

8% IN 2019

- FCAS
- SIDS
- BOTH

$1.2 B 6%

$282 M 1%

$207 M 1%

MAIN SECTORS

INFORMATION AND COMMUNICATION TECHNOLOGY	**$525M** 2 OPERATIONS
AGRICULTURE, NATURAL RESOURCES, AND RURAL DEVELOPMENT	**$414M** 5 OPERATIONS
ENERGY	**$192M** 6 OPERATIONS

of which **$76M 16%** SIDS COMMITMENTS SUPPORTING CLIMATE CHANGE ADAPTATION

PERFORMANCE OF COMPLETED OPERATIONS

COMPLETED FCAS OPERATIONS RATED *SUCCESSFUL*

73% IN 2016–2018

↓ **54% IN 2017–2019**

OVERALL SUCCESS RATE

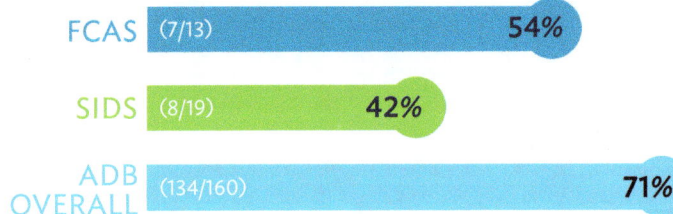

FCAS (7/13) **54%**

SIDS (8/19) **42%**

ADB OVERALL (134/160) **71%**

COMPLETED SIDS OPERATIONS RATED *SUCCESSFUL*

59% IN 2016–2018

↓ **42% IN 2017–2019**

ENHANCING ADB'S CAPACITY TO SUPPORT FCAS AND SIDS

16%

82 IN 2018

↑ **84 IN 2019**

In 2019, ADB had 84 budgeted staff positions in FCAS and SIDS field offices, of the total 539 budgeted international and national staff positions in operations departments' field offices

| RESIDENT MISSION | STAFF ALLOCATION |
| | FCAS SIDS FCAS/SIDS |

AFGHANISTAN
COOK ISLANDS
KIRIBATI
MARSHALL ISLANDS
MICRONESIA
MYANMAR
NAURU
PALAU
PAPUA NEW GUINEA

SAMOA
SOLOMON ISLANDS
FIJI (PACIFIC SUBREGIONAL OFFICE)
TIMOR-LESTE
TONGA
TUVALU
VANUATU

ADB = Asian Development Bank, B = billion, DMC = developing member country, FCAS = fragile and conflict-affected situation, M = million, SIDS = small island developing state.

A. OPERATIONAL FOCUS

171. **Fragile and conflict-affected situations.** Under Strategy 2030, ADB will provide long-term financing and capacity-development assistance to help build resilience and address the causes of fragility or conflict in countries experiencing fragile and conflict-affected situations (FCAS).[33] It will also continue its emphasis on gaining a full understanding of the local context to design the best response, making long-term commitments and ensuring country ownership so that development can be sustained, and maintaining the flexibility needed to adjust in often shifting FCAS conditions.

172. **Small island developing states.** When ADB was established, its charter accorded special attention to the needs of the region's small or less-developed member countries, which even then included most of the Pacific small island developing states (SIDS).[34] These developing member countries (DMCs) are remote and exceptionally vulnerable to natural hazards and to both the extreme weather events caused by climate change and the projected longer-term impacts on island environments.

As a result, among other development priorities, ADB support focuses on climate change adaptation, environmental sustainability, and disaster risk management, as well as connectivity.

173. **ADB financing in fragile and conflict-affected situations and small island developing states.** Nearly $1.7 billion, or 8%, of ADB's total commitments went to FCAS DMCs and SIDS in 2019. In FCAS DMCs, the largest share of financing committed was for operations in the information and communication technology (ICT) industries and ICT-enabled services (34%) followed by water-based natural resources management (18%). The large share of financing for ICT was primarily attributable to a $500 million nonsovereign commitment in Myanmar, which is expected to improve and provide gender-inclusive mobile telecommunications and broadband coverage. In SIDS, the largest share was for public expenditure and fiscal management (22%) and nonurban water transport (13%).

B. PERFORMANCE OF COMPLETED OPERATIONS

174. The annual success rates of sovereign operations in FCAS countries and SIDS are highly volatile because of the small number completed each year, but these rates have declined since 2016. Only two of the five operations in FCAS countries and three of the seven operations in SIDS were rated *successful* in reporting year 2019. Results from *successful* completed operations are highlighted in boxes 7.1 and 7.2. Four *less than successful* projects in the transport, water, and ICT sectors suffered from design flaws and weakness in the government plans and policies

to support them. ADB took several measures in 2019 to address these challenges. Of the 10 project-readiness financing facilities ADB committed in 2019, four are for SIDS and include project preparation and implementation capacity support for their government implementing agencies.[35] ADB also committed a regional technical assistance to help SIDS adopt longer-term planning horizons, promote cross-sector synergies, and support more programmatic approaches.[36]

C. ENHANCING ADB'S CAPACITY TO RESPOND

175. ADB increased the number of staff positions budgeted in FCAS DMCs and SIDS from 82 in 2018 to 84 in 2019. Responding to the needs of FCAS DMCs and SIDS, ADB introduced contingent disaster financing to support essential policy reforms for strengthened disaster resilience and

preparedness and to provide quick and flexible financing following disasters triggered by natural hazards. Contingent disaster financing was approved for the Cook Islands and Tonga in 2019, and for three FCAS countries— the Federated States of Micronesia, the Marshall Islands, and Solomon Islands.

Box 7.1: Transformed Roads in Kiribati

The Asian Development Bank (ADB) helped Kiribati carry out an overdue rehabilitation and upgrade of the land transport lifeline on the atoll of South Tarawa. More than two-fifths of Kiribati's people reside on the small, densely populated atoll. Most of them live, work, or study in homes, small businesses, and schools beside the single road that was worn, potholed, and a source of stagnant water and health hazards in the rainy season and of thick dust when it was dry.

The project linked communities to the city center, where better access to vital infrastructure, social services, and economic activities is available. It also improved the road joining the airport through the town of Bairiki with the seaport at Betio. The road's innovative design and structure mitigated a growing threat of damage from extreme spring tides and coastal erosion.

Source: ADB. 2018. *Completion Report: Road Rehabilitation Project in Kiribati*. Manila; Independent Evaluation Department. 2019. *Validation Report: Road Rehabilitation Project in Kiribati*. Manila: ADB.

Box 7.2: Enhanced Public Service Delivery and Economic Management in Solomon Islands

An Asian Development Bank (ADB) grant program provided budgetary support while also helping Solomon Islands develop policies to improve public service delivery and fiscal management. The program's policy actions led to tax reform, enhanced government budget reporting and cash management, and improved business registration processes that strengthened the enabling environment for private sector expansion. With the enactment of the 2014 Business Names Act supported by the program, annual business name registrations have increased annually by an average of 13%, with 1,954 business name registrations in 2017, compared with 1,455 in 2014.

The reforms and budget support addressed the deficit and reduced the need for the government to borrow or draw on reserves to meet its growing needs.

Source: ADB. 2018. *Completion Report: Economic Growth and Fiscal Reform Program in Solomon Islands*. Manila; Independent Evaluation Department. 2019. *Validation Report: Economic Growth and Fiscal Reform Program in Solomon Islands*. Manila: ADB.

D. IN FOCUS

1. A Country-Focused Approach to Progressing on the Fragility-to-Stability Continuum

176. **Implementing a country-focused approach.** A country experiencing FCAS confronts obstacles to development that another DMC may not face or may be better able to overcome. These constraints and special challenges can include violent conflict, political instability, weak governance, economic and social insecurity, and vulnerability to the effects of climate change. ADB recognizes that a one-size-fits-all operational approach will not work in FCAS countries because their needs, institutional capacities, and available resources are too varied. Experience has proven the benefits of using differentiated approaches that recognize the complex, multifaceted, and often interwoven dimensions of fragility and conflict (Figure 7.1).

177. Achieving development and progress on the fragility-to-stability continuum requires both basic fragility to be overcome and additional state capacity to be created to enable greater social and economic integration. In this vein, a $349 million investment program in Afghanistan aims to improve the availability and management of water resources in one of the most conflict-affected areas of the country, and an

umbrella facility of up to $100 million will help overcome constraints to private sector investment in renewable power projects in the Pacific DMCs.[37]

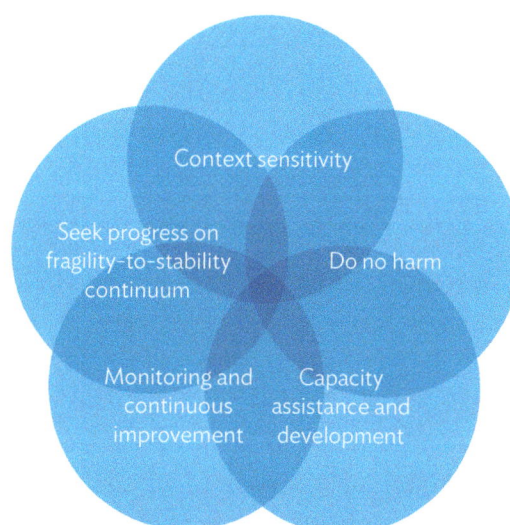

Figure 7.1: ADB's Approach to Fragile and Conflict-Affected Situations

Context sensitivity

Seek progress on fragility-to-stability continuum

Do no harm

Monitoring and continuous improvement

Capacity assistance and development

ADB = Asian Development Bank.
Source: ADB Sustainable Development and Climate Change Department.

2. Supporting Conflict-Affected Areas

178. **Empowering conflict-affected communities in Myanmar.** The 7-year Resilient Community Development Project, approved in 2019, incorporates participatory tools for analyzing the underlying factors and residual causes of conflict in Myanmar.[38] The project is designed to study and enhance local decision-making and resource allocation. Its conflict-sensitive approach aims to develop a

thorough understanding of the local context and needs through in-depth social preparation and broad outreach to villagers and the communities' most vulnerable groups. This is intended to help ensure sound decision-making on community infrastructure and livelihood investments. Flexibility has been built into the project's design and will continue through its implementation. Strong local ownership will be sought by securing the participation of villagers and developing the communities' abilities to implement and sustain project activities. Expected results include strengthened community resilience; poverty reduction and increased food security; and the expansion of local capacity and resources for sustainable investments in climate- and disaster-resilient, market-oriented infrastructure and livelihoods. Up to 1.8 million people are expected to benefit from the $243 million project, which is financed by ADB, the European Union, the Japan Fund for Poverty Reduction, and the Government of Myanmar.

179. **The role of civil society in fragile and conflict-affected situations.** Civil society organizations (CSOs) can sometimes navigate and operate in FCAS in ways that other actors cannot.[39] ADB recognizes the vital role CSOs can play to build bridges between people and communities, as well as between governments, development institutions, and aid agencies. The work of CSOs in promoting active citizenship, supporting social cohesion, facilitating dialogue, and creating networks and connections across boundaries helps identify, mitigate, and respond to local drivers of conflict.[40] In 2019, ADB's Myanmar Resident Mission drafted a comprehensive conflict-sensitive approach that integrated a strategy for civil society engagement. ADB exercises conflict sensitivity in each project and subproject in the country's conflict-affected areas. This includes recognizing and understanding the diversity of the area's ethnic groups, meeting with regional authorities, consulting with project-affected villagers, and engaging with local CSOs.

180. **Halting the conflict–fragility cycle in Afghanistan.** The vicious cycle of fragility, poverty, and conflict discourages investment that could create economic opportunities and spur socioeconomic recovery and growth. An investment agreed upon in 2019 by the Government of Afghanistan and ADB will work to help break this cycle in Kandahar Province, one of the country's least secure and most affected by

prolonged conflict. The Arghandab Integrated Water Resources Development Project, one of ADB's largest ever undertaken in Afghanistan, aims to provide Kandahar City with electricity and water-on-demand services in the province. The project will also introduce climate-smart irrigation systems and agricultural technologies and practices to boost legal crop production and sustainability and empower women farmers through training opportunities, scholarships, technology transfer, and farming advisory services.

181. Like similar previous ADB operations in Afghanistan, this project must deliver its outputs and outcome in a unique and challenging environment. ADB staff are employing the FCAS tools ADB has developed for guiding project design and implementation in Afghanistan, including a peace and conflict impact assessment.[41] The project's design is conflict-sensitive, based on a studied understanding of the project context, and the approach incorporates peace-building activities to strengthen connections, weaken divisions, and enhance social cohesion among communities in the project area.

182. **Actions taken to better monitor projects in conflict-affected areas.** Measuring and assessing the implementation status of projects in conflict conditions presents practical challenges. In Afghanistan, these can include poor security conditions. If its staff are prevented from undertaking review missions, ADB must rely on the progress reports of contracted supervision consultants to assess projects' progress. One solution ADB is now applying more widely in the country is the use of third-party consultant firms to visit sites, review the projects, and identify and recommend responses to key implementation issues. The short-term results have included better documentation of progress and an improvement in work quality at some project sites. ADB is now collaborating with executing agencies to fully implement the third-party reviewers' recommendations.

3. Addressing Sources of Fragility in the Pacific

183. **Targeting the common sources of fragility in the Pacific.** Fragility in eight small Pacific FCAS island countries is often driven by common factors. They are remote and have small populations and economies, governance and institutional capacity are weaker, infrastructure is lacking, and the delivery of basic and social services is limited. They are also extremely exposed to the adverse impacts of climate change and disasters triggered by natural hazards. ADB's Pacific Department began two new programs in 2019 to support its fragility-sensitive approach and a strategy to reduce the effects of these drivers.

184. **Building resilience to price shocks through renewable energy investment.** The small economies of the Pacific are open to external shocks, with fuel price spikes among the most economically damaging. Most electricity in the Pacific countries is generated using imported diesel fuel. Besides polluting the air, this dependence is a constant drain on scant foreign reserves and can affect economies, threaten energy security, and intensify fragility when international petroleum prices rise. The Pacific Renewable Energy Program, an umbrella facility of up to $100 million, intends to help offset this source of fragility by encouraging the development of alternative renewable energy supplies.[42]

185. The governments of Pacific FCAS countries are committed to developing renewable energy through public or private financing, but private investment is crucial in transitioning their economies away from fossil fuels. Such investments have so far faced several obstacles. Governments lack credit support for the payment obligations of power utilities and bankable power purchase agreements. Investors have been uncertain about the availability and convertibility of foreign currency and are wary of perceived political risks. The ADB Pacific Renewable Energy Program will provide loans, guarantees, and letters of credit to help overcome these constraints. Private investment in renewable energy undertakings will be encouraged through an innovative blend of direct ADB private sector lending, ADB guarantees for commercial bank loans, and development partner funds. These financing instruments will backstop the payment obligations of the power utilities, enhance their creditworthiness, and mitigate potential lenders' political concerns.

186. **Building disaster resilience in the Pacific.** Frequent disasters can perpetuate fragility. Statistically, the small economies and populations of SIDS suffer far more than their fair share. Delays in responding to disasters and launching early recovery in the post-disaster period drives up the indirect economic and social costs, worsens the ultimate effects, and compromises long-term fiscal balances. ADB's response has been to help these DMCs better prepare for such events and respond faster and more effectively after they strike.

187. ADB piloted contingent financing for disasters in the Cook Islands and Palau. Its Pacific Disaster Resilience Program did the same in Samoa, Tonga, and Tuvalu through a mechanism making timelier post-disaster financing available through policy-based loans and grants. The program's second phase, approved in September 2019, is providing a new round of contingent financing for Tonga and adding three FCAS countries—the Marshall Islands, the Federated States of Micronesia, and Solomon Islands. Participating governments have agreed on an ongoing, post-program partnership framework to strengthen their disaster risk management. Two countries have drawn down their contingent financing under the program: Tonga in February 2018, following Cyclone Gita; and Tuvalu in January 2020, after Cyclone Tino. ADB disbursed the funds for disaster response and early recovery within a few days.

Equal opportunities. Ziyagul Ismailova, beneficiary of the ADB-supported Skills for Inclusive Growth Sector Development Program in the Kyrgyz Republic, using a computer (photo by Danil Usmanov).

ACTIONS TO ADDRESS CHALLENGES

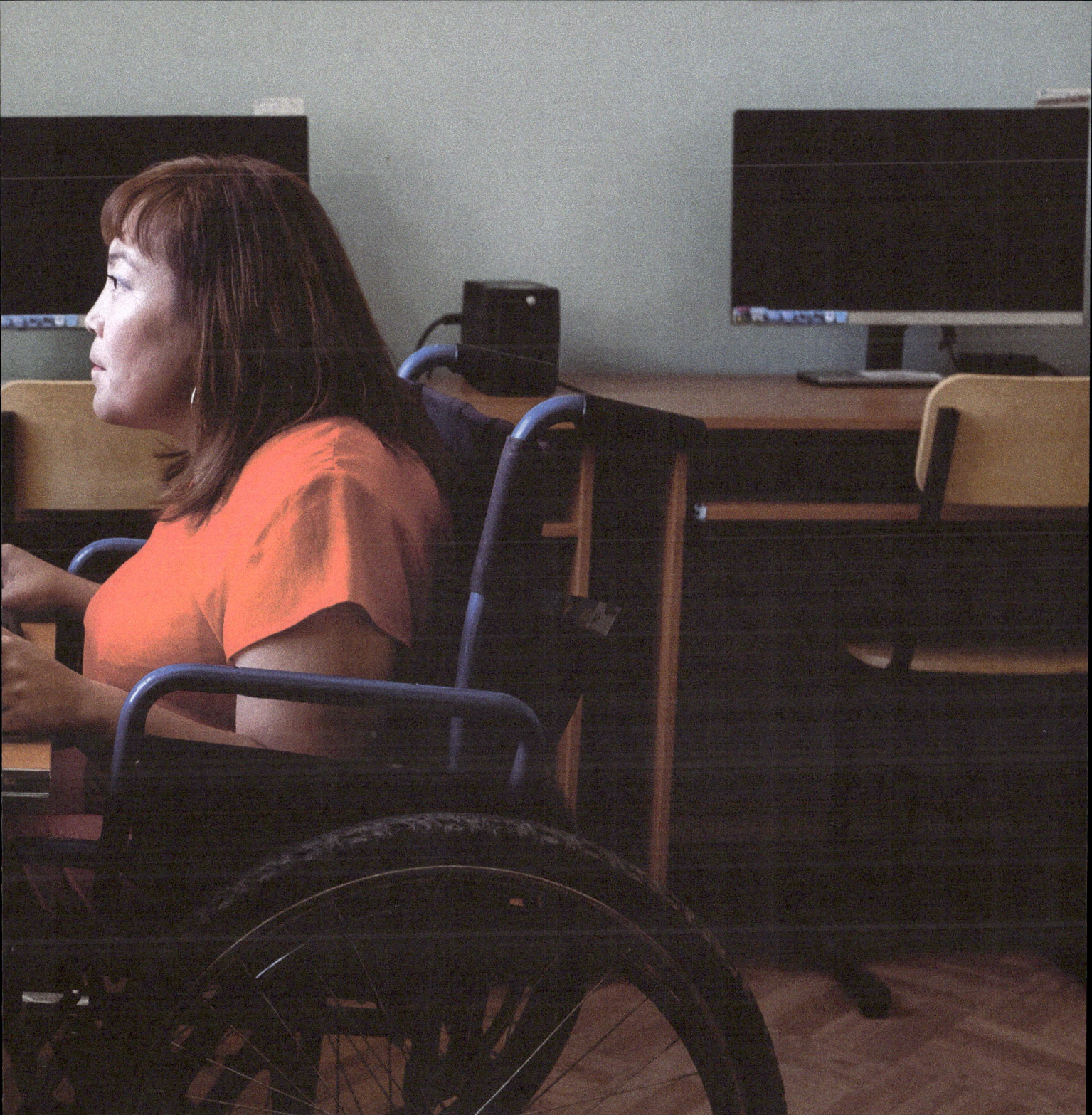

This section describes the systems and processes ADB has in place to identify and monitor actions to improve its performance, including the Management Action Record System. It summarizes the actions ADB took in 2019 in response to the challenges highlighted in the 2018 Development Effectiveness Review (DEfR) that pose barriers to implementing Strategy 2030, as well as to the challenges identified in the 2019 DEfR process that ADB needs to address in 2020 and beyond.

ACTIONS TO ADDRESS CHALLENGES

188. ADB's results-based management systems and processes are designed to formulate, communicate, mobilize, and monitor the actions ADB undertakes across the organization to tackle its operational and development effectiveness challenges. Challenges identified in the annual development effectiveness review (DEfR) are highlighted in the President's planning directions for the year, along with the corresponding strategic guidance and targets. These are then reflected in the annual work program and budget framework and cascaded down into the work plans of the individual departments and staff members to make performance expectations clear.

A. MANAGEMENT ACTION RECORD SYSTEM

189. ADB's electronic Management Action Record System (MARS) was introduced in 2009 to capture and monitor the implementation by Management of actions responding to the recommendations stemming from evaluations and reviews of ADB's Independent Evaluation Department (IED). Action plans needed to carry out these recommendations are uploaded by Management to MARS along with due dates for completing each action. Other multilateral development banks employ comparable tools for a similar purpose.[43]

190. **Action totals overall.** At the end of 2019, MARS held the records of 437 actions. Of the 378 actions due for implementation up to that point, 313 (83%) had been *fully* or *largely implemented,* 48 (13%) were *partly implemented,* and 17 (4%) were either *just started* or *not yet started.*

191. **Assessments of actions completed in 2019.** Of the 15 actions due in 2019, Management rated all 15 as *fully implemented* by the end of the year. These reflected recommendations from 10 IED evaluations uploaded to MARS from 2012 to 2018 that were scheduled for completion in 2019. Upon validation, IED assessed 10 of the 15 actions *fully* or *largely implemented* but downgraded the remaining five to *partly* or *not implemented.* The five downgraded actions related to the establishment of management systems, the use of a financing modality, strengthening organizational management, and improving the mobilization approach and measurement system for third-party financing.

192. **Actions added and action plan status in 2019.** The eight evaluation reports discussed by the Development Effectiveness Committee of the ADB Board in 2019 each made more than five recommendations. Of the 43 recommendations made overall, Management fully accepted 42 and partially accepted 1. As of March 2020, action plans responding to six of the eight reports had been uploaded, one was under discussion with IED, and one was not yet due to be uploaded. Eighteen action plans were originally scheduled to be completed in 2019. Of these, 13 were considered by Management to have been fully or largely completed and 5 were still ongoing.

193. **Challenges in designing actions.** One of the challenges faced in preparing actions is the need to strike a balance between specificity, measurability, and relevance. Although focusing an action on a particular recommendation might allow great specificity and ease of measurement, prioritizing the action's measurability may compromise its relevance or comprehensiveness to some extent. Not all the dimensions of some recommendations can be addressed by objectively verifiable actions. This often leads to trade-offs between the specificity and relevance of actions.

194. In 2019, ADB introduced internal learning events on all corporate, thematic, and sector evaluations where the MARS action plans were closed. ADB also plans to revisit the current 60-day timeline from Development Effectiveness Committee meetings for uploading action plans and will consider extending it to 90 days.[44] This would take into account the current practice of discussing action plans with IED after internal formulation and discussion by Management. It would also enable ADB to harmonize with other multilateral development banks that have adopted a 90-day timeline. Management will continue working closely with IED to improve the MARS process in 2020.

B. ACTIONS TO ADDRESS 2018 CHALLENGES

195. Three main performance areas that were rated *off track* in the 2018 DEfR scorecard remain relevant both to delivering Strategy 2030 and achieving targets in the new corporate results framework (CRF), 2019–2024. These are sovereign and nonsovereign success rates, and the share of operations supporting social protection. ADB started, continued, and completed initiatives to address these challenges during 2019. It will take time to see the full effects of these efforts. Sovereign and nonsovereign success rates remain *off track* in the 2019 DEfR, while support for social protection—which is monitored as a tracking indicator in the new CRF—did not increase from 2018's *off track* performance. This section summarizes the main actions taken during the year to address these challenges.

1. Actions to Improve Success Rates of Completed Sovereign Projects

196. **Challenge.** The success rate of completed sovereign projects remained unchanged in 2018 and below the 80% target at 74%. Of the four evaluation criteria, scores were lowest for sustainability, followed by effectiveness and efficiency. and financial sustainability. In addition, ADB developed and piloted a new methodology that includes sustainability alongside green, inclusion, and resilience criteria for screening the quality of infrastructure projects at the design stage (Chapter 2).

197. **Sustainability research informed design template and analysis enhancement.** To learn more about the causes of poor sustainability and derive lessons for improvement, ADB studied infrastructure projects in the road transport and water sectors (Chapter 3). Based on the lessons learned, several actions were taken. ADB added a new section in investment project approval documents to identify how project outcomes and outputs will be maintained over the project's economic life, as well as the mitigation measures planned to address related risks. The documents must also provide an analysis of the project's institutional, environmental, social, economic,

198. **Enhanced support to improve the quality of design and monitoring frameworks.** The most critical tool of ADB's self-evaluation system, the design and monitoring framework (DMF), has been the focus of ongoing improvement efforts. In 2019, ADB updated the DMF guidelines and expanded their scope from providing guidance on preparing the DMF to also covering good practices for using the DMF throughout the project cycle, including planning and budgeting for self-evaluation. The Strategy, Policy and Partnerships Department (SPD) collaborated with other ADB departments to scale up DMF training. A total of 682 people (452 ADB staff and 230 developing

member country officials) completed a DMF training workshop ranging in duration from 2 hours to 2 days. Of the 281 participants that completed a half-day or longer workshop, 145 ADB staff (79 women and 66 men) and 113 officials (46 women and 67 men) from implementing and executing agencies in DMCs indicated that they significantly improved their knowledge of and skills for preparing and using the DMF as a result of attending the workshop.[45] SPD, alongside teams comprising staff in the offices of the directors general of operations departments, continued to conduct quality reviews of operations before their submission for approval. These reviews are comprehensive and include a strong focus on the quality of the DMF.

199. ADB's efforts to improve the quality of its operations' DMFs are showing results. A comparative analysis of the quality of DMFs for operations committed in 2019 versus those committed in 2013 showed that 85% of the 2019 operations had high-quality DMFs, an improvement of 37 percentage points from 2013 when a DMF-specific quality control function was first introduced.[46] Substantially more 2019 DMFs had baseline values (90% versus 50%), target values (93% compared with 60% of 2013 DMFs), and sex-disaggregated baselines (75% versus 49%) for all indicators. The relevance of DMF indicators to measuring the intended outcome and outputs had also substantially improved.

200. **Implementation readiness and performance monitoring processes strengthened.** Other steps taken in 2019 to increase success rates included raising the share of infrastructure projects that are design- and procurement-ready (Chapter 3). The advance actions through which this has been achieved are expected to help inform the setting of performance targets and implementation timelines and arrangements that are realistic and ready to be carried out effectively and efficiently. ADB also developed and piloted an enhanced project performance rating methodology in 2019 to more accurately detect and flag issues with output delivery and compliance with safeguards and financial management covenants. Earlier flagging of such problems will allow ADB more time to work with clients on prompt solutions that ensure full and on-time delivery of the intended development benefits. The updated methodology will be fully rolled out in 2020.

201. **Complementary use of modalities to address effectiveness.** ADB made a more concerted effort to use the mix of ADB products and modalities that is most appropriate to fostering better development results. More policy-based lending operations were committed in sectors where investment loans are also undertaken, including in the education sector, which had comparatively low success rates in 2016–2018. This ensures that policy constraints on the achievement of intended development results, such as ensuring inclusive access to and use of services, are addressed by policy reforms.

2. Actions to Improve Success Rates of Completed Nonsovereign Operations

202. **Challenge.** The success rate of completed nonsovereign operations remained steady at 54% in 2016–2018. Low performance of finance sector projects, particularly private equity investments, contributed to the low success rate.

203. **Strategic guidance updated.** ADB prepared an operational plan for private sector operations that provides a strategic road map for how these operations will prioritize development impact and pursue the quality over the volume of investment.[47]

204. **Results management processes strengthened.** An expanded team of results management and social development specialists in the Private Sector Operations Department strengthened the focus on improving the quality of nonsovereign operation DMFs and results monitoring. In 2019, ADB developed and piloted a new CRF indicator for ongoing nonsovereign operations, which is intended to provide early warning of risks to the delivery of targeted development results. Development of a new ex ante impact assessment tool also began. The tool will make appraisals of proposed nonsovereign operations objective and will help set measurable and realistic targets for development results.

205. **Increased focus on quality in equity investments.** ADB established an equity investments unit in the Private Sector Operations Department, and began implementing actions based on the findings and recommendations of a corporate evaluation of private sector equity investments.[48] Actions specific to private equity fund operations, which historically have had low success rates, included an updating of the selection process to make assessments of their development impact and additionality more rigorous.

3. Focus on Social Protection

206. **Challenge.** The share of committed operations supporting social protection declined from 5.1% in 2015–2017 to 4.9% in 2016–2018. Strategy 2030 commits to increasing the share of operations in the social sectors as an important means to address poverty and inequality. This includes operations supporting social protection.

207. **Increased investment in capacity and building project pipeline**. The President's planning directions called on staff to prepare more operations supporting social protection in 2019. Ongoing ADB technical assistance (TA) projects helped operations departments expand their pipelines of social protection projects during the year and develop strategic frameworks for financing the expansion of social protection programs in selected DMCs. The TA projects also helped cultivate leadership in social protection, build a network of advocates and practitioners, and monitor regional progress in social protection through the Social Protection Indicator.[49] To inform and bolster the development of social protection in the region, ADB convened the Asia-Pacific Social Protection Week, a knowledge-sharing event for social protection experts and advocates in the region. ADB support enabled 18 government officials from 9 DMCs to complete training on public finance for social protection. The focus was on assessing financing options for social protection and developing tailored country financing plans. ADB also approved an additional 18 TA projects amounting to more than $18 million to support social protection initiatives in 10 DMCs, as well as regional initiatives in the Pacific and Central Asia.

C. KEY CHALLENGES TO ADDRESS IN 2020 AND ONWARD

208. **Decline in sovereign and nonsovereign operation success rates.** Sovereign and nonsovereign success rates are two areas in which the 2019 DEfR identified performance as *off track* or *on track but watch* to achieve the 2024 targets. Both indicators experienced further declines in 2017–2019 and require continuous attention. Sovereign operations in the transport, education, and finance sectors had the lowest scores. Of the four evaluation criteria, performance remained weakest on sustainability, followed by effectiveness. Among nonsovereign operations, lower performance by private equity funds was the main factor in the *off-track* performance. Development results ratings remain low. Underachievement against ambitious targets was among the causes, along with absent or insufficient data and other shortcomings in the DMFs. ADB work quality was the weakest of the other evaluation criteria for nonsovereign operations.

209. **Three other areas merit close attention in 2020.** Financing for education, achievement of gender results, and on-time completion of sovereign projects also require careful monitoring. The share of ADB financing committed for education operations was lower than targeted in 2019 and rated *off track*, although it only dropped by 0.2 percentage points from its record performance in 2018.

210. The share of completed operations assessed as having achieved their envisaged gender equality results remained roughly consistent and was rated *on track but watch* to meet the 2024 target. Better performance in this area requires proactive efforts from project teams. Reviews of completion reports reveal a need to enhance the capacity of executing and implementing agencies, borrowers, and clients in routine collection of sex-disaggregated data and for regular discussions about the status of gender action plan implementation. In 2019, fewer sovereign projects closed on time. Delays were mainly caused by issues related to procurement and the performance of contractors and consultants. However, design readiness was rated *on target* and procurement readiness *on track*, which should support more timely completion in the future (Chapter 3).

211. Future editions of the DEfR will take stock of how ADB is adapting its operations to respond to the changing development needs and context of the region as tracked by Level 1 indicators. This will include ADB's responses to new shocks and stresses that affect the region's development trajectory and prospects for achieving the Sustainable Development Goals.

Handled with care. The owner of a ceramics shop in Tashkent, Uzbekistan arranges her merchandise (photo by Relisa Granovskaya).

APPENDIXES

Swinging high. A child at play on the west coast of Funafuti Island in Tuvalu, one of the world's most isolated countries (photo by Lester Ledesma).

APPENDIX 1: INDICATOR INDEX

1.   The tables below indicate where to find details on each results framework indicator and tracking indicator discussed in this report. Some indicators are featured across several chapters. Data for the remaining indicators is in the scorecard that accompanies this report.

Table A1.1: Development Progress in Asia and the Pacific (Level 1)

RFI No.	TI No.	Regional Progress Indicator	Page / Paragraph
1		**Population living on less than $1.90 a day** (%, number)	**p. 11, para. 13; p. 20, para. 56; p. 26**
	1	Population living on less than $3.20 a day (%, number)	p. 11, para. 13; p. 20, para. 56; p. 26
	2	Youth not in education or training (%)—a. Female; b. Male	p. 11, para. 14; p. 20, para. 58; p. 21, para. 59
	3	Lower secondary education graduation rate (%)—a. Female; b. Male	p. 11, para. 13
	4	Universal health care coverage service index (%)	p. 11, para. 13; p. 20, para. 58
	5	Proportion of adults (15 years and older) with an account at a bank, financial institution, and/or mobile money service provider (%)—a. Female; b. Male	p. 21, para. 60; p. 26
2		**Growth rates of household expenditure or income per capita among the bottom 40% and the total population** (percentage point difference)	**p. 11, para. 13; p. 20, para. 57**
	6	Income inequality (average Gini coefficient)	p. 20, para. 57
3		**Annual growth rate of real GDP per capita in 2010 constant United States dollars (%)**	**p. 11, para. 13; p. 20, para. 56**
4		**Unemployment rate (%) a. Female; b. Male**	**p. 11, para. 14; p. 21, para. 59**
	7	Labor force participation rate (%)—a. Female; b. Male	p. 21, para. 59; p. 26
	8	Proportion of time spent on unpaid domestic and care work (%)—a. Female; b. Male	p. 11, para. 14; p. 21, para. 60
5		**CO_2 emissions per unit of GDP** (kg per $ constant 2010 PPP GDP)	**p. 11, para. 15; p. 22, para. 61; p. 26**
	9	Forest area as a proportion of total land area (%)	p. 11, para. 15; p. 22, para. 61
	10	Coverage of protected areas in relation to marine areas (%)	p. 11, para. 15; p. 22, para. 61
6		**Deaths attributed to climate-related and geophysical hazards** (number)	**p. 11, para. 15; p. 22, para. 61**
	13	Access to social protection—social assistance (%)	p. 11, para. 13; p. 20, para. 58; p. 26

continued on next page

112

Table A1.1 *continued*

RFI No.	TI No.	Regional Progress Indicator	Page / Paragraph
7		**PM2.5 air pollution, mean annual exposure** (micrograms per cubic meter)	**p. 12, para. 16; p. 22, para. 63; p. 27**
	14	Proportion of population with primary reliance on clean fuels and technology for cooking (%)	p. 22 para. 63; p. 23, Box 1.1
8		**Prevalence of stunting among children under 5 years** (%)	**p. 12, para. 17; p. 23, para. 64**
9		**Worldwide Governance Indicators** (average score)	**p. 12, para. 18; p. 23, para. 65; p. 24; p. 27**
	16	Tax revenue (% of GDP)	p. 24, para. 66; p. 27
10		**Regional cooperation and integration index** (average score)	**p. 12, para. 19; p. 24, para. 67; pp. 25, 27**
	18	Regional cooperation and integration index—Money and finance (average score)	p. 24, para. 67
	19	Proportion of population with access to electricity (%)	p. 11, para. 13; p. 12, para. 17; p. 23, Box 1.1; p. 27
	20	Proportion of population using basic drinking water services (%)—a. Rural; b. Urban	p. 11, para. 13; p. 12, para. 17; p. 23, Box 1.1; p. 27
	21	Proportion of population using basic sanitation services (%)—a. Rural; b. Urban	p. 11, para. 13; p. 12, para. 17; p. 23, Box 1.1; p. 27

CO_2 = carbon dioxide, GDP = gross domestic product, kg = kilogram, PM2.5 = atmospheric particulate matter with a diameter of less than 2.5 micrometers, PPP = purchasing power parity, RFI = results framework indicator, TI = tracking indicator.

Table A1.2: Results from Completed Operations—Strategy 2030 Operational Priority Results (Level 2A)

RFI No.	TI No.	Indicator	Page / Paragraph
		OP 1: Addressing Remaining Poverty and Reducing Inequalities	
1.1		**People benefiting from improved health services, education services, or social protection** (number)	**pp. 26, 28**
	1.1.1	People enrolled in improved education and/or training (number)	p. 28
	1.1.2	Health services established or improved (number)	pp. 26, 28
	1.1.3	Social protection schemes established or improved (number)	p. 26

continued on next page

Table A1.2 *continued*

RFI No.	TI No.	Indicator	Page / Paragraph
1.2		**Jobs generated** (number)	**p. 28**
1.3		**Poor and vulnerable people with improved standards of living** (number)	**pp. 26, 28**
	1.3.1	Infrastructure assets established or improved (number)	p. 28
		*OP 2: Accelerating Progress in Gender Equality*	
2.1		**Skilled jobs for women generated** (number)	**p. 30**
	2.1.2	Women opening new accounts (number)	p. 26
2.2		**Women and girls completing secondary and tertiary education, and/or other training** (number)	**pp. 26, 30**
2.3		**Women represented in decision-making structures and processes** (number)	**p. 30**
2.4		**Women and girls with increased time savings** (number)	**pp. 26, 30**
2.5		**Women and girls with increased resilience to climate change, disasters, and other external shocks** (number)	**p. 30**
		*OP 3: Tackling Climate Change, Building Climate and Disaster Resilience, and Enhancing Environmental Sustainability*	
3.1		**Total annual greenhouse gas emissions reduction** (tCO_2e/year)	**pp. 26, 32**
	3.1.3	Low-carbon infrastructure assets established or improved (number)	p. 32
	3.1.5	Low-carbon solutions promoted and implemented (number)	p. 32
3.2		**People with strengthened climate and disaster resilience** (number)	**p. 32**
	3.2.1	Area with reduced flood risk (hectares)	p. 32
	3.2.4	National and subnational disaster risk reduction and/or management plans supported in implementation (number)	pp. 26, 32
3.3		**People benefiting from strengthened environmental sustainability** (number)	**pp. 26, 32**
	3.3.1	Pollution control enhancing infrastructure assets established or improved (number)	p. 32
		*OP 4: Making Cities More Livable*	
4.1		**People benefiting from improved services in urban areas** (number)	**p. 32**
	4.1.2	Urban infrastructure assets established or improved (number)	p. 34
4.2		**Entities with improved urban planning and financial sustainability** (number)	**p. 34**
	4.2.1	Measures to improve regulatory, legal, and institutional environment for better planning supported in implementation (number)	p. 34
4.3		**Zones with improved urban environment, climate resilience, and disaster risk management** (number)	**pp. 27, 34**
	4.3.1	Solutions to enhance urban environment implemented (number)	p. 34

continued on next page

Table A1.2 *continued*

RFI No.	TI No.	Indicator	Page / Paragraph
OP 5: Promoting Rural Development and Food Security			
5.1		**People benefiting from increased rural investment** (number)	**pp. 27, 36**
	5.1.1	Rural infrastructure assets established or improved (number)	p. 36
	5.1.4	Rural economic hubs supported (number)	p. 36
5.2		**Farmers with improved market access** (number)	p. 36
	5.2.2	Storages, agri-logistics, and modern retail assets established or improved (number)	p. 36
5.3		**Land with higher productivity** (hectares)	**pp. 27, 36**
OP 6: Strengthening Governance and Institutional Capacity			
6.1		**Entities with improved management functions and financial stability** (number)	**pp. 27, 38**
	6.1.1	Government officials with increased capacity to design, implement, monitor, and evaluate relevant measures (number)	p. 38
	6.1.2	Measures supported in implementation to improve capacity of public organizations to promote the private sector and finance sector (number)	p. 38
	6.1.4	Transparency and accountability measures in procurement and financial management supported in implementation (number)	p. 27
6.2		**Entities with improved service delivery** (number)	**p. 38**
	6.2.1	Service delivery standards adopted and/or supported in implementation by government and/or private entities (number)	p. 38
	6.2.3	Measures to strengthen state-owned enterprise governance supported in implementation (number)	p. 38
OP 7: Fostering Regional Cooperation and Integration			
7.1		**Cargo transported and energy transmitted across borders** ($)	p. 40
	7.1.2	Measures to improve the efficiency and/or productivity of cross-border connectivity supported in implementation (number)	pp. 27, 40
	7.1.3	Clean energy capacity for power trade installed or improved (megawatt equivalent)	p. 40
7.2		**Trade and investment facilitated** ($)	**pp. 27, 40**
7.3		**Regional public goods initiatives successfully reducing cross-border environmental or health risks, or providing regional access to education services**	**p. 40**
	7.3.4	Regional or subregional mechanisms created or operationalized to enhance coordination and cooperation among DMCs on regional public goods (number)	p. 40

DMC = developing member country, OP = operational priority, RFI = results framework indicator, tCO$_2$e/year = tons of carbon dioxide equivalent per year, TI = tracking indicator.

Table A1.3: Results from Completed Operations—Quality of Completed Operations (Level 2B)

RFI No.	TI No.	Indicator	Page / Paragraph
1		**Completed operations rated *successful* (%) (sovereign)**	**p. 12, para. 22; p. 56; p. 57, para. 96; p.58, paras. 99–100; p. 62, para. 112; p. 105, para. 196; p. 108, para. 208**
	1	Completed operations rated *successful* (%) (sovereign)—a. Investment projects; b. Policy-based operations; c. FCAS DMCs; d. Small island developing states	p. 13, paras. 23, 25; p. 56; p. 57, para. 96; p. 96; p. 97, para. 174
	2	Completed operations rated *successful* (%) (sovereign)—a. Relevance; b. Efficiency; c. Effectiveness; d. Sustainability	p. 13, para. 24; p. 56; p.57, para. 97; p. 59, Box 3.1; p. 59, para. 101; pp. 60–62, paras. 102–111
2		**Projects closed on time (%) (sovereign)**	**p. 13, para. 26; p. 56; p. 61, para. 108; p. 62, para. 113; p. 108, para. 208**
3		**Completed operations rated *successful* (%) (nonsovereign)**	**p. 13, para. 27; p. 66; p. 67, para. 119; pp. 70–71, paras. 128–131; p. 107, para. 202; p. 108, para. 208**
	3	Completed operations rated *successful* (%) (nonsovereign)—a. Development results; b. ADB's additionality; c. ADB's investment profitability; d. ADB's work quality	p. 13, para. 28; p. 66; p.67, para. 121; pp. 71–73, para. 132–133
4		**Completed operations delivering intended gender equality results (%) (sovereign and nonsovereign)**	**p. 13, para. 29; p. 31; p. 57, para. 98; p. 108, para. 209**
5		**Clients satisfied with the use of ADB knowledge products (%)**	**p. 76, paras. 137–138**
	4	Web-distributed knowledge solutions (number of downloads)	p. 77, para. 141
	5	Engagement on social media (number)—a. Subscribers and followers; b. Active engagement	p. 77, para. 142
	6	Event participants reporting increased knowledge and/or skills (number)	p. 76, para. 139
	8	Completed technical assistance projects rated *successful* (%) (sovereign and nonsovereign)	p. 76, para. 140
	10	Impact evaluations completed (number)	p. 78, para. 145

ADB = Asian Development Bank, DMC = developing member country, FCAS = fragile and conflict-affected situation, RFI = results framework indicator, TI = tracking indicator.

Table A1.4: ADB's Operational Management (Level 3)

RFI No.	TI No.	Indicator	Page / Paragraph
		Level 3A. Design and Implementation Quality	
1		**Infrastructure projects that are design-ready** (%) (sovereign)	p. 14, para. 31; pp. 56–57, para. 93; p. 106, para. 200
2		**Infrastructure projects that are procurement-ready** (%) (sovereign)	p. 14, para. 31; p. 56–57, para. 93; p. 106, para. 200
3		**Performance of operations at implementation rated** *satisfactory* (%) (sovereign)	p. 14, para. 32; pp. 56–57, para. 95; p. 106, para. 200
	1	Performance of operations at implementation rated *satisfactory* (%) (sovereign)–a. Output; b. Contract award; c. Disbursement; d. Financial management; e. Safeguards	pp. 56–57, para. 95
4		**Operations at risk of not achieving development results** (%) (nonsovereign)	p. 14, para. 32; pp. 66–67, para. 117; p. 107, para. 204
		Level 3B. Development Finance	
	2	Time from concept approval to first disbursement (months) (sovereign)—a. From concept approval to loan fact-finding; b. From loan fact-finding to approval; c. From approval to commitment; d. From commitment to first disbursement	p. 15, para. 38; pp. 88–89, para. 159
	3	Time from concept approval to first disbursement (months) (nonsovereign)—a. From mandate approval to project approval; b. From approval to signing; c. From signing to first disbursement	p. 15, para. 38; pp. 88–89, para. 160
5		**Disbursement rate** (%) (sovereign)	p. 14, para. 33; p. 44, para. 70
	4	Overall disbursement ($ billion) (sovereign)	p. 44, para. 70
	5	Disbursement ratio (%) (sovereign)	p. 44, para. 70
	6	Approvals ($ billion) (sovereign and nonsovereign)	p. 44, para. 69
	7	Commitments ($ billion) (sovereign and nonsovereign)	p. 44, para. 69
	8	Commitments in concessional assistance countries (group A + group B) (%) (sovereign and nonsovereign)	p. 44, para. 69
	9	Commitments in FCAS DMCs and SIDS (%) (sovereign and nonsovereign)	p. 14, para. 37; pp. 96–97, para. 173
6		**Cofinancing ratio** (%) (nonsovereign)	p. 14, para. 34; p. 45, para. 71; p. 49, para. 81; p. 67, para. 116

continued on next page

Table A1.4 *continued*

RFI No.	TI No.	Indicator	Page / Paragraph
7		**Financing for education** (%) (sovereign and nonsovereign)	**p. 14, paras. 30, 35; p. 50, para. 83; p. 108, para. 208**
8		**Financing for health** (%) (sovereign and nonsovereign)	**p. 14, para. 36; p. 50, para. 84**
		Level 3C. Strategic Alignment	
9		**Committed operations classified gender equity theme or effective gender mainstreaming** (%) (sovereign and nonsovereign)	**p. 16, para. 41; p. 45, para. 71; p. 46, para. 73**
	12	Committed operations that promote gender equality (%) (sovereign and nonsovereign)—a1. GEN—sovereign operations; a2. GEN—nonsovereign operations; b1.EGM—sovereign operations; b2. EGM—nonsovereign operations; c1.SGE—sovereign operations; c2. SGE—nonsovereign operations; d1.NGE—sovereign operations; d2. NGE—nonsovereign operations	p.16, para. 41; p. 46, para. 74; p. 47
10		**Committed operations classified gender equity theme, effective gender mainstreaming, or some gender elements** (%) (sovereign and nonsovereign)	**p. 16, para. 41; p. 45, para. 71; p. 46, para. 73; pp. 66–67, para. 115**
	13	Financing for gender equality (%) (sovereign and nonsovereign)	p. 16, para. 41; p. 46, para. 73
11		**Committed operations that support climate change mitigation and adaptation** (%) (sovereign and nonsovereign)	**p. 16, para. 42; p. 45, para. 71; p. 48, para. 78**
	14	Committed operations supporting climate change (%) (sovereign and nonsovereign)–a. Mitigation; b. Adaptation; c. Both	p. 16, para. 42; p. 48, para. 78
12		**Financing for climate change mitigation and adaptation** ($ billion, cumulative) (sovereign and nonsovereign)	**p. 16, para. 43; p. 45, para. 71; p. 48, para. 79; pp. 66–67, para. 115**
	15	Financing for climate change ($ billion, cumulative) (sovereign and nonsovereign)–a. Mitigation; b. Adaptation; c. Both	p. 16, para. 43; p. 48, para. 79
13		**Nonsovereign operations as a share of total ADB operations** (%, number) (nonsovereign)	**p. 16, para. 44; p. 45, para. 71; p. 66; p. 68, para. 122**
	16	Nonsovereign operations as a share of total ADB operations (%, $) (nonsovereign)	p. 16, para. 44; p. 68, para. 122
14		**Operations in frontier economies and/or in new sectors** (%) (nonsovereign)	**p. 16, para. 45; pp. 66–67, para. 115; p. 69, para. 124**
15		**Operations supporting poverty reduction and inclusiveness** (%) (sovereign and nonsovereign)	**p. 15, para. 40; p. 51, para. 86**
	17	Operations or transactions supporting inclusive business (number) (nonsovereign)	p. 66–67, para. 115; p. 70, para. 127

continued on next page

Table A1.4 *continued*

RFI No.	TI No.	Indicator	Page / Paragraph
	18	Knowledge products and services delivered (%)	p. 78, para. 144
	19	Operations that are green, sustainable, inclusive, and resilient (%) (sovereign and nonsovereign)	p. 52, para. 89
	20	Operations contributing to each of seven operational priorities (%) (sovereign and nonsovereign)	p. 15, para. 39; pp. 26– 28, 30, 32, 34, 36, 38, 40; p. 45, para 72
	21	Operations contributing to social protection (%) (sovereign and nonsovereign)	p. 15, para. 40; p. 26; p. 50, para. 85; p. 107, paras. 206–207
	22	Disability-inclusive operations (%) (sovereign and nonsovereign)	p. 15, para. 40; pp. 51–52, paras. 87–88
	23	Operations aligned with Sustainable Development Goals (sovereign and nonsovereign)—a. (%, number); b. (%,$)	p. 53, paras. 91–92
	24	Operations using country procurement systems (%) (sovereign)	pp. 90–91, para. 168
	25	Contracts using government e-procurement systems ($ billion) (sovereign)	pp. 90–91, para. 168
	26	Innovative operations and technical assistance projects (%) (sovereign and nonsovereign)	pp. 78–79, paras. 146–148
	27	Civil society organizations' participation (% of committed operations) (sovereign)	pp. 92–93, para. 170

ADB = Asian Development Bank, DMC = developing member country, EGM = effective gender mainstreaming, FCAS = fragile and conflict-affected situation, GEN = gender equity theme, NGE = no gender elements, RFI = results framework indicator, SGE = some gender elements, SIDS = small island developing state, TI = tracking indicator.

Table A1.5: ADB's Organizational Effectiveness (Level 4)

RFI No.	TI No.	Indicator	Page / Paragraph
		Level 4A. Organizational Systems and Processes	
1		**Quality of budget management** (%)	**p. 17, para. 46; pp. 88–89, para. 162**
	1	Equity–loan ratio (%) (sovereign and nonsovereign)	p. 17, para. 47; pp. 86–87, para. 153
	2	Impaired loans ratio (%) (nonsovereign)	p. 17, para. 48; pp. 66–67, para. 118; pp. 86–87, para. 153
	3	Weighted average risk rating of the nonsovereign portfolio (%) (nonsovereign)	p. 17, para. 48; pp. 66–67, para. 118; pp. 86–87, para. 153

continued on next page

Table A1.5 *continued*

RFI No.	TI No.	Indicator	Page / Paragraph
	4	Internal administrative expenses per $1 million disbursement ($'000)	pp. 88–89, para. 162
	5	Internal administrative expenses per project under administration ($'000)	pp. 88–89, para. 162
	6	Internal administrative expenses per project approved ($'000)	pp. 88–89, para. 162
2		**Procurement contract transactions of $10 million or more with processing time of 40 days or less** (%) (sovereign)	p. 17, para. 49; pp. 90–91, para. 165
	7	Procurement time from advertisement to contract signing, $10 million or more (days) (sovereign)	pp. 90–91, para. 166
	8	Consulting services recruitment time for ADB-administered contracts, from consulting services recruitment notice to consultant contract signing (days) (sovereign)	pp. 90–91, para. 167
	9	Audited financial statements reviewed on time (%) (sovereign)	pp. 88–89, para. 161
3		**Representation of women in the international staff category** (%)	p. 17, para 50; pp. 86–87, para. 154
	10	Representation of women in the international staff category (%)—a. Levels 4–6; b. Levels 7–8; c. Levels 9–10	p. 17, para 50; pp. 86–87, para. 154
4		**Projects or transactions with sovereign–nonsovereign collaboration** (number, cumulative) (sovereign and nonsovereign)	p. 17, para. 51; pp. 92–93, para. 169
		Level 4B. Organizational Capacity	
	13	Digital products completed (number)	p. 17, para. 52; pp. 90–91, para. 164
	15	Internal training budget (average $ per staff)	pp. 86–87, para. 155
	16	Departments with documented and tested business continuity plans in place (number)	pp. 88–89, para. 163
7		**Budgeted international and national staff positions in field offices** (% of total operations departments)	p. 17, para. 53; pp. 86–87, para. 156
	17	Budgeted international and national staff positions in FCAS DMCs and SIDS field offices (number)	p. 17, para. 53; pp. 86–87, para. 157; pp. 96–97, para. 175
	18	Operations administered in field offices (%) (sovereign)	pp. 86–87, para. 158
8		**Staff rating ADB as an effective knowledge and learning organization** (%)	p. 17, para. 54; pp. 80–81, paras. 149–151
	20	Knowledge products and services drawn from k-Nexus (number)	p. 78, para. 143

ADB = Asian Development Bank, DMC = developing member country, FCAS = fragile and conflict-affected situation, RFI = results framework indicator, SIDS = small island developing state, TI = tracking indicator.

APPENDIX 2: SELECTED RESULTS OF 2019 COMPLETED OPERATIONS BY SUSTAINABLE DEVELOPMENT GOAL

1 NO POVERTY
- **7,784,000 people benefiting from improved health services, education services, or social protection**
- **1,742,000 poor and vulnerable people with improved standards of living**
- **Eight social protection schemes established or improved**
- Nine measures to improve regional public health and education services supported in implementation

4 QUALITY EDUCATION
- **76,000 people enrolled in improved education and/or training**
- **67,000 women enrolled in TVET and other job training**
- 179,000 women and girls completing secondary and tertiary education, and/or other training
- 220 women and girls enrolled in STEM or nontraditional TVET

8 DECENT WORK AND ECONOMIC GROWTH
- **313,000 jobs generated**
- **Two enhanced labor policies or standards implemented**
- **Four new financial products and services made available to the poor and vulnerable**
- **1,772,000 women opening new accounts**
- 59,000 skilled jobs for women generated
- 28 business development and financial sector measures supported in implementation

11 SUSTAINABLE CITIES AND COMMUNITIES
- **25 national and subnational disaster risk reduction and/or management plans supported in implementation**
- **2,783,000 people benefiting from improved services in urban areas**
- 98 entities with improved urban planning and financial sustainability
- 37 zones with improved urban environment, climate resilience, and disaster risk management

2 ZERO HUNGER
- **176,000 hectares of land with higher productivity**
- **610 rural infrastructure assets established or improved**
- 6,628,000 people benefiting from increased rural investment
- 62,000 farmers with improved market access
- 4,000 storages, agri-logistics, and modern retail assets established or improved
- 23,000 hectares of land improved through climate-resilient irrigation infrastructure and water delivery services

5 GENDER EQUALITY
- **14,000 women represented in decision-making structures and processes**
- **2,084,000 women and girls with increased time savings**
- 459,000 women-owned or -led SME loan accounts opened or women-owned or -led SME end borrowers reached
- 963,000 women and girls benefiting from new or improved infrastructure
- 2,800 women with strengthened leadership capacities

10 REDUCED INEQUALITIES
- Two measures for increased inclusiveness supported in implementation

13 CLIMATE ACTION
- **3,161,000 people with strengthened climate and disaster resilience**
- **1,588,000 women and girls with increased resilience to climate change, disasters, and other external shocks**
- 12,778,000 tCO_2e/year total annual greenhouse gas emissions reduction

3 GOOD HEALTH AND WELL-BEING
- **38 health services established or improved**
- **Two health services for women and girls established or improved**
- 26 pollution control enhancing infrastructure assets established or improved

6 CLEAN WATER AND SANITATION / 7 AFFORDABLE AND CLEAN ENERGY / 9 INDUSTRY, INNOVATION AND INFRASTRUCTURE
- **75,000 MW renewable energy capacity installed**
- **720 infrastructure assets established or improved**
- **18 low-carbon infrastructure assets established or improved**
- **Six new and existing infrastructure assets made climate- and disaster-resilient**
- **Six transport and ICT connectivity assets established or improved**
- 16 measures to improve the efficiency and/or productivity of cross-border connectivity supported in implementation
- 1,000 MW of clean energy capacity for power trade installed or improved

12 RESPONSIBLE CONSUMPTION AND PRODUCTION / 14 LIFE BELOW WATER / 15 LIFE ON LAND
- **870 hectares of terrestrial, coastal, and marine areas conserved, restored, and/or enhanced**
- **Nine solutions to conserve, restore, and/or enhance terrestrial, coastal, and marine areas implemented**
- 5,137,000 people benefiting from strengthened environmental sustainability

16 PEACE, JUSTICE AND STRONG INSTITUTIONS
- 1,700 entities with improved management functions and financial stability
- 390 entities with improved service delivery
- 70,000 government officials with increased capacity to design, implement, monitor, and evaluate relevant measures
- 33 transparency and accountability measures in procurement and financial management supported in implementation
- Eight citizen engagement mechanisms adopted

17 PARTNERSHIPS FOR THE GOALS
- $237,434,000 trade and investment facilitated
- 120 measures supported in implementation to improve capacity of public organizations to promote the private sector and finance sector
- 23 regional or subregional mechanisms created or operationalized to enhance coordination and cooperation among DMCs in trade, finance, or multisector economic corridors

DMC = developing member country; ICT = information and communication technology; MW = megawatt; SME = small- and medium-sized enterprise; STEM = science, technology, engineering, and mathematics; tCO_2e/year = tons of carbon dioxide equivalent per year; TVET = technical and vocational education and training.
Note: Indicators in bold are derived from or aligned with official Sustainable Development Goal indicators. Others are linked to the goal and associated targets.

APPENDIX 3: ADB DEVELOPING MEMBER COUNTRIES

Table A3.1: ADB Developing Member Countries

Afghanistan	India	Mongolia	Solomon Islands
Armenia	Indonesia	Myanmar	Sri Lanka
Azerbaijan	Kazakhstan	Nauru	Tajikistan
Bangladesh	Kiribati	Nepal	Thailand
Bhutan	Kyrgyz Republic	Niue[a]	Timor-Leste
Cambodia	Lao People's Democratic Republic	Pakistan	Tonga
China, People's Republic of	Malaysia	Palau	Turkmenistan
Cook Islands	Maldives	Papua New Guinea	Tuvalu
Fiji	Marshall Islands	Philippines	Uzbekistan
Georgia	Micronesia, Federated States of	Samoa	Vanuatu
			Viet Nam

ADB = Asian Development Bank.
Note: Five developing members—Brunei Darussalam; Hong Kong, China; the Republic of Korea; Singapore; and Taipei,China—have graduated from regular ADB assistance and are not included in this table.
[a] Niue became an ADB member country on 11 March 2019.

Table A3.2: 2018 Classification of ADB Developing Member Countries

Regular OCR-Only Countries (group C)	CA Countries		FCAS	SIDS
	OCR Blend Countries (group B)	CA-Only Countries (group A)		
Armenia [a]	Bangladesh	**COL-only countries**	Afghanistan	Cook Islands
Azerbaijan [b]	Mongolia [e]	Cambodia	Kiribati	Fiji
China, People's Republic of	Pakistan	Myanmar	Marshall Islands	Kiribati
Cook Islands	Palau	Nepal	Micronesia, Federated States of	Maldives
Fiji	Papua New Guinea	**ADF blend countries**	Myanmar	Marshall Islands
Georgia [c]	Sri Lanka [f]	Bhutan	Nauru	Micronesia, Federated States of
India [d]	Timor-Leste [g]	Kyrgyz Republic	Papua New Guinea	Nauru
Indonesia	Uzbekistan	Solomon Islands	Solomon Islands	Niue [k]
Kazakhstan	Viet Nam [h]	Vanuatu	Timor-Leste	Palau
Malaysia		**Grants-only countries**	Tuvalu	Papua New Guinea
Philippines		Afghanistan		Samoa
Thailand		Kiribati		Solomon Islands
Turkmenistan		Lao People's Democratic Republic		Timor-Leste
		Maldives		Tonga
		Marshall Islands [i]		Tuvalu
		Micronesia, Federated States of [j]		Vanuatu
		Nauru		
		Samoa		
		Tajikistan		
		Tonga		
		Tuvalu		

ADB = Asian Development Bank, ADF = Asian Development Fund, CA = concessional assistance, COL = concessional ordinary capital resources lending, FCAS = fragile and conflict-affected situation, OCR = ordinary capital resources, SIDS = small island developing state.

Notes:

[a] ADB. 2014. *Armenia: Review of Classification under ADB's Graduation Policy.* Manila (R77-14).

[b] ADB. 2013. *Azerbaijan: Review of Classification under ADB's Graduation Policy.* Manila (R89-13).

[c] ADB. 2013. *Georgia: Review of Classification under ADB's Graduation Policy.* Manila (R78-14).

[d] India is classified under group B but has no access to concessional assistance based on OM Section A1 (23 April 2019).

[e] ADB. 2011. *Review of the Classification of Mongolia under the Asian Development Bank's Graduation Policy.* Manila (115-11).

[f] ADB. 2017. *Sri Lanka: Review of Classification under ADB's Graduation Policy.* Manila (R67-17). Sri Lanka's reclassification to group C (regular OCR-only) was effective from 1 January 2019.

[g] ADB. 2011. *Review of the Classification of Timor-Leste under the Asian Development Bank's Graduation Policy.* Corrigendum 1. Manila (172-11).

[h] ADB. 2017. *Viet Nam: Review of Classification under ADB's Graduation Policy.* Manila (R66-17). Viet Nam's reclassification to group C (regular OCR-only) was effective from 1 January 2019.

[i] ADB. 2013. *Marshall Islands: Review of Classification under ADB's Graduation Policy.* Manila (R61-13).

[j] ADB. 2017. *Federated States of Micronesia: Review of Classification under ADB's Graduation Policy.* Manila (R1-17).

[k] Niue became an ADB member country on 11 March 2019. Assessment of its lending eligibility is ongoing.

Sources: ADB. 2013. *Operational Plan for Enhancing ADB's Effectiveness in Fragile and Conflict-Affected Situations.* Manila; ADB. 2018. Classification and Graduation of Developing Member Countries. *Operations Manual.* OM A1/BP. Manila; and ADB Strategy, Policy and Partnerships Department.

APPENDIX 4: UPDATES TO THE CORPORATE RESULTS FRAMEWORK, 2019–2024

1.   This appendix contains the Corporate Results Framework, 2019–2024, as approved by the Asian Development Bank (ADB) Board of Directors in 2019. Baseline values have been revised where relevant to reflect the latest values; these changes are flagged in red font.

Table A4.1: Development Progress in Asia and the Pacific (Level 1)

RPI	Regional Progress Indicator[a]	Baseline Year	Baseline	
			ADB DMCs Overall	ADB Concessional Assistance Countries
1	Population living on less than $1.90 a day (%, number)	2015	6.96	8.29
2	Growth rates of household expenditure or income per capita among the bottom 40% and the total population (percentage point difference)	2000–2017	(0.12)	0.13
3	Annual growth rate of real GDP per capita in 2010 constant United States dollars (%)	2017	~~5.40~~ 5.54	~~4.55~~ 4.48
4	Unemployment rate (%) a. Female b. Male	2018	~~4.03~~ 3.49 ~~4.40~~ 3.79 ~~4.01~~ 3.51	~~3.86~~ 3.13 ~~5.47~~ 4.38 ~~3.32~~ 2.68
5	CO_2 emissions per unit of GDP (kg per $ constant 2010 PPP GDP)	2014	~~1.09~~ 1.04	~~0.77~~ 0.64
6	Deaths attributed to climate-related and geophysical hazards (number)	2018	~~7,655~~ 8,761	~~1,062~~ 397
7	PM2.5 air pollution, mean annual exposure (micrograms per cubic meter)	2016	~~59.81~~ 60.07	~~65.72~~ 49.39
8	Prevalence of stunting among children under 5 years (%)	2006–2016	28.93	~~37.05~~ 37.00
9	Worldwide Governance Indicators (average score)	2017	(0.32)	~~(0.344)~~ (0.34)
10	Regional cooperation and integration index (average score)	2010–2015	~~0.362~~ 0.43	~~0.355~~ 0.424

( ) = negative, ADB = Asian Development Bank, CO_2 = carbon dioxide, DMC = developing member country, GDP = gross domestic product, kg = kilogram, PM2.5 = atmospheric particulate matter with a diameter of less than 2.5 micrometers, PPP = purchasing power parity, RPI = regional progress indicator.

Note: All baseline values were updated to reflect most recently available data.

[a] Level 1 indicators are renamed "regional progress indicators," and since ADB reviews regional development progress against baselines, they remain under the umbrella of results framework indicators.

Table A4.2: Results from Completed Operations—Strategy 2030 Operational Priority Results (Level 2A)

RFI	Results Framework Indicator	ADB Operations Overall			Operations Financed by Concessional OCR Loans and ADF Grants		
		No. of PCRs/ XARRs/TCRs	Results Achieved	Achievement Rate (%)	No. of PCRs/ XARRs/TCRs	Results Achieved	Achievement Rate (%)
OP 1: Addressing Remaining Poverty and Reducing Inequalities							
1.1	People benefiting from improved health services, education services, or social protection (number)	...	...	...	...	...	...
1.2	Jobs generated (number)[a]	...	...	...	...	...	...
1.3	Poor and vulnerable people with improved standards of living (number)	...	...	...	...	...	...
OP 2: Accelerating Progress in Gender Equality							
2.1	Skilled jobs for women generated (number)	...	...	...	...	...	...
2.2	Women and girls completing secondary and tertiary education, and/or other training (number)	...	...	...	...	...	...
2.3	Women represented in decision-making structures and processes (number)	...	...	...	...	...	...
2.4	Women and girls with increased time savings (number)	...	...	...	...	...	...
2.5	Women and girls with increased resilience to climate change, disasters, and other external shocks (number)	...	...	...	...	...	...

continued on next page

Table A4.2 *continued*

RFI	Results Framework Indicator	ADB Operations Overall			Operations Financed by Concessional OCR Loans and ADF Grants		
		No. of PCRs/ XARRs/TCRs	Results Achieved	Achievement Rate (%)	No. of PCRs/ XARRs/TCRs	Results Achieved	Achievement Rate (%)
OP 3: Tackling Climate Change, Building Climate and Disaster Resilience, and Enhancing Environmental Sustainability							
3.1	Total annual greenhouse gas emissions reduction (tCO_2e/year)[a]	...	...	...	...	...	...
3.2	People with strengthened climate and disaster resilience (number)	...	...	...	...	...	...
3.3	People benefiting from strengthened environmental sustainability (number)	...	...	...	...	...	...
OP 4: Making Cities More Livable							
4.1	People benefiting from improved services in urban areas (number)	...	...	...	...	...	...
4.2	Entities with improved urban planning and financial sustainability (number)	...	...	...	...	...	...
4.3	Zones with improved urban environment, climate resilience, and disaster risk management (number)	...	...	...	...	...	...
OP 5: Promoting Rural Development and Food Security							
5.1	People benefiting from increased rural investment (number)	...	...	...	...	...	...
5.2	Farmers with improved market access (number)	...	...	...	...	...	...
5.3	Land with higher productivity (hectares)	...	...	...	...	...	...

continued on next page

Table A4.2 *continued*

RFI	Results Framework Indicator	ADB Operations Overall			Operations Financed by Concessional OCR Loans and ADF Grants		
		No. of PCRs/ XARRs/TCRs	Results Achieved	Achievement Rate (%)	No. of PCRs/ XARRs/TCRs	Results Achieved	Achievement Rate (%)
OP 6: Strengthening Governance and Institutional Capacity							
6.1	Entities with improved management functions and financial stability (number)	...	...	...	...	...	...
6.2	Entities with improved service delivery (number)	...	...	...	...	...	...
OP 7: Fostering Regional Cooperation and Integration							
7.1	Cargo transported and energy transmitted across borders ($)	...	...	...	...	...	...
7.2	Trade and investment facilitated ($)	...	...	...	...	...	...
7.3	Regional public goods initiatives successfully reducing cross-border environmental or health risks, or providing regional access to education services (number)	...	...	...	...	...	...

... = 2019 data will be available in 2020, ADB = Asian Development Bank, ADF = Asian Development Fund, No. = number, OCR = ordinary capital resources, OP = operational priority, PCR = project completion report or program completion report, RFI = results framework indicator, tCO_2e/year = tons of carbon dioxide equivalent per year, TCR = technical assistance completion report, XARR = extended annual review report.

Note: "Achievement rate" represents a percentage of total "results achieved" of the total, aggregate planned outputs and outcomes as reported in the reports and recommendations of the President for the same operations. An annual achievement rate of 80% will be used as a benchmark for satisfactory performance.

[a] Results framework indicator that is harmonized or for which at least three multilateral development banks and/or international finance institutions have a similar or equivalent indicator.

Table A4.3: Results from Completed Operations—Quality of Completed Operations (Level 2B)

RFI	Results Framework Indicator	Baseline Year[a]	ADB Operations Overall		Operations Financed by Concessional OCR Loans and ADF Grants	
			Baseline Value	2024 Target	Baseline Value	2024 Target
1	Completed operations rated *successful* (%) (sovereign)[b]	RY2016–RY2018	77	80	77	80
2	Projects closed on time (%) (sovereign)	2016–2018	40	45	~~39~~ 40[d]	45
3	Completed operations rated *successful* (%) (nonsovereign)[b]	RY2016–RY2018	~~56~~ 54[c]	70		
4	Completed operations delivering intended gender equality results (%) (sovereign and nonsovereign)	RY2016–RY2018	75	80	76	80
5	Clients satisfied with the use of ADB knowledge products (%)[b]	2016	78	80 ◉		

◉ = periodic performance target, ADB = Asian Development Bank, ADF = Asian Development Fund, OCR = ordinary capital resources, RFI = results framework indicator, RY = reporting year.

Notes:

1. Indicators with periodic performance targets have minimum and/or maximum threshold values that need to be satisfied every measurement period up to 2024.
2. Gray shading in cells indicates that the column head does not apply.
3. RY is used instead of the calendar year to allow the Independent Evaluation Department an additional 6 months to prepare validation reports on project or program completion reports and extended annual review reports.
4. Baseline values cover 3-year periods, e.g., RY2016–RY2018 refers to 1 July 2015–30 June 2018.

[a] RY covers 1 July–30 June and will be based on the circulation year of the documents reviewed.

[b] Results framework indicator that is harmonized or for which at least three multilateral development banks and/or international finance institutions have a similar or equivalent indicator.

[c] A project performance evaluation report with a *less than successful* rating for a nonsovereign operation that had no previous validation report was made available in September 2019 and was included in RY2018.

[d] Two sovereign operations were reclassified from being policy-based operations only to also become investment projects because of their grant components.

Table A4.4: ADB's Operational Management (Level 3)

RFI	Results Framework Indicator	Baseline Year[a]	ADB Operations Overall		Operations Financed by Concessional OCR Loans and ADF Grants	
			Baseline Value	2024 Target	Baseline Value	2024 Target
3A. Design and Implementation Quality (high-quality operations prepared and satisfactorily implemented)						
1	Infrastructure projects that are design-ready (%) (sovereign)	2018	80.0	Maintain ⊙	76.5	Monitor
2	Infrastructure projects that are procurement-ready (%) (sovereign)	2018	46	60	37	Monitor
3	Performance of operations at implementation rated *satisfactory* (%) (sovereign) [a]			Monitor		Monitor
4	Operations at risk of not achieving development results (%) (nonsovereign)			Monitor		
3B. Development Finance (developed finance mobilized and transfered)						
5	Disbursement rate (%) (sovereign)	2018		90 ⊙		
6	Cofinancing ratio (%) (nonsovereign)	2018	120	200		
7	Financing for education (%) (sovereign and nonsovereign)	2016–2018	5.43	6–10		
8	Financing for health (%) (sovereign and nonsovereign)	2016–2018	1.75	3–5		
3C. Strategic Alignment (Strategy 2030 priorities promoted)						
9	Committed operations classified *gender equity theme* or *effective gender mainstreaming* (%) (sovereign and nonsovereign)[a]	2016–2018	47	50	62	Monitor
10	Committed operations classified *gender equity theme, effective gender mainstreaming,* or *some gender elements* (%) (sovereign and nonsovereign)[a,b]	2016–2018	70	71	82	Monitor
11	Committed operations that support climate change mitigation and adaptation (%) (sovereign and nonsovereign)[a]	2016–2018	56	65	~~54~~ 58[d]	Monitor

continued on next page

Table A4.4 *continued*

RFI	Results Framework Indicator	Baseline Year[a]	ADB Operations Overall		Operations Financed by Concessional OCR Loans and ADF Grants	
			Baseline Value	2024 Target	Baseline Value	2024 Target
12	Financing for climate change mitigation and adaptation ($ billion, cumulative) (sovereign and nonsovereign)[a]	~~2016–2018~~	0	35		
13	Nonsovereign operations as a share of total ADB operations (%, number) (nonsovereign)[c]	2018	~~19.3~~ 20[d]	33 ~~.0~~		
14	Operations in frontier economies and/or in new sectors (%) (nonsovereign)	2016–2018	48	55		
15	Operations supporting poverty reduction and inclusiveness (%) (sovereign and nonsovereign)			Monitor		

⊙ = periodic performance target, ADB = Asian Development Bank, ADF = Asian Development Fund, OCR = ordinary capital resources, RFI = results framework indicator.

Note: Gray shading in cells indicates that the column head does not apply. For indicators 3, 4, and 15, data that will be used to set the baseline will be available by 2020.

[a] Results framework indicator that is harmonized or for which at least three multilateral development banks and/or international finance institutions have a similar or equivalent indicator.

[b] The performance of this indicator is conditional on the performance of results framework indicator 3C.9. If 3C.9 is rated *on track but watch* or *off track,* 3C.10 will take the same rating. If 3C.9 is rated *on track*, 3C.10 will be rated independently.

[c] In this indicator, nonsovereign operations is synonymous with private sector operations, as per Strategy 2030, para. 69 (ADB. 2018. *Strategy 2030: Achieving a Prosperous, Inclusive, Resilient, and Sustainable Asia and the Pacific.* Manila).

[d] Change is due to updated 2018 commitment values.

Table A4.5: ADB's Organizational Effectiveness (Level 4)

RFI	Results Framework Indicator	Baseline Year[a]	ADB Operations Overall		Operations Financed by Concessional OCR Loans and ADF Grants	
			Baseline Value	2024 Target	Baseline Value	2024 Target
4A. Organizational Systems and Processes (organizational systems and processes improved)						
1	Quality of budget management (%)	2018	5.4	5.0 or less ⊙		
2	Procurement contract transactions of $10 million or more with processing time of 40 days or less (%) (sovereign)	2017–2018	67	80	60	80
3	Representation of women in the international staff category (%)[a]	2018	36.3	40.0		
4	Projects or transactions with sovereign–nonsovereign collaboration (number, cumulative) (sovereign and nonsovereign)	2016–2018	2	18		
4B. Organizational Capacity (organizational capacity increased)						
5	Staff rating ADB's effectiveness in digital transformation (%)	2018	68	75		
6	Staff rating ADB as providing enabling culture for Strategy 2030 implementation (%)	2018	58	70		
7	Budgeted international and national staff positions in field offices (% of total operations departments)	2018	48	Monitor		
8	Staff rating ADB as an effective knowledge and learning organization (%)	2018	63	75		

⊙ = periodic performance target, ADB = Asian Development Bank, ADF = Asian Development Fund, OCR = ordinary capital resources, RFI = results framework indicator.

Note: Gray shading in cells indicates that the column head does not apply.

[a] Results framework indicator that is harmonized or for which at least three multilateral development banks and/or international finance institutions have a similar or equivalent indicator.

ENDNOTES

1 ADB. 2018. *Strategy 2030: Achieving a Prosperous, Inclusive, Resilient, and Sustainable Asia and the Pacific.* Manila; and ADB. 2019. *ADB Corporate Results Framework, 2019–2024.* Manila.

2 Concessional assistance is the subset of ADB's overall operations financed by concessional ordinary capital resources loans and Asian Development Fund grants.

3 United Nations Economic and Social Commission for Asia and the Pacific. 2019. Asia and the Pacific SDG Progress Report 2019. Bangkok. https://www.unescap.org/publications/asia-and-pacific-sdg-progress-report-2019.

4 International Labour Organization. 2018. *Women Do 4 Times More Unpaid Care Work than Men in Asia and the Pacific.* News release. 27 June.

5 Global Carbon Project. Carbon Budget and Trends 2018. http:/www.globalcarbonproject.org/carbonbudget (accessed 20 February 2020).

6 United Nations Environment Programme. 2019. *UNEP Report Warns Plastic Policies Lagging Behind in South-East Asia.* News release. 13 November.

7 Sarah Ruiz and Andika Putraditama. 2019. *Will the Start of Forest Fires Season Hamper Indonesia's Progress in Reducing Deforestation?* World Resources Institute. https://www.wri.org/blog/2019/07/will-start-forest-fires-season-hamper-indonesia-s-progress-reducing-deforestation.

8 IQAir AirVisual. World's Most Polluted Cities 2019 (PM 2.5). https://www.iqair.com/us/world-most-polluted-cities (accessed 20 February 2020).

9 ADB. 2018. *Mainstreaming Air Quality in Urban Development through South–South Twinning.* Consultant's report. Manila (TA REG-8751).

10 International Fund for Agricultural Development. 2019. *Rural Poverty in Developing Countries: Issues Policies and Challenges.* https://www.un.org/development/desa/dspd/wp-content/uploads/sites/22/2019/03/Rural-poverty-EGM_IFAD-overview.pdf.

11 Food and Agriculture Organization of the United Nations, World Health Organization, World Food Programme, United Nations Children's Fund. 2019. *Asia and the Pacific Regional Overview of Food Security and Nutrition.* https://www.unicef.org/eap/media/4526/file/Asia%20and%20Pacific%20food%20security.pdf. Wasted children have a low weight for their height. Children who experience stunting early in life often go on to struggle with challenges, including poor cognition and educational performance, low wages, and lost productivity.

12 Food and Agriculture Organization of the United Nations. 2019. *The State of Food and Agriculture 2019: Moving Forward on Food Loss and Waste Reduction.* http://www.fao.org/3/CA6030EN/CA6030EN.pdf.

13 ADB. 2020. *2019 Annual Portfolio Performance Report.* Manila.

14 ADB. 2018. *Strategy 2030: Achieving a Prosperous, Inclusive, Resilient, and Sustainable Asia and the Pacific.* Manila.

15 ADB. 2015. *ADB to Double Annual Climate Financing to $6 Billion for Asia-Pacific by 2020.* News release. 25 September.

16 ADB. 2019. *Report and Recommendation of the President to the Board of Directors: Proposed Loan to the People's Republic of China for the Demonstration of Guangxi Elderly Care and Health Care Integration and Public–Private Partnership Project.* Manila.

17 Organisation for Economic Co-operation and Development–Development Assistance Committee. 2019. *Handbook for the Marker for the Inclusion and Empowerment of Persons with Disabilities.* http://www.oecd.org/officialdocuments/publicdisplaydocumentpdf/?cote=DCD/DAC/STAT/RD(2019)1/RD1&docLanguage=En; United Nations Economic and Social Commission for Asia and the Pacific. 2019. *Incheon Strategy to "Make the Right Real" for Persons with Disabilities in Asia and the Pacific and Beijing Declaration and Action Plan to Accelerate the Implementation of the Incheon Strategy.* https://www.unescap.org/resources/incheon-strategy-make-right-real-persons-disabilities-asia-and-pacific-and-beijing.

18 ADB. 2019. *Report and Recommendation of the President to the Board of Directors: Proposed Loan to India for the Mumbai Metro Rail Systems Project.* Manila.

19 ADB. 2018. *Report and Recommendation of the President to the Board of Directors: Proposed Loan and Technical Assistance Grant, and Administration of Technical Assistance Grant to the Democratic Socialist Republic of Sri Lanka for the South Asia Subregional Economic Cooperation Port Access Elevated Highway Project.* Manila.

20 All success rates reported in this chapter are based on ratings by ADB's Independent Evaluation Department (IED) in project completion report validation reports or project performance evaluation reports. The reporting year is based on the project completion report circulation dates and ends on 30 June, e.g., the 2019 reporting year is 1 July 2018–30 June 2019.

21 In addition to rating their overall satisfaction, respondents were asked to assess such KPS as flagship publications, technical studies, working papers, policy briefs, op-eds, policy dialogue, capacity building and training, ADB processes and project management, and seminars and workshops.

22 Knowledge-related events include forums, conferences, seminars, meetings, workshops, and training programs in which DMCs participate.

23 This includes followers on Facebook, Instagram, LinkedIn, and Twitter.

24 In early 2019, Facebook and Twitter changed their algorithms to prioritize personal and popular content, and this reduced the visibility of, and engagement in, content from organizations such as ADB.

25 ADB. Technology Innovation Challenge (Energy). https://www.adb.org/news/events/technology-innovation-challenge-energy.

26 The count is based on staff participants and includes training expenses directly managed by the Budget, Personnel, and Management Systems Department.

27 Field offices include resident missions, regional offices (i.e., the Pacific Liaison and Coordination Office in Sydney and the Pacific Subregional Office in Suva), and country offices in the Pacific. The figure refers to budgeted international and national staff as of 31 December each year.

28 The 2019 sample for sovereign operations comprises 60 projects.

29 The 2019 sample for nonsovereign operations comprises 29 projects.

30 These are Budget, Personnel, and Management Systems Department; the Controller's Department; the Department of Communications; the Information Technology Department; the Office of Risk Management; the Office of Administrative Services; and the Treasury Department.

31 The new procurement framework was rolled out in 2018 along with new guidance notes and instructions for staff. Processing time is the period from the time ADB receives a bid evaluation report to the time it approves it. While a significant percentage of transactions are recorded in the Procurement Review System, in some instances regional departments record them only in their own systems. The new procurement framework will encourage most transactions to be processed using the Procurement Review System.

32 ADB's definition of CSOs includes groups organized as cooperatives or for self-help groups and very formally as nongovernment organizations, professional associations, and chambers of commerce.

33 ADB. 2018. *Strategy 2030: Achieving a Prosperous, Inclusive, Resilient, and Sustainable Asia and the Pacific.* Manila. As of January 2019, ADB classified 10 developing member countries (DMCs) as FCAS, of which 2 were affected by conflict in parts of the country (Afghanistan and Myanmar). The remaining eight are Pacific small island developing states (SIDS) and demonstrate the effects of fragility. In addition, Vanuatu had country performance assessment scores just slightly above the 3.2 cutoff for FCAS, and ADB's operations in this country continue to pay due attention to issues of fragility.

34 ADB. 1966. *Agreement Establishing the Asian Development Bank.* Manila.

35 Project readiness financing facilities were committed for the Federated States of Micronesia, Solomon Islands, Tonga, and Vanuatu.

36 ADB. 2019. *Technical Assistance for Implementing a Differentiated Approach to Urban Development in the Pacific.* Manila.

37 ADB. 2019. *Report and Recommendation of the President to the Board of Directors: Proposed Grant and Administration of Grant to the Islamic Republic of Afghanistan for the Arghandab Integrated Water Resources Development Project.* Manila; and ADB. 2019. *Report and Recommendation of the President to the Board of Directors: Proposed Pacific Renewable Energy Program.* Manila.

38 ADB. 2019. *Report and Recommendation of the President to the Board of Directors: Proposed Loan, Grant, and Administration of Grants to the Republic of the Union of Myanmar for the Resilient Community Development Project.* Manila.

39 ADB. 2012. *Working Differently in Fragile and Conflict-Affected Situations: The ADB Experience.* Manila.

40 British Council in partnership with INTRAC. 2017. Building Civil Society Capacity in Fragile and Conflict-Affected States. https://www.intrac.org/resources/policy-brief-building-civil-society-capacity-fragile-conflict-affected-states/.

41 The toolkit used in the Afghanistan operations consists of the FCAS Handbook for ADB Projects in Afghanistan, the FCAS Assessment Guideline, the FCAS Action Plan, the FCAS Monitoring and Evaluation Guideline, the Community Engagement Guideline, the FCAS Project-Community Agreement Guideline, the Community-Driven Development Component Guideline, the FCAS Capacity Development Tool, and the FCAS Conflict-Sensitive Procurement Guide.

42 ADB. 2019. *Report and Recommendation of the President to the Board of Directors: Proposed Pacific Renewable Energy Program.* Manila.

43 These include the Inter-American Development Bank, the International Monetary Fund, and the World Bank.

44 Only the recommendations of IED reports that are discussed at the Development Effectiveness Committee are uploaded to MARS. Management is required to upload its action plan no later than 60 days after each committee meeting.

45 Results were based on data collected in post-training surveys, which asked participants to rate their knowledge and skills both before and after the workshop (as "poor," "fair," "good," or "very good") for nine subtopics. Participants are counted as having increased their DMF knowledge and skills if they reported at least a 2-level improvement on average across the nine subtopics (e.g., from "poor" to "good"). Of the 281 participants, 258 (92%) reported significant improvement in knowledge and skills from the workshop. The remaining participants either somewhat improved their knowledge and skills or reported that they already had "good" or "very good" knowledge and skills prior to attending the workshop. In 2019, ADB delivered 2-day DMF workshops to DMC officials in Bhutan, the People's Republic of China, Mongolia, and Nepal.

46 SPD assessed the quality of DMF indicators of all 108 operations committed in 2019 using the same criteria used for its 2013 assessment of 105 projects approved in 2013. The assessment used the following criteria to assess the quality of DMF indicators, with each criterion assigned a corresponding weight (Table 1).

Table 1: Criteria for Assessing the Quality of Design and Monitoring Framework Indicators

Criteria	Weight (%)
Describes how impact, outcome, or output [will be] achieved	5
Describes what is to be measured	20
Identifies how much, by when	20
Baseline data in evidence	25
Target value is provided	25
Gender-disaggregated baseline and target	5

Each DMF indicator was assigned a pass or fail rating for each of the six criteria. SPD then obtained a project's "passing rate" for each criterion (i.e., the total number of "passed indicators" over the total number of DMF indicators). The passing rate was then classified based on the categories used in SPD's 2013 assessment to determine whether all, most, few, or none of the DMF indicators passed each criterion (Table 2). SPD then obtained the average passing rate for all projects using the weights identified in Table 1.

Table 2: Scale for Passing Rate

Reporting Scale	Description
All	100% of DMF indicators were assigned a "pass" rating
Most	75%–99% of DMF indicators were assigned a "pass" rating
Few	25%–74% of DMF indicators were assigned a "pass" rating
None	0%–24% of DMF indicators were assigned a "pass" rating
NA	Projects that do not have any gender-disaggregated indicator

DMF = design and monitoring framework, NA = not applicable.

47 ADB. 2019. *Operational Plan for Private Sector Operations, 2019–2024.* Manila.

48 Independent Evaluation Department. 2019. *Corporate Evaluation of ADB Private Sector Equity Investments.* Manila: ADB.

49 ADB. 2019. *The Social Protection Indicator for Asia: Assessing Progress.* Manila.

2019 DEVELOPMENT EFFECTIVENESS REVIEW

SCORECARD AND RELATED INFORMATION

APRIL 2020

ASIAN DEVELOPMENT BANK

CONTENTS

SIGNALS AND SCORING METHODS

Alignment with the Sustainable Development Goals..2
Results Framework Indicators Level 1: Signals..2
Results Framework Indicators Levels 2–4: Signals...3
Results Framework Indicators Levels 2–4: Composite Signals 4
Results Framework Indicators Levels 2–4: Scoring Methods for 2019–2023.....................4
Results Framework Indicators Levels 2–4: Scoring Methods for 2024 5

RESULTS FRAMEWORK INDICATORS

Level 1: Development Progress in Asia and the Pacific 8
Level 2: Results from Completed Operations 12
Level 3: ADB's Operational Management 18
Level 4: ADB's Organizational Effectiveness...22

TRACKING INDICATORS

Level 1: Development Progress in Asia and the Pacific 26
Level 2: Results from Completed Operations 32
Level 3: ADB's Operational Management 48
Level 4: ADB's Organizational Effectiveness...56

Notes:
1. In this report, "$" refers to United States dollars.
2. The Asian Development Bank's Strategy, Policy and Partnerships Department is the source of all information in tables, figures, boxes, and infographics in this report, unless otherwise stated.
3. Totals may not sum precisely because of rounding.